Sheldon Amos

Political and Legal

Remedies for War

Sheldon Amos

Political and Legal
Remedies for War

ISBN/EAN: 9783337071479

Printed in Europe, USA, Canada, Australia, Japan

Cover: Foto ©ninafisch / pixelio.de

More available books at **www.hansebooks.com**

POLITICAL AND LEGAL

REMEDIES FOR WAR

BY

SHELDON AMOS, M.A.
BARRISTER-AT-LAW
LATE PROFESSOR OF JURISPRUDENCE IN UNIVERSITY COLLEGE, LONDON

NEW YORK
HARPER & BROTHERS, FRANKLIN SQUARE
1880

To My Wife

TABLE OF CONTENTS.

CHAPTER I.

OF THE CHARACTER OF MODERN WARS, AND THE POSSIBILITY OF PERMANENT PEACE.

THREE LEGITIMATE AIMS OF LAWS OF WAR: PAGE
(1) To Mitigate its Severity 9
(2) To Reduce its Frequency 9
(3) To Pave the Way to its Abolition 9

ABOLITION NOT IMPOSSIBLE, SINCE—
1. Private Wars, Judicial Combat, and Duelling have disappeared . 11
2. War itself has undergone a Sweeping Change of Character . . 12
3. The Progress of Civilization is Antagonistic to War 17
4. Economic Facts, newly recognized, are against it 18
5. Public Sentiment is increasingly influenced by—
   (1) Diffusion of Education, especially as to Social and Economical Matters 21
   (2) The Press, which, through its War Correspondents, reveals what War actually is 26
   (3) Growth of Liberal Principles 29
   (4) Philosophical Theories Antagonistic to War 33
   (5) Religious Principles Antagonistic to War 35
   (6) Habits of International Co-operation and Association . . 42

CHAPTER II.

OF SOME OF THE CAUSES OF MODERN EUROPEAN WARS.

DOCTRINE OF LEGAL EQUALITY OF STATES 48
POLITICAL INEQUALITY OF STATES 49
FLUCTUATION OF CONDITIONS ON WHICH THIS DEPENDS 50

CAUSES OF MODERN WARS: PAGE
  1. Internal Development of any State outgrowing its External Relations 51
  2. Peculiar Mutual Sensibilities of States 55
  3. Intervention 57
  4. Systems of Policy 61
  5. Defective State of International Morality 68
  6. Standing Armies 79
  7. State of International Law 84

CHAPTER III.

OF SOME POLITICAL REMEDIES FOR WAR.

SECTION   I. Of the Nature and Possibility of Political and other Remedies for War 96
SECTION II. Of Intervention and Non-intervention 101
SECTION III. Of Mediation and Arbitration 117
SECTION IV. Of Treaties, and especially Treaties of Peace 123
SECTION V. Of Great and Small States; and of the Equilibrium of States 133
SECTION VI. Of the Neutralization of States, Seas, and Canals . . . 143
SECTION VII. Of Standing Armies 160
SECTION VIII. Of International Conferences and Congresses 182

CHAPTER IV.

OF LEGAL REMEDIES FOR WAR.

SECTION I. Of the Legal Operation of War on Trade; and more especially of the proposed Exemption of Private Persons and Property from Maritime Capture 196
SECTION II. Of the Laws of War in their bearing on Peace 216

INDEX 247

POLITICAL AND LEGAL REMEDIES

FOR WAR.

CHAPTER I.

OF THE CHARACTER OF MODERN WARS AND THE POSSIBILITY OF PERMANENT PEACE.

IF the International Lawyer confines himself to his own proper task, and does not usurp the functions of the International legislator, of the moralist, or of the philanthropist, he is only concerned with War as a means, however violent and irregular, for the support of legal rights, or with the restrictions which civilization has introduced into the exercise of what are sometimes called the extreme rights of War. He is called upon only to register and expound the practical rules based upon the tacit or express consent of nations, and conformable to the dictates of abstract justice, so far as these can be ascertained; and he is not entitled to impair the simple treatment of a subject, engrossing enough in itself, by speculations on a remote future, or even by benevolently suggested reforms for the immediate present.

Function of the International Lawyer.

Not, indeed, that the writers of text-books on International Law have generally exercised the self-restraint here commended. On the contrary, they have all but universally assumed the character of legislators as well as lawyers. Nor have they even confined themselves to the

Its limits not sufficiently observed.

moderate course of hinting at what, in their opinion, the law ought to be, while explaining what it actually is. Their views of what the law is have been largely colored by what they have wished the law to be, and, too often, by what they have conceived the interests of their own States demanded it should be. Some writers, indeed, by publishing Codes of International Law, have combined inextricably together the treatment of the law as it is, and that of the law as, in their opinion, it ought to be. They have given definiteness and precision to principles which are, as yet, of most fluctuating authority, and are only creeping on toward general recognition. They have imparted clearness and simplicity to rules the true import and circumscription of which can only be understood by laying side by side a long series of treaties, despatches, judicial decisions, and desultory utterances of eminent statesmen. They have everywhere substituted order for disorder, the rule of right for that of might, and the claims of humanity for the traditional assumptions of egotistic self-interest.

But, though the motives of these philanthropic legislators have been of the noblest, and the results of their efforts, no doubt, widely beneficent, their method has been one of the causes which has discredited International Law as a system of actually binding rules. It has come about that neither the subject of the law as it is, nor that of the law as it ought to be made, has been adequately treated; and, when those who professed to be teachers of the law acknowledged themselves uncertain as to the existence of any rules at all wholly out of the region of further debate, there might be an excuse for those who were interested in prolonging a period of uncertainty and confusion in declaring there was no law at all.

Uncertainty of rules of International Law.

The Laws relative to War afford a good illustration of these remarks. There is no part of International Law in which the rules are, almost from day to day, undergoing more rapid vacillations; and the proceedings of the Brussels Conference, in 1874, display at once the

Laws of War in course of formation.

number of points in respect of which the law is unsettled, and the extraordinary amount of interest which attaches to their settlement. Thus it might be expected that here, perhaps more than elsewhere, the function of the lawyer would almost unavoidably have slidden into that of the legislator. In fact, the two functions cannot be wholly kept apart, because it sometimes happens that the existing rule can only be understood by examining its reasons, or even by setting forth in full the controversies amidst which it hardly maintains its existence. Nevertheless, it is desirable to separate the legislative function from the strictly legal one where it is possible; and this is especially important in respect of a question like that of War, in which so many strong passions, and generous, though uninformed, instincts, are wont to divorce the discussion of it altogether from a regard to the practical difficulties of national life.

There are three distinct aims which are usually regarded as being legitimate objects of concern on the occasion of making a proposed change in International Law, or on that of giving increased definiteness and validity to a rule of law which has hitherto been imperfectly apprehended and recognized. These aims are (1) mitigation of severity in carrying on War; (2) a reduction in the length and frequency of Wars; (3) preparation for a time when War shall become obsolete. Though all these aims are recognized as worthy ones, and the pursuit of the first two of them has undoubtedly operated largely in the reform of the law, yet they have been hitherto treated of after a very desultory fashion; they have rarely been handled in relation to each other; the proportionate claims of each have been rarely ascertained, or, when conflicting, reconciled; the importance of these, especially of the last, has not been rated highly enough—so much so, that many readers of standard text-books would be of opin-

Sidenote: Three legitimate aims of Laws of War. (1) To mitigate severity of War; (2) to reduce its frequency; (3) to pave the way to its abolition.

ion that the authors held War to be little more of an evil than a civil lawsuit, and the acquisition of territory, or of a commercial advantage, happily and honorably purchased by War.

Owing to this levity or confusion of treatment, the whole topic of Neutral rights and duties, with which about a third part of International Law is concerned, has been treated far too exclusively, and far more often, from the point of view of Neutral and Belligerent interests than from its bearing on the length of the War, on the probability of the recurrence of War, or on the promotion of a permanently pacific state of society. Of course, the latter considerations have been adverted to, and the consideration of Neutral and Belligerent interests ought to have its weight in the inquiry. The complaint here is that writers on the subject either do not adjust competing classes of considerations, or adjust them in a way which nothing but an habitual indifference to the evil of War in itself, or inattention to its true nature, could explain or excuse.

It will be replied that a time when War shall become obsolete, or the frequency of its recurrence much reduced, is too distant to furnish any guide to the conduct of the practical politician, or legal reformer.

Ultimate abolition of War not impossible.

The prospect of such a time may invigorate the hopes of the philanthropist, and even console the despondent misgivings of the moral philosopher; but there is much on the face of the civilized world to point to the speedy advent of a season of warfare on an unprecedented scale, and little to suggest the hope of its speedy abolition.

If it were conceded that, however distant the time of general and permanent Peace now seems, yet that time *may* come, and that it should be one of the objects of the International Law Reformer to make that time a reality and to hasten its arrival —so far as he could work in this direction without jeopardizing nearer and more certainly attainable ends of true value—enough would be admitted for the present purpose. But this concession is not a hard one to make, as a little examination into the facts will make clear.

1. In the first place, the teachings of history certainly are to the effect that practices and institutions, which at one time seem to be necessary conditions of the social and political condition of all people, and yet which stand condemned as counter to principles of morality, justice, and political expediency, vanish in an almost inconceivably short space of time, and become so far obsolete as to be with difficulty revived, even in imagination.

Some mischievous practices, once prevalent, have disappeared.

The interminable, and seemingly irrepressible, private wars which marked the middle period of the Feudal system, and against which the abler Kings and Popes so perseveringly struggled by the use of such devices as the "King's Peace,"* and the "Truce of God,"† are remarkable quite as much for the completeness with which they were superseded by the supremacy of Law and Courts of Justice, as for the complexion they imparted to the whole of the nascent political life of Europe. The judicial combats, again, which took so deep a hold of the legal and political mind of the Normans, and obtained a firm footing in England, passed away, for all practical purposes, as it would appear, in the course of the single reign of Henry II. The more recent experience of the rapid decay of the practice of duelling is still more instructive, as the practice is still honored in some countries, while in not more civilized countries it is already placed on a par with the most abominable crimes. These instances, at least, prove that there is nothing in the mere popularity, diffusion, or antiquity of a practice, itself abhorrent to humanity, which can secure for it a lasting endurance.

Private Wars.

Judicial Combat.

Duelling.

---

* See Stubbs's Constitutional History, vol. i. pp. 179-183.
† See Ward's History of the Law of Nations, vol. ii. pp. 21-23.

2. Again, it is especially difficult to prophesy perpetuity of an institution or practice which is essentially protean in character, and has undergone, and is still undergoing, manifold changes in its most distinguishing features. It is hardly possible to embrace under the same name the sort of incessant feuds between tribe and tribe which prevail at a time when union for purposes of conflict is the main basis of national association, and actual conflict is at once the absorbing occupation and the chief stimulus of life, and the occasional wars which interrupt the equable progress of a society uniformly given to pacific pursuits. Between these two extremes, again, there is the stage, such as was represented in the middle Feudal period, when military and pacific interests equally divide men's thoughts and lives.

Change in the character of War.

To each of these conditions of War correspond varieties in the mode of conducting War, and in the moral aspect under which it is viewed. In the most primitive period, scarcely any distinction can be drawn between the form and spirit of the contests and the unrestricted ferocity which marks the internecine struggles of wild beasts. The object of the fight is one little short of mutual extermination, and the conduct of it is marked throughout with personal vindictiveness and bloodthirsty hatred. In the next stage, War begins to be regarded as a means to an end outside itself, and more lasting than itself. The notion of national right, as a legal conception, has begun to disclose itself, and War is regarded as merely a temporary suspense of well-ascertained relationships. Under some such forms as those of chivalry, or of religious obligations enforced, perhaps, by the head of a common spiritual community, restrictive measures are introduced into the modes of conducting War, especially in relation to the treatment of prisoners, and the observance of positive engagements. At a still later stage, the laws which regulate the conduct of War have become almost as numerous and cumbrous as those which ascertain the relations of peace: War is conducted after the most highly systematized methods, and with the help of the most finely organized and expensive military and naval equipments; the scale of operations is enormous; the armaments so prodigious in times of Peace, as well as of War, as to encroach perilously on the labor needed to provide means of subsistence; the objects of War are increasingly complex and manifold; and yet, withal, it is theoretically held that War is (at best) nothing but a disastrous means to an indispensable end; that no greater injury ought to be done an enemy than is needed to attain this end, and that it is the imperative moral duty of statesmen to exhaust every pacific resource before plunging their country into War.

These successive changes of practice and belief indicate, first, Changes indicate non-permanence of War. that there is no fixed character appertaining to War which seems to promise it a permanence superior to that which might, at one time, seem to have attached to institutions now obsolete and discredited; and, secondly, that, in all ages and states of society, the appetite for War, and the methods of conducting War, have reflected, with considerable exactness, the aggregate features and tendencies of the then existing civilization, though the extraordinary energy which, at the present day, enriches every field of exertion, availing itself of the latest physical innovations and discoveries, seems to impart to War, among other things, an appearance of freshly-springing activity, which may be wholly an hallucination, and in no way an augury of its longevity.

Again, War, in modern times, assumes a great variety of aspects from the condition of relative civilization, or Diverse forms of War in modern times. War of a strong State against a weak. political weight, which happens to characterize the parties to it. Thus, when a State, possessed of enormous political influence, material strength, and unlimited resources, makes war upon a weak, disorganized, and impoverished State, the conflict is called War, but it is, in reality, a mere exercise of superior force, whether for purposes of tyranny, self-defence, or executive justice. The rules of War, for instance, common among European States, may or may not be observed and enforced when England is at war with China, or Turkey, or Persia, and the outward formalities may be more or less rigorously complied with. But the result is, from the very commencement, a foregone conclusion; and the only issue involved for the more powerful State is that of the expediency of inflicting the chastisement, the expense its infliction will involve, and the moral propriety of the action proposed. There is no hazard or speculation in the enterprise. It is from first to last a mere question of moral right and political exigency, as apprehended by the more powerful State.

Very similar is the case of warlike expeditions conducted by a powerful and highly-civilized State against a feeble, imperfectly civilized, or semi-barbarous State. Such have been the military enterprises in which England has, during the last century and a half, incessantly engaged against small Indian States and the native tribes of Australasia and Western and Southern Africa; the United States, against the infirm and disorganized communities within its reach, as Texas and Mexico; Russia, against refractory political aggregates bordering on its territory in Western Asia, as Khiva and Khokand; and (perhaps) Egypt, against recalcitrant and more barbarous neighbors on the south and west, as Abyssinia and Zanzibar.

<small>War between civilized and uncivilized States.</small>

In such enterprises as these the forms of civilized War seem to be only observed as a matter of mere gratuitous courtesy, and usually only to such an extent that they do not involve the slightest interference with the plenary success, at every point, of military operations, carried out with the utmost despatch and the most inflexible resolution. The grounds of the War are of the most various kinds, and admit of every shade of justification. Among these grounds are the alleged ill-treatment of the citizens of the more powerful States; alleged offences committed by citizens of the weaker State; the necessity of intervention in the cause of humanity, for the purpose of promoting internal peace and orderly government; alleged territorial aggressions, or possible aggressions in the future; alleged infractions of implied or express engagements, especially as to the payment of money or the facilitation of commerce. Whatever justification these grounds really admit of, the openly-avowed grounds are seldom the true ones, and, whether true or not, they are only very slightly subjected to criticism at the hands of civilized governments, or public opinion in civilized States. The result is that the enterprise is nothing more than a voluntary act of force, in which the whole and undivided responsibility rests, from first to last, with the stronger State. This class of so-called Wars differs from the former class mainly in the less amount of deference to the public opinion of, and in, other States, which is acknowledged on entering upon them, and which regulates the conduct of them.

Another class of Wars of a wholly peculiar kind, and presenting problems quite diverse from those inherent in the last two classes, are those designated as "Civil Wars," and which, through the tendency they have to diffuse themselves and to promote general War, demand especial attention. These Wars admit of a great variety of forms, from the armed insurrection of a portion of a perfectly harmonized and seemingly well organized State, as that of the Confederate States of America in 1861–'65, to the final stroke of practical emancipation of Servia in 1862, and the portentous and not unsuccessful struggles for independence which have since manifested themselves in the loosely-attached provinces of the Turkish Empire. Whatever sanguine or despondent theories may prevail as to Wars of this sort ever becoming obsolete—a subject which will be treated farther on—it is at least obvious that the stimulus and the obstacles to Wars of this class are of a totally different

Civil Wars.

kind from those present in the case of Wars of other sorts. These Wars are, at the outset, closely connected with the internal government and organization of a particular State, and are, presumedly and primarily, owing to defects either in the form or in the administration of a political constitution. Thus it may be expected, even on the face of the inquiry, that these Wars will decrease as the knowledge of the science and practice of the art of government progresses, though, of course, their entire disappearance (if ever it can be attained) will depend largely upon general causes, unfavorable to the resort to armed force for any purpose whatever.

The remaining class of Wars, that between States at the same *Wars between equal States.* pitch of civilization, and recognized as politically equal and independent, presents War in what may be termed its most characteristic shape, and that in which all the difficulties which beset the annihilation of War are at a climax. The grounds, objects, and causes of Wars of this kind have little parallelism with those of the three kinds just adverted to. Strong passions are stimulated, keen and competing interests are involved, notions of dignity and honor are concerned, a military and naval organization, long and unremittingly perfected, is ready, on each side, to be turned to instant account, in a way and to a degree which, in the circumstances attending a one-sided War between a great European and a petty Eastern State, or a suddenly fermented insurrection of a wide-spread character in a single State, finds little resemblance.

The causes, real and apparent, near and remote, which in modern times promote Wars between highly civilized and politically equal States will, shortly, be enumerated and critically examined, with a view to determining how far existing rules of International Law tend to aggravate or to reduce them. In the mean time, it is here asserted that War between these States is, so far as its causes and conditions go, extremely unlike what is called War in every other case; that the reasons for one class of Wars becoming less frequent, or vanishing altogether, are different from, and stronger or weaker than, those which may be assigned in the case of another class of Wars; and that, in a word, War, as a general fact, is a product of such multiform and yet clearly distinguishable influences, of a transient and perishable sort, that perpetuity can no more be predicted of War than of any one of these influences, or of all of them.

3. A further reason why no prediction can be ventured upon as to the endurance of warfare among civilized States is that, for some hundreds of years past, the modes of conducting Wars between such States have been steadily undergoing changes in one continuous direction, the object of these changes being the diminution of the miseries inherent to warfare, the limitation of its area, and the alleviation of the evils incidentally occasioned by it to Neutral States. What is the actual bearing, in this respect, of past or proposed reforms will be the topic of special inquiry farther on. They are now only adverted to as affording an index of a sort of instinctive resolution on the part of civilized States to reduce, in every way that from time to time seems practicable, the parts of warfare which are least in harmony with the demands of the current civilization.

<small>Progress of civilization antagonistic to War.</small>

These changes have proceeded far more rapidly and decisively in the case of land warfare than of sea warfare; though in this latter they have advanced most conspicuously of late years, and there are symptoms that very shortly the Laws of War by land and by sea will, so far as the difference of material permits, be identical. It is a common complaint with respect to some of these changes—as those of the exemption from capture of enemy's goods in neutral ships, the abandonment of the use of privateers, the strict protection of private property on land owned by the citizens of a Belligerent State, the growing disrepute attaching to the appropriation by a victor of territory at the close of the War, and the constantly enlarged security afforded to neutral commerce—that they tend to make the trial by battle increasingly uncertain, perplexed, and in every way unsatisfactory. This may or may not be the case; but, at any rate, it is clear that changes of this sort have all been gradually forced upon Belligerent States by an aggregate of civilizing influences unfavorable to War of any sort, and that it must be quite impossible to anticipate how far these and similar influences may hereafter operate so as to preclude recourse to War under any circumstances whatever.

4. This consideration of the presumption that may be reasonably based on changes which have hitherto been inevitably brought about in the mode of conducting War, leads to another class of considerations, suggested by the economical and moral condition of society in the leading States of the world.

<small>Advance of Economic Science opposed to War.</small>

In the present aspect, it is impossible to estimate too highly the momentousness of the change that has been brought about, during the past century, in the economical doctrines and policy professed by the politicians of Europe. It is not only that Navigation Laws, a selfish and suicidal colonial system, and recourse to protective taxation, have been, in England and many other European countries, discredited and renounced, but, even in countries where, for the sake of stimulating local manufactures, protection still exists, the essential meaning and spirit of Free-trade are more and more adequately appreciated, and converted into practical action, in a variety of unconscious ways. It is not merely professed, but widely believed, that each State profits by the wealth, and not by the poverty, of surrounding States; that each State, from its climate, situation, or special opportunities of all sorts, is likely to have, and, in fact, has superior advantages in some certain kinds of production, manufacture, or trade; and that a State becomes

<small>Free-trade principles.</small>

rich and prosperous in proportion as it buys all things, in respect of which it has not that advantage, as cheaply as possible, and finds the greatest demand in other countries for the things which itself most economically produces or prepares.

Though these truths are occasionally clouded from view, owing to a passing spasm of national distrust or impatience—the result of exceptional economical perplexities—yet they are not seriously contested in any quarters worthy of attention, and, in fact, are already raised to the dignity of universal dogmas or axioms. They not only guide the statesman in devising schemes of taxation and arranging commercial treaties, but they have entered deeply into the popular thought and feeling on all international topics, and they create that sort of secondary consciousness toward foreign nations which, in the long run, determines the attitude toward them of all popular assemblies, whether strictly political or not.

This notion of the benefit to all States of the wealth and prosperity of each, and the loss to all caused by the poverty or depression of any one, marks a complete transformation of the aspect under which foreign nations have, up to very recent times, been invariably regarded, and in which they are still regarded in only partially civilized communities. It is not confined to purely mercantile matters. In every field of activity and interest it translates rivals into co-operative laborers, and jealous foes into helpful and sympathetic allies. It has manifold indirect influences on social life, as between the citizens of different States. Not only does the stimulus given to trade directly promote and endlessly multiply association of all sorts, but one sort of association always produces another, and constant familiarity begets friendliness, and banishes suspicion and vague dislike. It thus may be expected that the new era of Free-trade will have consequences to the relations between the citizens—and ultimately the governments—of different States, of a kind wholly new and incalculable.

Amicable intercourse between nations.

Some of these consequences have already manifested themselves in the actual changes made in favor of the freedom of commerce in time of War. Other consequences are beginning to make themselves felt in the same direction, and it must be quite impossible to fix an arbitrary limit to the extent to which such causes may hereafter operate.

Anyway, it is clear that War, and all it presupposes, is diametrically opposed—and is now beginning to be felt to be so as never before—to the modern spirit and doctrines of international trade. This is not only the case because War springs out of, or is inflamed by, sentiments of personal rivalry and animosity between the citizens of different States, which are incompatible with wide-spread trade relations, but because War, more than any other event, is fatal to the course of trade. It occasions interruptions, sudden, perplexing, and incalculable; it forces ordinary trade into unnatural and uncongenial channels; it calls into existence a bastard sort of trade, based on nothing but the artificial exigencies of War, and which the chance of a single battle, or a turn in diplomatic negotiation, may instantly wither. For these and the like reasons it is obvious that War must be recognized, more and more distinctly, as implacably alien to the most characteristic tendencies of modern society. Of course this fact can, in itself, furnish no ground for hope of its speedy abolition. But it at least suffices to rebut any presumption that War must, of necessity, be coeval with the life of civilized States; and if no such presumption can be fairly made, then it is legitimate for the reformers of International Law to include among their objects the hastening of the time for the final abolition of War.

5. Another reason, or class of reasons, for holding the extinction of War beween civilized States to be a reasonable object of concern at the present time is, that a diffused apprehension of the evils and, in some respects, of the moral anomalies of War, is distinctly

Growth of dislike to War on various grounds.

traceable, of a kind which seems to be without precedent. Part of this phenomenon is, no doubt, connected with the class of facts just noted; that is, the recognized incongruity between War and the maintenance of a finely organized commercial system. These facts have, no doubt, attracted attention to evils greater even than themselves, and they have encouraged free speech and unfettered criticism. But the growing dislike to War, on social and purely ethical grounds, certainly has an independent origin of its own, and is connected with an aggregate of social, moral, political, and religious influences which are only very remotely connected with commercial considerations.

(1.) The most prominent influences of this sort are those which may be described as being due to the extraordinary impulse which has of late years been given to popular education, and to the general diffusion of knowledge. The work which has thus been started is, of course, as yet extremely incomplete in all countries, and a persistent controversy is everywhere being waged as to the true and best mode of carrying it forward, both in its higher aspect, as bearing on the promotion of science and erudition, and in its lower aspect, as securing a minimum of general knowledge to every citizen of the State. This work has been largely favored by the diffusion of literature, the study of foreign languages, and all those forms of International co-operation which will have, on their own account, to be separately adverted to lower down.

A public opinion opposed to War favored by diffusion of education.

The direct and increasingly familiar result of this educational stir is a popular appreciation of the true bearing and significance of the common facts of daily life. The conditions of national wealth, the causes of high and low wages, the theory of prices, the relation of population to material well-being, the distinction between productive and unproductive labor, the problem of pauperism and its reme-

Popular interest in social questions.

dies, and even the general principles of equitable and economical taxation, are now no longer topics only for the abstracted student or philosophical statesman, but are "common coin" for every school-boy, as well as for the husbandman and the artisan. True it is that the knowledge abroad on all these points is at present of the crudest description, and gross fallacies are in the mouth of almost every one who, without a special and even technical training, aspires to instruct his fellows in reference to them. But what is to be noticed is that these topics are, and will be, discussed in the public thoroughfares of the world in a way they never yet have been; and a true light will gradually displace the flickering false lights, which have rather revealed than illumined the long night of ignorance. As the true light becomes broadened over the whole field of economic science, the relation of War to material wealth and prosperity must be everywhere steadily scrutinized and thoroughly understood. No longer will the false glare of military glory intercept the true view of the bearing of the enormous organization which War presupposes on national prosperity.

There are two causes which will help to enforce this sort of instruction. One is the constantly-increasing scale on which military and naval preparations are, in most of the leading States of the world, being conducted, with an activity of competition to which no pacific industry presents a parallel. The other is the operation of the pacific tendencies now being reviewed, which, by making Wars less frequent, and shorter in duration, brings into sharper contrast the enormous expenditure of all sorts on War, entailed in times of Peace, with the product of the expenditure, reaped in the brief and more and more rarely-recurrent time of actual War.

It would not be relevant to the present inquiry into the effect of popular education on the prospects of permanent Peace, to examine in detail the sort of lessons on the economic loss entailed by War which an increased and deepened study of such subjects is likely to spread abroad on every side. The main facts are gathered up in the obvious phenomena that, during the time of the most unruffled Peace in Europe, some millions of men, selected from the healthiest part of the population of the different countries, and at the maturest period of human life, not only are withdrawn from all productive occupations, but luxuriously, not to say extravagantly, subsist upon, and thereby divert to their own support, the productive labor of a proportionate number of other persons. This, however, only represents a single item in the cost of modern War. New ships, new artillery, new fire-arms, new projectiles and engineering apparatus, are daily displacing the old; and no State believes it can afford to be outdone in its speed to adopt, at any expense, in the process of complete reconstruction of its armament, an invention which at any moment may be accidentally discovered by another State.

<small>Obvious evils of military establishments.</small>

This Governmental activity in the department of warlike preparation is incessantly going on, and necessarily creates a factitious demand for a certain sort of manufacturing skill and device which the best scientific energy of the day finds it well worth its while to satisfy, even at the price of withdrawing itself from remunerative fields of ordinary industrial activity. Thus the latest scientific researches, the finest artistic contrivances, the most exact mechanical appliances are, at the first moment of their discovery, pressed into the service of War. It need not be pointed out how great a consumption of precious material, and diversion of ingenuity and labor, all this involves, when it is multiplied over so many countries, and has to be repeated over again so many times in such interminable succession.

<small>Scientific and mechanical knowledge diverted to military purposes.</small>

There is, again, the expense and loss entailed by the mere extravagance of War; by the necessity of borrowing money, under the pressure of a sudden emergency, in any market and at any price; by the speed with

<small>Waste of national wealth.</small>

which it has to be obtained, and by the small security that can ever be afforded for even ordinary prudence or economy in its distribution. In addition to all these sources of expense, incurred either in time of profound Peace or in time of War, there are special, but often enormous, expenses incurred through the momentary alarm produced by an apprehension of War. Alarms of this sort, sometimes so slight as scarcely to deserve the name, are constantly going on; and even an accidental turn in the style of a diplomatic correspondence, or a local political movement, or even a manifestation of mere political excitement in some known centre of disorder, are enough to call for the presence of a small fleet of iron-clads, or the mobilization of a considerable body of troops. This involves immense expense, and often enough no small part of the cost of an actual War is incurred simply by the expectation of one.

It must be remembered that this cost of War is being, and

War an obstacle to schemes of Social Reformers. will be increasingly, studied and appreciated, at a time when questions respecting the growth and distribution of national wealth and the causes of pauperism are becoming of the most absorbing interest, and felt to be of the most urgent importance. Two objects are being kept steadily in view, not only by theoretical reformers, but by the constantly growing number of thoughtful persons who are concerning themselves in the welfare of the laboring classes in all European countries. One of these objects is the reduction, or even (if possible) the extinction, of pauperism. The other is the elevation of the condition of the laborer by raising his wages and shortening his hours of work. These two objects are drawing more and more attention to themselves; and it would seem as if one of the earliest fruits of a systematic extension of popular education would be shown in a spirited and unanimous resolution to grapple with the most obvious and remediable of the causes of destitution, and to raise the lower class of laborers in the scale of cultivation.

One of the most formidable obstacles to all such schemes at once presents itself in the recurrent fact of War, and in the assiduous and universal preparations for it. Even the States which, like Germany, conceive themselves unable to dispense with their gigantic armaments confessedly groan under the economic burden, and almost regret the victories which have imposed new military responsibilities upon them.

> "Mortgaged States their grandsires' wreaths regret,—
> From age to age in everlasting debt."

The undoubted tendency at present, in the central States of Europe, is toward an enlargement, and not a contraction, of military resources, and there does not appear to be any limit at which this ceaseless production and reproduction of soldiers must necessarily stop short. It is plain, then, that the conflict between what are called military exigencies and the demands for a better economical condition, as above alluded to, is every day becoming more momentous, and must some day assume so monstrous a form as either to be no longer tolerated, or to be tolerated only at the price of the inanition of what are now the most powerful States.

Anyway, the growth and diffusion of knowledge cannot permit the true character of the economic ruin involved in the vast preparations which modern War seems to entail, to be kept out of sight. It must be, and will be, sifted to the bottom, deeply pondered upon, and publicly discussed, in all circles, great and small. It is quite impossible to predict what may be the final results of a conviction on this subject, wrought into the deepest consciousness, and expressed in the common speech, of the bulk of the populations of all European countries. Certainly, it cannot be predicted, in view of these facts, that War is, and must be, eternal.

(2.) Akin to the influence of education and of popular knowledge directed to the economic anomalies resulting from War, and co-operating with this influence, is the power of the newspaper press in modern times. This power might seem almost too light and superficial to deserve the prominent place here accorded to it. But as a vehicle of the truth about War, the power of the press ranks among the very highest.

<small>War correspondence of Daily Papers.</small>

It has been the instinctive policy of those who are concerned in sustaining the war spirit, and obtaining ever new resources to satisfy the exhaustless cravings of a military system, to gloss over and hide out of sight the real evils of War, and to surround all that concerns it with a dazzling radiance of so-called "glory." This has been effected in a multitude of ways, some of them consciously, and others of them unconsciously, pursued. The gay dress of soldiers, the flying colors, the caparisoned horses, the orderly processions and movements, the very sound of the artillery turned to festive uses, are all ingenious devices, more or less consciously resorted to, for the purpose of imparting a glamour of fascination to the calling of a soldier. For the same purpose, military distinction and preferment is usually made to have an advantage over civil honors; and in almost all European States the most illustrious potentates, by their personal pretensions to the highest military rank, do their utmost to impart to this rank dignity of the most exalted kind. In the same way, heraldry, and even literature and the popular speech, are laid under tribute, or rather corrupted to sinister uses, by being tempted to impart to all the incidents of War, and to the occupation of a soldier, a romantic lustre, and even a grandeur, which no other facts or pursuits are allowed to carry with them.

<small>War spirit fostered by military splendor.</small>

The direct influence, however, of the extraordinary powers of rapid, facile, accurate, and extensive communication which the modern newspaper press possesses and habitually exerts, must result in making every one see War and battles just as they are, and picture to themselves all the circumstances and incidents of every stage of a campaign, divested of all the adventitious drapery wherewith the seductive language of romance and the artful machinations of Government officials have succeeded in investing it. The newspaper press in England and the United States, and to an increasing extent in Continental countries, involves an elaborate mechanism, having wide ramifications everywhere, and supported by a keen spirit of competition and honorable *esprit de corps*. The result was signally witnessed in the War of 1870 between France and Germany, and still more in the War of 1877–'78 between Russia and Turkey. Special correspondents of superior intelligence and tried capacity, representing each of the leading English daily papers, accompanied the staff of both the opposed armies—as they were treated on the most honorable and even friendly and familiar footing by the officers on each side, and every opportunity was afforded them for making themselves masters of all the events as they happened, and rapidly transmitting their communications—often by a special service—homeward.

The result was that, for thousands upon thousands of readers in the most tranquil, though industrially active, towns, and even in the most sequestered villages, the whole story of the conflict, as it raged from day to day, was told with almost unerring accuracy and clearness, by a chosen body of eye-witnesses, in amicable competition with one another. Not only the actual battle, but the preparations and the waiting for it, the quickened march, the camp life, the mode of intercourse with invaded villagers and towns-people, the very conversation and moral tone of the soldier on either side at each turn of the campaign, were made to live before men's eyes in such pomp and circumstance as literary skill could impart to them.

Horrors of War revealed by newspaper correspondents.

What the story was, and what a ghastly contrast it presented to the idealized nobility of War, many will recall with shuddering. There was a picture of men chosen, often out of pure and honorable homes, and consecrated to brutal practices, and such forms of (perhaps) mitigated savagery as man is compelled to put on when he is taught it is his duty first to destroy, and only secondarily to save alive. No doubt the order, the precision, the very comprehensiveness of military action did much, as it always does, to give dignity, and even lustre, to barbarities exercised on defenceless towns-people, erring on the side of patriotism, or making honest mistakes as to their technical duties in respect of either their own Government or an invading Army. But the individual life, given to rapine, and more and more habituated to dispense with the most ordinary moral obligations; reckless of all claims but those of so-called military necessity; blunted and hardened against the commonest sensibilities, and merging all the finer responsibilites of humanity in the one overbearing duty of military obedience — all this was brought into clear relief by the searching eye of the Special Correspondent; and it was generally felt and believed that, if it be true that self-sacrifice, patriotism, and military skill form one side of War, it is also true that individual demoralization, and the suspense of all customary moral obligation, form the other side.

Of course this picture is not here recurred to for the purpose of branding one side in certain special Wars with infamy rather than the other, or even of doing any dishonor to the undoubted courage, the endurance, and even the forbearance of the mass of the men and officers engaged on both sides. These qualities were conspicuous enough, and have everywhere had justice done them. But what the daily memoirs from the seat of War brought out was, that the ordinary result of War, as it proceeded, was for passions to become roused on both sides with ever growing intensity; for the legal restrictions on the exercise of the extreme (so-called) Rights of War to become increasingly disregarded; for the gentle to become harsh, the harsh brutal;

and for all the most attractive and ennobling features of civilized humanity to fail to be recognized.

This influence of the Daily Press in laying bare the truth about War is, of course, supported by more permanent literature, of which in this aspect the fictions of M.M. Erckmann-Chatrian are remarkable specimens. The true life of the soldier in times of Peace and of War, and his experiences and conduct before, during, and after battle, are growing to be just as essential a part of the conception of warfare as the flag, the uniform, and the roar of artillery. Here, then, again, as with the other signs of a new era previously adverted to, it is quite impossible to predict how far this improved knowledge may operate in breeding a wholly novel aversion to War. Nor is it saying too much to allege that those who have labored so much to make the occupation of War seem attractive and glorious have been truly wise in their generation; because, if once the popular imagination, aided by common language, took a new turn, and regarded the occupation of a soldier as one so morally difficult as to be unfit for any men but the very best, and, even in their case, to be so surrounded with special temptations of the worst sort as to afford occasion for unremitting anxiety and watchfulness, large standing armies would become an impossibility, and the area of War would soon be reduced to insignificance.

Knowledge of War derived from literature.

(3.) A further ground for resisting the presumption that War must ever, hereafter as heretofore, be looked upon as a permanent necessity, is discoverable in the constitutional changes, resting upon what are called liberal political principles, which have been operating to so large an extent of late years in nearly every European State. These changes have manifested themselves under a variety of forms, but there are certain general features in them which are conspicuous everywhere. Such are, for instance, the responsi-

Spread of liberalism in Europe.

bility of the Executive Authority to the Legislative Authority, and of the Legislative Authority to the people; the creation of a broad basis of representation, by which the claims, sentiments, and desires of every class of the people will secure attention at the hands of the Legislative Assemblies; and the enforcement of doctrines, somewhat vague in terms, but forcible enough in practical cogency, to the effect that Government is to be conducted in the interests of the whole people, and not of any fractional part of it; that personal liberty is to be respected and hedged round with adequate guarantees; that taxation and representation are to be coextensive; and that the rights of free public meeting, free discussion, and a free press are to be jealously guarded against legal or executive encroachments.

Perhaps there is not a single country where, as yet, all these requirements can be said to be satisfactorily attained, though the constitutions of England, the United States, the Swiss Confederation, and the Kingdoms of Belgium and Holland approach nearest to the ideal type; while France, Italy, Germany, and Austria are constantly approaching nearer, and Spain, and even Russia, are making intermittent and tentative, but distinct, movements in the same direction. On the other hand, there are abundant indications, in almost every country, that the moderate constitutional programme above sketched out is by no means the limit of the aspirations of large classes of persons in each country. There are those who seek and work for an entire reconstruction of the political and social institutions around them, and who hold that the past is too rotten and discredited to afford a worthy structure for building upon in the future. These persons admit, of course, of endless subdivisions among themselves, some of them advocating doctrines only slightly removed from anarchy, others being only a little more pronounced than their sober "constitutional" brethren in calling for systematic and comprehensive reforms. It is especially noticeable, however, that the reformers of various grades in different countries are, for the most part, in close sympathy with one another, are generally desirous of overcoming the narrow prejudices which are often mistaken for patriotism, are sincerely eager to assimilate the better institutions of other countries, and are eminently favorable to every form of political and commercial union between their own States, and States in the enjoyment of more advanced institutions than those at home.

The bearing of these unquestionable facts on the tendency to War in modern society is obvious enough. The mere fact that it is impossible for a modern civilized State to go to War, or at least to maintain a War, unless the Government can so far conciliate a popularly-constituted Assembly as to procure the necessary supplies, has the effect of launching the vital topic of how the War arose into the field of public discussion of the most serious and responsible kind, and also of making every War, in reality as well as in form, to be waged by the whole people, acting through their freely elected representatives, and not by the Government alone. These two facts cannot but have a most decisive influence on the frequency and on the duration of Wars, though the character of the influence may undoubtedly for a time be somewhat ambiguous. It is no doubt true that where a Government can shift its responsibility on to a large political Assembly, in which its own influence is at once concealed and overwhelming, it may be more ready to engage in a hazardous War than where itself must bear the whole onus of responsibility from first to last. It is also true that the War-fever can be very easily roused in a country, and in no way can the rhetoric of daily journals and platform orators be turned to more successful and pernicious use than in that of creating a maddening fanaticism for War. A partially civilized people is perhaps quite as warlike as the most bellicose of Governments.*

Though the passion for War is easily stirred in a nation, yet—

---

* The following remarks of the Duke of Argyle may here be appositely

But—what is alone relevant here—though the influence of an era of constitutional Government and liberal policy is likely to be, for a time, ambiguous, yet its weight must at last be felt far more against War than for it, and some day may prove fatal to its continued existence. All the forces of civilization tend to draw together the populations of different countries, to make them eager for each other's welfare and happiness, sympathetic for each other's sufferings, disposed to co-operate in each other's schemes. The result must be that it will become increasingly difficult for interested persons to crush the pacific spirit, which will increasingly assert itself throughout each population, and to fan to the necessary heat the flame of warlike enthusiasm. The proposition to fight will seem more and more unnatural, irrational, and impious, and the only Government which can maintain its ground will be the one which has a character

Constitutional Government must ultimately tend to Peace.

---

quoted: "It is always in the power of any Executive Government to get the country into a position out of which it cannot escape without fighting. This is the terrible privilege of what, in the language of our Constitution, is called the Prerogative. It is, in reality, the privilege of every Executive, whether of monarchial or of popular origin. I am not one of those who are of opinion that it could be lodged elsewhere with advantage, or even with any safety. The majorities which support a strong Government in power are invariably more reckless than the Ministry. In this Eastern Question, wrong and injurious as I think their policy has been, it has been wise and moderate as compared with the language of many of its supporters in both Houses of Parliament. I have too vivid a recollection of the difficulty which was experienced by the Cabinet of Lord Aberdeen in moderating within reasonable bounds the excitement of the country, to place the smallest confidence in any scheme for checking, through some popular agency, the action of the responsible advisers of the Crown. They are always, after all, through a process of 'natural selection,' the ablest men of the party to which they belong. Except under very rare conditions, they are more disposed, and are more able, to look all round them than any other body in the State."—*The Eastern Question, from* 1856 *to* 1878, *and to the Second Afghan War.* By the Duke of Argyle. Vol. ii. p. 519.

for peacefulness. The public discussion, to which every War must hereafter be subjected, will bring to the front all economic aspects of War which have previously been dilated upon; while free speech also gives an opportunity for an appeal to the national conscience of a kind to which the Wars which lived, breathed, and had their being in the cabinets of statesmen and diplomatists were wholly strangers.

(4.) A yet further reason for taking a sanguine view as to the possible extinction of War may be found in the influence, at the present day, of a variety of diverse philosophical schemes and religious ideas. Of course the degree in which abstract philosophical notions affect practical politics is difficult *Recent philosophy antagonis-* at any moment to assign, and it is still more diffi- *tic to War.* cult to prophesy how far and at what rate even the best accepted theories may operate in the future. But it is undeniable that the philosophical persuasion of the few in one generation becomes the common belief of the second generation, and the axiom, if not the truism, of the third.

There are three streams of philosophical thought, entirely dis- *Three lead-* tinct from each other, and having a totally inde- *ing schools.* pendent origin, which may be said to represent the latest and most powerful products of the German, the French, and the English mind. The German stream starts from the double fountain of Kant and Hegel; the French stream starts in, and seems to be absorbed by the philosophy, ethical and political, of Auguste Comte; the English stream flows from the utilitarian philosophy of Bentham, based upon that of Locke and Hobbes, and developed by James Mill and his son, the late John Stuart Mill. It is by no means asserted here that this compendious summary of recent philosophical history does any more than recall the most superficial and obvious phenomena, and still less that the classification of the several schemes of philosophic thought here adverted to is true and sufficient, merely because it happens conveniently to gather up under a few heads a number of contemporary tendencies. For the present purpose the superficiality of the description is part of its value, if it has any, and questions of the accuracy of the arrangement, and of the inherent truth of one or another philosophical system, are irrelevant. What is important to notice is that every one of the leading thinkers and original founders of these several schools— as Kant, Hegel, Comte, Bentham, and the two Mills—devoted a prominent place in his system to the moral duties arising from International relations, and sketched out, with greater or less distinctness and minuteness, the lineaments of a great international Society, of which permanent Peace should be the essential basis and most beneficent feature. Each of them treated of politics as the climax of ethics, and International politics as the sublimest department of general politics. Each of them conceived man as gifted with a nature which can only find its adequate development and satisfaction in reciprocal intercourse, extending over the widest field, and directed to purposes conterminous with man's habitations on the face of the earth.

These thinkers differed much from one another, and some of them had little in common with any of the rest. The English Utilitarians, especially, exhibited the most striking opposition, or even antagonism, at almost every point, to the metaphysical spirit of Kant and Hegel, and to the intensely moralizing and systematizing habits of Comte. But in respect of the claims of a true international morality, of the possibility of constructing a true Society of States, of the conception of a human intercourse overstepping the limits of any purely national society, and which would be wholly incompatible with the interruptions of War—they were absolutely at one. Whatever the general influence of these writers may have been, and may yet be, the weight of that influence is likely to be greatest where it is all in the same direction, and this is against War, and in favor of lasting Peace. As

Pacific tendency common to different schools of thought.

this influence filters down to larger classes of society, it is not possible to assign a limit to the practical consequences which may ensue from it. It is the philosophers who teach the school-masters, and the school-masters who educate the public writers and politicians.

(5.) With respect to the influence of religious ideas, it is more difficult to speak with confidence, because it may truly be said that religion in Europe has undergone no remarkable transformation of late years, and that the past experience of professed Christianity certainly shows it to be compatible with every phase of the warlike spirit, and, indeed, to afford the occasion, or the pretence, for the bitterest of all Wars. Nevertheless, it will not be denied, at any rate by professed Christians, that it is mainly due to Christianity and its ecclesiastical institutions that those modifications have been introduced into the practice of War which nobly distinguish the Wars waged by European States—at least as among themselves—from the Wars waged among more backward communities. Mr. Ward, in his "Origin and History of the Law of Nations," has described in glowing terms the services which the organization of the Christian Church rendered in the Middle Ages to the cause of humanity, in taming the ferocity of warriors, protecting prisoners of War, and enforcing the observance of treaties. Indeed, the efforts and Institutions of the Christian Church are always, and properly, ranked among the most notable of the sources of the Modern Law of Nations.

Religion antagonistic to War.

Christianity has modified the character of War.

It also must be confessed that the essential doctrines and principles of Christianity, as held by almost every Christian sect, tend far more to draw men and nations together than to dissociate them, though no doubt a sad experience has shown that there is also a centrifugal tendency, due to minute variations of belief or practice. But

Christian principles must ultimately tend to Peace.

professed Christians, at least, must hold that, as time goes on, the essentially pacific principles of their religion must dominate over, and finally expel, the accidental, bellicose, and separative accretions to it, and that every genuine religious effort for good of any sort, whether private or public, makes the hour of this victory nearer at hand.

The position taken up by the Friends, or Quakers, though hard to adapt to the actual exigencies of modern States, cannot be charged with being an illogical consequence of the theory that the populations and Governments of Christian countries are, what they call themselves, Christian, and bound to save each other's lives, even at the sacrifice of their own, and not to destroy them. The truth is that the populations and Governments are the reverse of what they call themselves, and a truly Christian population and Government have yet to be seen—if, indeed, they ever can be seen. But, so far as people believe in the ultimate, and not indefinitely remote, triumph of Christian principles, and also hold that such a triumph cannot be reconciled with the permanence of War, to that extent must it become a fixed conviction that War must some day cease. There are, no doubt, at the present moment large classes of persons to be found who, simply on such religious grounds as these, pertinaciously uphold this belief, and, in fact, indignantly resent the opposite of it. If these classes of persons grow in numbers and influence—as there is every sign they will—it may be found that—while economists are hesitating, oppressed men and women are impotently complaining, statesmen are debating and faltering—another War has already become impossible, simply because a dominant section of European society in all countries have unanimously declared that War is morally wrong, and, therefore, no longer defensible.

Before quitting the subject of the relation of Christianity to War, it is necessary to notice certain strange vagaries of religious opinion in reference to War, which owe their existence to causes wholly independent of the religious character of those who profess them, but which undoubtedly derive no small weight and influence from that religious character.

It is needless to point out that the policy of the Roman Cath-
<small>Attitude of the Roman Catholic Church toward War.</small> olic Church on the Continent at the present day, when it no longer has that undisputed predominance which in the Middle Ages made it free to give reins to its unsuppressed Christian instincts, is of so unaccountable and incalculable a nature that it may be expected, in the case of a warlike policy, to throw its sympathies on the side of Peace or of War, and on one side or another of the struggle, without reference to any considerations other than those which actuate the most keenly diplomatic secular government.

The Established Church of England occupies a very different
<small>Sympathy with the War spirit among the English clergy.</small> position; and yet, from causes peculiar to itself, and in some measure the product of the history of the Christian Church, its most eminent authorities are often found to be as eager in favor of prosecuting a war as the leaders of the Government who advocate it; and generally, in discussing the fortunes of a War, or the prospects of Peace, it will be found that, whereas with Non-conformists an almost overwhelming presumption is always admitted in favor of any policy which will terminate hostilities, or prevent them, in the case of ordinary clergymen the prospects of prolonged War are not more morally unattractive than those of any other assigned political condition.

In proof of some of these statements it may be noted that, in spite of the presence of the Bishops in the House of Lords, a public remonstrance on the part of any one of them against entering on War from some regard to the general interests of religion and humanity is, it is believed, unknown. In the case of the China War of 1857, there were only four bishops who sided with the majority against Lord Palmerston's Government, which had initiated as reckless and needless a War as England had ever committed itself to. Some of the most eminent bishops of the present day, as the Bishop of Gloucester (Ellicott) and the Bishop of Peterborough (Magee), have, on well-known occasions, gone out of their way to protest against the intrusive rhetoric of philanthropic advocates of Peace, and to call especial attention to the virtues and excellences incident to War and to the military profession. The late Professor Charles Kingsley, full of enthusiasm at the time of the Crimean War for the self-denying spirit and energy which it revealed, as still existing in aristocratic, and even in commercial, circles of society, in one passage of a playful kind ranks "peace-mongers" with the most odious of mankind. The late Professor Mozley, of Oxford, in a remarkable lecture which attracted great attention—and which for its logical and comprehensive survey of the subject deserved that attention—entered upon an elaborate defence of War on purely Christian grounds. He intimated that the scheme of Christianity distinctly contemplated War as an essential remedial agency in the progress of society; that the existence of War was a necessary complement to the existence of government and organized society; and that in the struggle of War the human conscience was destined to find the same healthy nutriment as it discovers in the spectacle of a Court of Justice distributing, with authority delegated from on High, such penalties as human skill and wisdom, with all their imperfections, unhesitatingly assign.

The causes of this state of mind must be briefly examined, or else the arguments of such men would be fatal to much of the reasoning which has been here conducted. In the first place, the Church of England, especially in reference to the institution of the Episcopate, is not only a State Church, but is a State Church the traditions of which have bound it up in a peculiar and personal connection with the Monarchy, and by means of a tie which owes much of

Relation of the Church to the State favors a taste for War.

its closeness and familiarity to the fact of past and common adversities, struggles, failures, successes, and, unfortunately, also animosities. The Church of England, in fact, so far as it is an Established Church, is thus not only bound by the closest ties to the State, but it is bound to the State on what may be called its side of pugnacity, and of ostentatious display of power. For the average Churchman, the State means restrictions on the advances of non-conformity, and a display of magnificence, in all the outward signs of which the Church, and the Church alone, has a prominent share.

That the ordinary temper of Churchmen is conservative rather than radical, and that the Bishops in the House of Lords, as a body, have invariably resisted every reform which has been finally accepted by the whole country, are only parts of this phenomenon. The inherent temptation of Churchmen is to prefer order and quiet to right. The pursuit of right, as such, is always a restless search; it may lead to strange companionships; it may land the seeker in circumstances of temporary isolation; it may even, for many anxious moments, seem to point in the direction of anarchy or disorder. But the seeker knows that Right implies at length the highest order; and that to rest anywhere short of obtaining the object of the search is to live, or rather slumber, in a dream-land of shadows, which may at any moment flee away, and leave him homeless and heartless.

Thus, mentally, morally, and historically, the English Churchman starts with a presumption in favor of what is called strong government, both at home and abroad. And if he likes strong government — which, by-the-way, is often the weakest of all governments — he must needs see it visibly before him in order to believe in it. But it is in War, more than in any other condition, that the State caparisons itself with a sort of festal garment which can be seen of all men. In police, in taxation, even in the homely struggles of common Parliamentary life, political existence is tamely and obscurely conducted, and almost shrinks out of sight altogether. But when the State goes to War, the ear, the eye, the heart, not to say the passions, of all men and women are roused into activity, and the State is seen to be, for a moment, a real and living organ of the national life. Those who need the reassurance of its presence for their own security are never more at rest than in such a moment as this; for whatever purpose the War is waged, or however it is conducted, there are those who will cling to it simply because, apart from War, the State seems, for them, to vanish altogether. Thus their love of War is a token of loyalty and patriotism. Those who abstractedly declaim in favor of Peace are traitors, or cosmopolitan "patriots," "loving every country but their own."

But, apart from the special circumstances of the Church of England, there is much in Christianity itself and its history which affords an excuse for much confused sentiment on the subject of War. The Christian dispensation was the child and logical outcome of the Jewish; and the history of Judaism, as detailed in the Old Testament, resembles the history of every other people struggling out of barbarism into civilization, and obtaining a national life for itself, in being largely occupied with the story of War. Thus, military analogies, metaphors, anecdotes, images, and heroes crowded on the minds of the early Christian writers, and competed with their thoughts of a kingdom which was not of this world, and which was to be governed by the new principle that he who takes the sword shall perish with the sword.

Warlike temper of Judaism, and of Church History.

Christian history soon became merged in the history of the European world; and while Christianity did much to introduce Peace into War, the secular world around it did far more to introduce War into the kingdom of Peace. Nevertheless, the combined influence of two such strong passions as military ardor and religious zeal induced the Christian Church not only to recognize War as a salutary and necessary instrument, but to propagate doctrines which extolled "a just War" with all the fanatical credulity with which the Mohammedan leader applauded an expedition against the infidel.

It is also true that there are real vices peculiar to a time of Peace, and to persons engaged in the occupations of Peace, which disappear in time of War, and are the reverse of the vices of those engaged in War.

There are military virtues, and vices peculiar to times of Peace.

There are also real virtues peculiar to a time of War, to a nation at War, and to the soldiers who personally engage in War. It is not in the least necessary to cloak over the selfishness, the apathy, the want of patriotism, the commercial greed, the cowardice, the unsocial instincts, the depression of national self-consciousness, which are besetting temptations at all times to men and nations, in order to denounce the notion that War is the only possible issue from them. Nor is it necessary to deny the real magnificence of a great nation, teeming through its length and breadth with a new-formed enthusiasm —when the enthusiasm is genuine, and something other than a brutal and fitful fever for fight—and going forth, in an unaccustomed outburst of faith and hope, to perils and sufferings only dimly imagined, but none the less cheerfully contemplated, because a belief in right and justice occupies the whole heaven; nor to ignore the obscure virtues and graces of the humblest soldier who simply does his work because it is before him to do, and who asks no other reward than that he may be held one day in indiscriminate remembrance with others who died in obedience to their country's laws. There need be no exaggerations on one side or the other. The issue is far too momentous to admit of any other treatment than one based on the most severe and exact truth. The Christian minister must reply to the question whether the Christian Church is too feeble, too poorly furnished with a Divine instrumentality, too much of an anachronism for the needs of modern society, to reform society without relying on the co-operation of War.

It is one thing to say that, in the mysterious course of the government of the world, War has been a necessary agent in the evolution of national life, and in preserving distinction between the nations of the earth. It is quite another thing to say that War is to be consciously consecrated by Christian people as an everlasting agent for advancing the Kingdom of Heaven. It is true that nations have struggled upward by the help of atrocious institutions and practices, which can only be tolerated in the retrospect by remembering that they were the only substitutes for something worse. But because trial by battle, the ordeal, private wars, cruel sports, inhuman punishments, and duelling have all had their part in building up the nations of Europe, this is no argument for prolonging their existence into a time when their work is done, and when the microscopic good some of them might yet achieve would be out of all proportion to the terrible blight which the revival of any of them would cast upon the whole field of human affairs.

The good wrought by War no ground for perpetuating it.

The time has not yet come when even the Christian vision is cleansed enough to look upon War as it is, and as dissociated from one and another of the petty gains of a moral kind which it seems to bring with it. But, while the Church of England, or rather a considerable portion of its ministers, is, for the reasons above noted, still in the rear-guard, the strong and united voice of those to whom the Christian life is in verity the best and the only life is giving no uncertain sound. In quarters not to be despised for their influence, the disposition for War is already being classed with the habit of drunkenness and the taste for blood.

(6.) If further proof were needed of a change coming over the spirit of European life and thought in reference to War, which may have issues in the future to which no limit can be assigned, it would suffice to refer to the extraordinary development of International as-

Pacific effect of International association.

sociation and co-operation for all sorts of purposes, the most solemn and the most trivial, of which the present age is a witness. This development is, no doubt, to a great extent a direct consequence of some of the other circumstances of modern society just enumerated, and, therefore, might be held to be not fairly adducible as a distinct ground for faith in the advent of a new order of ideas inimical to War. But this growing habit of International co-operation, whatever its causes, is a phenomenon deserving attention on its own account, and one which every day is manifesting itself in more various and noticeable forms.

There is scarcely a portion of the whole field of Government Administration, scientific research, religious and philanthropic effort, or economical enterprise, in which, by means of so-called "International" conventions, congresses, conferences, associations, leagues, societies, or occasional exhibitions, the citizens of all civilized States are not learning to organize themselves, in exactly the same fashion in which the inhabitants of each country originally trained themselves, and were trained, to harmonize their erratic pursuits and desires, and submit to a common Government. The process of combination is likely, indeed, to be more rapidly effected as between the citizens of different States than, in primitive times, between the inhabitants of the same country seeking to organize themselves as a State, inasmuch as culture has now explained the benefits of union, and long habits of national existence have accustomed all persons to the discipline which union imposes. On the other hand, there is in International efforts at union the absence of any central force, such as exists in a community forming itself into a State, by which desultory efforts are made continuous, recalcitrant members compelled into obedience, and stability insured for all deliberately concerted schemes. This want can only be supplied by a higher spirit of moral self-abnegation, and a greater consecration of mind and purpose to the achievement of complete International union.

How far this work will proceed, and how rapidly, can only be a matter of conjecture, and opinions in respect of it will differ widely. But there can be no doubt that such projects for reducing national distinctions to the smallest point are becoming more and more conspicuous, and are assuming a very practical shape, while their general tendency to promote lasting Peace is unquestionable.

From the review of some of the phenomena of modern society as exhibited among the States of Europe, it must at least be gathered that it is not an irrational faith to hold that some day War between civilized States must become obsolete, and that there are sufficient novel indications, even at the present day, to justify the hope that, in spite of the most glaring symptoms to the contrary, the day may not be very remote. Of course, it is not here for a moment pretended that there are no reasons for fearing that War may yet have a long tenure of existence before it; or that a solution can be given off-hand to all the difficult problems which may be suggested as likely to arise when the differences of States have to be settled otherwise than by War; or, still less, that any one State can, at the present moment, righteously or expediently resolve never to go to war again. All these matters, deserving as they are of the most serious attention in the proper place, are irrelevant here. The only purpose in this place is to establish the very moderate proposition that the object of hastening the day when War shall become extinct is a rational and legitimate end (among others) for the reformer of International Law; and as every writer on International Law becomes, often unconsciously, a reformer of it, then every International Lawyer and Law Student is bound to comprehend this object of ultimately securing permanent Peace among the purposes he has in view.

Permanent Peace a rational aim for International lawyers.

CHAPTER II.

OF SOME OF THE CAUSES OF MODERN EUROPEAN WARS.

AN account of the causes of War might be held properly to include a research into a large portion of human history, accompanied by some curious processes of psychological analysis. The word "cause," however, is one of those words which must await its explanation from the surrounding subject-matter, as, in itself, it implies any one of a long train or large assemblage of antecedents, which, with or without the presence of other favoring causes, and in the absence of counteracting causes, is invariably, and therefore, as it is said, necessarily, followed by a definite consequence, which is spoken of as the "effect" of the cause. Thus, when the word *cause* is used in reference to any event, or class of events, any one of a number of invariable antecedents will satisfy the meaning of the word; and it is of no import how numerous such antecedents are, how complicated they are with one another, or how remote they are in the order of time and sequence from the happening of the event.

<small>Causes of War too numerous and complicated for complete investigation.</small>

Thus an account of the causes of War in Europe, if unlimited by the purpose in hand, might include all such facts as the temper and manners of the tribes which founded the States of Europe, the geographical situation of the territory of those States, all the past relations of the several States to each other, and all the leading events of European history. It might be safely predicted that—the character of the populations being such as it was and is, the territory of the different States being assigned to them as it came to be, the reciprocal relations and general events and ideas being of the kind they have been for the last thousand years and more—the occurrence of occasional Wars must be a certainty, unless some counteracting cause, or assemblage of counteracting causes, intervene to prevent it.

<small>Principles of selection.</small> Interesting as the inquiry might be, it would be quite beside the present purpose to enter upon the investigation, curious rather than profitable, into all the antecedents of the indeterminate class just mentioned, from which modern War results. There are, however, some antecedents which seem to stand apart from the rest, on the ground both of their more general and comprehensive character, and of their being open to the direct influence of International Law. There must, necessarily, be something arbitrary in this process of selection; but, inasmuch as the purpose is to fix attention upon facts which are not so much denied as accidentally overlooked, and not to enforce questionable theories about facts, there is little room for serious differences of opinion. The argument will proceed rather by the collection and arrangement of thoroughly admitted phenomena, and not by hunting out of their ambush facts of obscure and ambiguous import.

<small>The true reason for declaring War seldom alleged.</small> In speaking of the causes of War, an essential distinction has to be made at the outset between the real and the apparent causes of any particular War. It is very seldom that the real ground of a War—that which has brought matters to the state at which War seems the only and inevitable solution—is that which is publicly alleged to be so by the diplomatists and statesmen who are concerned with it. Indeed, these persons, on one side at least, are always interested in glossing over the reasons which seem to have compelled their State to take the final step of declaring War. If the assertions of the diplomatists of a Belligerent State were to be believed, such an event as the occurrence of an unjust or needless War would be impossible. Each War, they say, is waged

either in defence of a threatened right, or in order to avenge and punish a violated right; and the existence of the right, and the fact of actual or apprehended violation, are matters upon which they are prepared to offer evidence to all the world. This evidence may seem more or less cogent to different persons or Governments; but respect for European opinion, and the hope of obtaining sympathy, if not co-operation, are always potent enough to lead to the evidence being prepared as skilfully as possible.

Thus there is almost always an *ex post facto* element in the causes of War as alleged by the contemporary diplomatists of the Belligerent States. It usually happens that on one side, at least, if not on both sides, the resolution to go to War has been long formed and, indeed, matured, a suitable occasion only being waited for; or it may be that it has only been foreseen that a War is probable, or no more than possible, and yet this probability or possibility may involve quite as much preparation as a War actually determined upon, and it will only depend upon very minute accidents whether the occasion for actual War is really held to have arrived or not.

In order, then, to understand the causes of modern War, it will not suffice to rely exclusively upon the despatches of diplomatists and the speeches of responsible statesmen, as illustrated by the abstract doctrines of International Law that no War can be lawfully entered upon, except in defence of an ascertained right, either violated or menaced. This doctrine, valuable as it is, is rather a standard and a limiting rule, to which it has been attempted to make warlike States conform, than an expression of a subsisting practice. The doctrine, no doubt, has considerable influence, and, at least, cuts away the possibility of waging War on palpably unjust grounds, while it obliges statesmen always to shape their public apologies in conformity with the requirements of a legal rule. This is, no doubt, a gain in the direction of substituting legal methods for mere violence, and so deserves every encouragement. But the real causes of modern War are usually far deeper than the assigned ones, and are of a strictly political or moral, and not of a legal character.

It is well known that the established doctrine of International Law is that all States are equal. This is a doctrine which can only be made intelligible by tracing its actual legal consequences, as exhibited, for instance, in the identical rights of the smallest and the largest States to exemption from foreign interference, to the free use of the open sea, to the observance of treaty engagements, to the fair treatment of its citizens when abroad, to the immunity of its ambassadors, and to due ceremonial courtesy and respect.

All States are regarded as legally equal.

The validity of these rights is confessed on all hands, though momentous discussion often arises on two questions: first, whether a particular State claiming its exercise of these rights is, for all purposes, a true sovereign and independent State; and, secondly, whether the admitted right does or does not comprehend certain specific claims, alleged on any particular occasion to be contained in it.

Nevertheless, discussion arises upon claims to equal rights.

The first of these questions is suggested by the various aspects which a State is apt to present, according as it has bound itself temporarily to another State by conventional ties, or has entered into a permanent league with other States; or, as in the case of Hungary and Austria, Prussia and the German Empire, Turkey and Egypt, is associated with another State through anomalous dynastic or constitutional relations. It is also presented in the case of a portion of a State becoming detached from the parent State, whether by successful insurrection or colonization, or, as in the case of Greece and Turkey, Belgium and Holland, by more or less voluntary separation. In all these cases difficult problems are apt to arise as to the condition of the offshoot community, or of the two parties to the separation, while yet the whole proceedings are incomplete; and as to the finality and stability of the new Constitution, when they are alleged to be complete. Thus, in respect of the first of the questions implied in the general axiom that "all States are equal," it is seen that the most complex questions of law and of fact are apt to be involved, and to obstruct, at the outset, the direct application of a rule of law.

In respect of the second question—what is the measure of the rights which the equality carries with it, and what acts are or are not infringements of them—these topics, of course, are matters for fine legal argument; and are likely to give rise to just the same amount of forensic debate, and to remain often as unsettled, as the ordinary legal points which are daily discussed in national Courts of Justice.

Thus the abstract doctrine that "all States are equal" goes a very little way, of itself, in solving the political problems of international life, and preventing the sort of quibbles and evasions which the interpretation of the doctrine itself must needs involve, and which may be, and has been, the fruitful source of overbearing injustice. The difficulties in the way of solving purely legal questions, of the sort above described as arising between different States, are inherently great, and, so far as they directly operate to cause War, will be separately considered lower down. In the mean time they are only referred to here in order to show that a purely legal dogma of an abstract equality cannot take the place of true political equality.

Theoretical equality avails little against practical inequality.

Setting for a time out of account the more antiquated causes of European War—which, however, cannot be held to have, as yet, quite exhausted their efficacy—such as religious differences, disputed dynastic successions, and commercial rivalry, the most familiar cause of recent and threatened War in Europe is the political in-

Political Inequality of States the main cause of modern Wars.

3

equality of the States of Europe, as looked upon in connection with the historical circumstances to which the inequality in the case of any particular State is owing in the past, and with the probable consequences which seem likely to result from it in the future. The meaning of political equality and inequality must here be subjected to a careful analysis.

It is evident that, in one sense, equality between States is im-

Exact equality can never be ascertained or asserted.

possible, or rather that the term, as applied to such complex institutions as States, based as they are partly on material, partly on personal, and wholly on moral ideas, and having relation at once to the past, the present, and the future, is meaningless. There is no conceivable standard by which the equality or the inequality of States can be tested. It is not true that Russia is a greater State than Germany, because of its vaster extent of territory; or Spain than Switzerland or Belgium, because of its more numerous population; or England than Germany or France, because of its greater pecuniary and commercial resources; or Germany than France, England, or Italy, because of what would seem to be, at the present moment, its incontestable military supremacy.

It is customary, indeed, to speak of first, second, or third rate

Relative power of States fluctuates with their internal condition.

powers, and to speak of a State passing from a higher to a lower, and from a lower to a higher, position in the scale. No doubt there is before men's minds an impalpable measuring-rod, by which the moral and material elevation of States is habitually measured, and in accordance with the register of which they are said to be equal or unequal. A number of ingredients, such as population, extent of territory, commercial advantages, wealth, military strength for defensive and offensive purposes, diplomatic resources and skill, historical antecedents, moral reputation, and actual political influence, must be weighed together and looked at in relation to each other in order to ascertain the true place any given State will be held to occupy in the scale of States;

and, in proportion to the difficulty of correctly calculating the value of these different, delicate, and shifting elements, it is obvious that the result must be of a very arbitrary and fluctuating kind.

It is evident, then, first, that no State, in any precise political sense, can be said at any given moment to be exactly equal to any other State; and, secondly, that the political relations of States to each other, as measured by the subtle and varying elements above enumerated, are likely to undergo constant and even rapid change. It is in the constant flux and change of these elements, without adequate constitutional provision for recognizing and incorporating them in their constantly modified form, that the main cause of European Wars will be found to exist. It is precisely the same story as that of the growth of a nat'onal society into a true and fully developed State. In this latter region the old forms show extraordinary tenacity of life, and a contest ensues between the exuberant life of the people and the fast and tight leading-strings in which the primitive constitution seeks to confine it. A dilemma is presented in which either the constitution must be modified peaceably, as has generally been the case in England; or violently, as was the case in France in 1789; or the popular life must be suppressed and the nascent State crushed out with it, as in the Asiatic States which have succumbed beneath the weight of military and despotic Governments.

1. Nor is it merely that the elements above enumerated undergo incessant change in all States which have any progressive character at all, but the rate and mode of change is different in different countries. The result is that there arrives a time, by no means the same for all States, at which a sort of antagonism is experienced between what may be called the variable and the fixed elements of national existence. The variable

Wars are caused by: (1) The internal development of any State outgrowing its external relations.

elements are those which have been just described. The fixed elements are territorial boundaries, subsisting political relations with other States, and treaty engagements. When all considerations of mere passion, injustice, or transparent illegality are removed, there remains, as the most permanent cause of War between civilized States, and the main cause of all the European Wars of the present century, the necessity of providing some practical solution for the problem here presented—that is, the problem of adjusting the territorial limits, the political relations, and the ties resulting from the voluntary engagements of States, to the manifold changes, in material condition and inherent physical strength, which every progressive State ceaselessly undergoes.

That this is at least presumedly true will be clear from even a cursory view of the direct connection between great internal constitutional changes of some State or other, and the occurrence of every European War of the last one hundred years, commencing with the Seven Years' War, including the Wars of the French Revolution, and terminating with the War of 1877–'78 between Russia and Turkey. The Seven Years' War was the direct product and expression of the rapid political development of Prussia as a European State. The Wars of the French Revolution, and the Napoleonic Wars which succeeded them, were, of course, the effect, direct and indirect, of the spasm of constitutional change, and of unlimited political aspirations, generated by the events of the Revolution. The Crimean War undoubtedly marked the first step in the internal reconstitution of the Russian Empire, and the assumption by it of a new political vantage-ground in reference to the other States of Europe — an assumption which, though successfully contested for the time, has been, through a fresh War, practically conceded. The internal reconstruction of the provinces which now form the Kingdom of Italy gave occasion to one War. The extraordinary new birth

Instances during last one hundred years.

and reorganization of Germany are directly responsible for three Wars directed by Prussia against Austria, Denmark, and France.

With the single exception of the Wars of the French Revolution and the Napoleonic Wars—an exception which can be easily accounted for—all these Wars were successful in vindicating, sooner or later, for the State, the internal changes of which seem to have led to the War, a superior political position, or in releasing it from fettering obligations by which its progress had, previously to the War, been impeded. It is impossible to question the fact that Prussia owes the eminent political position occupied by herself, and by Germany, to four or five Wars, extending over a century, in spite of her misfortunes in the Napoleonic period. The Kingdom of Italy has been created by War. Russia has gained more than she has lost by War. If quasi-civil Wars are taken into account, it is undoubted that the flourishing Kingdoms of Belgium and Holland, Greece, Switzerland, and the United States, in their reconstituted forms, are all the offspring of successful Wars.

Necessary re-adjustments have been effected by means of these Wars.

These facts certainly raise a presumption that most of the Wars of the last century have been, in one sense of the word, necessary; that is, if no other mode of adjusting formal relationships and conditions of existence to the progressive elements of national life could be discovered, a choice must have been made in all these cases between War and national stagnation or extinction.

So far as recent history can throw any light on the investigation, it appears that one cause of modern European Wars is the struggling effort which a State is induced to make when its internal constitution or material resources are undergoing a rapid, progressive development, disproportionate to the pressure, of one kind and another, which the State suffers at the hands of surrounding States.

This cause is often disguised by the presence of one or other of two different causes, which must be carefully distinguished from it. One of these is the natural resistance which any State makes to novel though almost imperceptible pretensions, not to say aggressions, on the part of surrounding States.

<small>Efforts after natural progress to be distinguished from resistance to aggression, and from Wars of ambition.</small>

The other is the ambition and covetousness of a State which is bent on overtly claiming for itself far more than is legally or morally due to it. The prospect of the necessity of resistance, at an early date, to the pretensions either of a single State or a group of States, whether manifested in silent encroachments or in publicly maintained claims of an unjust sort, will often precipitate the commencement of a struggle from the side of a peaceable and wholly unoffending State.

In some cases, as in the Franco-German War of 1870, it is difficult even for contemporaries to decide to which of the three causes—that is, natural efforts after increased liberty and security proportioned to the growth and the consolidation of the internal resources of one of the Belligerent States, or resistance, by anticipation, to future aggressions, or direct ambition and political acquisitiveness—the War is to be attributed. Nor was it easy to say in the case of that War—though later events have thrown some light on the subject—to what extent each of these different causes was conjoined with the rest in impelling both France and Germany almost simultaneously into War.

Thus, it is one thing to separate the causes of War from each other, in thought, for purposes of analysis, and another to discriminate the actual share which each has taken in bringing about a particular War. For the present purpose, however, which is a practical and not a historical one, it is of less importance to ascertain how many causes are present in the case of any particular War, and in what degree they are mixed with each other, than to enumerate all the possible causes, and to ascertain generally which of them are likely to prove the most lasting or the least remediable.

2. Apart from the special and temporary circumstances affecting the political relations of two States which urge them into War, it always happens, and must happen in the case of European Wars, that the true ground of War can only be understood by conducting a lengthened and exact historical inquiry into the past relations to each other of the two Belligerent States. These relations have not only produced, in the way of direct parentage, the existing relations, for the explanation of which they must needs be adduced, but they have evolved a peculiar class of national sentiments in each State, and have, as it were, imparted to each a special aspect or characteristic moral bearing in regard to the other. The result is that each State has, in respect of every other one, a definite kind and amount of sensibility, shared in both by the citizens and the Government, which is the product of innumerable events in the past, as well as of the reciprocal influences of the national character of the two countries. This sensibility is at once a source and a kind of incubating medium of all the strong feelings of irritation, impatience, rivalry, dislike, malice, revenge, which incite to War and make it popular.

Hereditary jealousies and antipathies between States.

This assertion needs little proof, or it would be easy to establish it in the case of any pair of the civilized States of the world. All other circumstances being equal, the sensibility of England, and English citizens, in respect of any dispute which might present itself between England, on the one hand, and (say) Germany, France, Italy, Russia, Belgium, Switzerland, and the United States, is different for every one of these States. No doubt the mere magnitude and political importance of some of these States, and the insignificance of others, may have something to do with this feeling. But many of these States which seem small are stronger, in some points, than larger ones, through their guaranteed independence or neutrality; and this sensibility survives many alternations of strength and weakness, and various political vicissitudes. Not that it is by any means unchangeable, as is manifested in the improved moral relations subsisting of late years between the French and English people, and the secular oscillations of sentiment which England, France, and Germany respectively undergo in respect of such a country as Russia.

The national sensibility is determined by a variety of independent causes, generally of a somewhat subtle kind, and not always easy to explore and set forth in any particular case. Among these causes are past Wars and their consequences; harsh terms imposed in Treaties of Peace, especially such as involve the alienation of territory; habitual encroachments or political assumptions, venting themselves in chronic diplomatic discourtesy; mere partial quarrels or imbroglios between the cliques of the two States; and still less palpable or intelligible grounds of animosity, such as are implied in mere differences of manners, religion, political institutions, and even language, out of which, however, real misunderstandings are peculiarly apt to grow. On the contrary, an opposite class of causes is apt to counteract the grounds of discord, or, at least, of want of harmony, and to generate permanent sentiments of friendliness. Such counteracting causes are gratitude; the recollection of past alliances and mutual services of all sorts; a sense of common sufferings in the past, or of a common national origin or race; and identity of language, or of religion, or of political institutions.

Reasons for mutual animosity or amity of States.

The above would generally be styled predisposing causes to War or to Peace, and their operation is too obvious to need illustration. There are some States with which it would be next to impossible to make England go to War, quite apart from all political objects or considerations. There are countries between which it has needed all the efforts

War often the direct result.

of the statesmen of both countries, for years, to maintain peace from day to day. These causes, so far as they produce War, are thus often far more than predisposing. They rank with the most direct and potent causes of War, though they are not susceptible of being openly alleged, or of becoming the basis of negotiation. They can only be indirectly met, and gradually reduced in strength, by a long line of efforts, more of a moral than of a political or legal character. Actual War, of course, only inflames and exaggerates them for the future.

These impalpable impulses to War are apt to prevail among some classes of society more than others; and it will often depend upon the political preponderance, at the moment, of the classes which favor War, whether War results or not. It is also obvious that the general tendencies of civilization are in the direction of reducing this class of causes, by making reason take the place of blind animosity, and accustoming the whole national mind habitually to balance the evils of War against the satisfaction of a vague and brutal instinct. On the other hand, the friendlier sentiments are likely to grow in strength, based as they are on true and lasting human relationships, on constantly growing memories of the reciprocal services which States at peace must render each other, and on an advancing and widening conception of the benefits to be obtained from the closest union and co-operation.

<small>These causes of War will become less active as civilization advances.</small>

3. There is another cause of War which, in the present condition of the States of Europe, seems likely, for a time, to attain greater proportions even than heretofore, and to outlive some of the other causes. This is the disposition, on the part of the more powerful States, to intervene, at certain emergencies, in the affairs of the less powerful, whether the occasion is presented within the limits of Europe or elsewhere.

<small>Doctrine of Intervention.</small>

3*

The topic of Intervention, and the legal grounds of it, form an interesting chapter in the history of International Law. The most striking form the doctrine of Intervention has taken is that of the Balance of Power, as it was understood in the sixteenth, seventeenth, and part of the eighteenth century, and according to which a certain relative and existing political situation of the States of Europe was to be definitely guaranteed to each State, and any political assumption or encroachment incompatible with this situation was ground for War to be waged by any or all of the other States.

The Balance of Power.

An exceptional, though very remarkable, manifestation of a tendency to intervention was the Holy Alliance,* which resulted from the Wars of the French Revolution, and in accordance with which certain leading States allied themselves together, with the avowed purpose of making War on any State which should adopt institutions uncongenial to themselves.

The Holy Alliance.

It is well known that a number of distinct influences—political, economical, and philosophical—have of late years been tending to discredit the practice of Intervention in the internal affairs of foreign States. England, especially, from her insular position, and her complicated commercial system, has been prominent in advocating doctrines of so-called "Non-intervention," which present a curious contrast to the intricate foreign policy which has for centuries distinguished her career. Not, indeed, that England has been entirely of one mind on this subject; and political parties differ from one another, at any rate, as to the mode of applying the novel doctrine; while, in actual practice, England has not shrunk from sharing the responsibility of actual Intervention—as in the case of the establishment of the kingdom of Greece, of the principality of

England has recently advocated Non-intervention.

Instances in which England has nevertheless intervened.

---

* See, for a full account of this, Manning's Law of Nations, p. 488 *seq.*

Servia, of the kingdoms of Belgium and Holland, and, pre-eminently, in the case of the maintenance of the integrity of the Turkish Empire.

The doctrine of Non-intervention is further professed as a tenet even by those States which are most habitually tempted to intervene. An apology—often very much labored and tortuous — is always alleged in the diplomatic correspondence which accompanies every occasion of the sort. Each case is treated as exceptional, and as justifying special measures, which must not be turned into a precedent. Either the circumstances are those of the alleged oppression of a nationality, or religious persecution, or a mere succession of brutal outrages, due to a tyrannical or incompetent government, or apprehended danger to neighboring States; and a State representing persons having a common nationality or religious creed with the oppressed, or bound by historical ties of various sorts, conceives itself entitled to interfere in the avowed behalf of humanity or abstract justice, if not of obvious self-interest.

Pretexts for Intervention are found by States which disavow the principle.

Such an occasion has long been pending in the case of the United States and Cuba, and the position is constantly referred to in the Messages of the President to Congress. The condition of the European provinces of the Turkish Empire has also long been such as to invite or compel interference from Russia and Austro-Hungary on one or other of the above grounds. Austria and France have, within the last twenty years, vied with each other in interfering in the internal struggles of Italy; and France, Italy, and Germany have each held themselves, and would again doubtless hold themselves, on one ground or another, entitled to intervene in the case of serious internal discord in Switzerland.

Thus it appears that the indisposition to intervene in the affairs of a foreign State, when a sufficient exigency seems to call for it, is far more nominal than real; and, in fact, the complicated system of International politics, which the settlement of the Treaty of Vienna, as modified by later Treaties (as the Treaty of Paris of 1856, and the Treaty of Berlin of 1878), at once presupposes and substantiates, renders it practically impossible for any State honorably to stand aloof when events are happening which seem likely seriously to impair, to the detriment of other States, or of any single other State, the terms of the existing settlement. By the operation of these treaties Europe has become, for better or worse, a corporate union of States; and it is equally impossible, by any single act, to readjust in a day the written and unwritten terms of the union, and for any particular State to evade the moral and legal responsibilities thereby cast upon it. This "solidarity" of the States of Europe would, if appreciated and acted on to the full, carry with it a cure for the dangers to public peace it undoubtedly conceals. As it is, it exists to the extent needed to create mutual sensitiveness and irritability, and to furnish, ever and anon, plausible excuses for interference; but—as was shown in the various unsuccessful efforts to obtain European concert for the readjustment of the mutual relations of the Turkish provinces in 1876—it does not exist in sufficient strength to insure an effective combination of States, out of which the blessings of orderly government would naturally flow.

Non-intervention made practically impossible by—

complications of European Politics.

Solidarity of States not sufficiently recognized.

The main difficulty connected with Intervention is the following. It may be admitted that there are possibilities of tyrannical usage, barbarous practices, or persistent and hopeless anarchy, out of which the friendly aid of a generous, impartial, and truly disinterested by-stander may be the only way to a deliverance. But two cautions have to be interposed. First, it has to be provided that the aid is accorded at a time and under circumstances which do not in any way prejudge the issue of a struggle yet

Two necessary cautions in admitting Right of Intervention.

undetermined, and which ought, in the interests of the State concerned, to be decided by the real and internal, and not by the factitious and external, elements of victory. The importance of this consideration was signally illustrated in the late insurrection of the Southern States of the American Union, and in the controversy that long hung round the questions whether England had chosen the proper moment for according to the Southern Confederacy the rights of a Belligerent State, and what was the meaning and political significance of recognition for belligerent purposes only.

A second caution in respect of Intervention is, that, admitting the propriety and duty of Intervention in certain extreme crises, it is always open to a State, influential, designing, and unscrupulous, to foster in another State, subject to its moral control, the very condition of things which will, sooner or later, bring about a fit opportunity for its own overt interference. Whether Russia was guilty of this conduct in the case of the late Servian War and the Herzegovinian Insurrection, is of less importance here than the fact that she was constantly reproached with it. It is a danger which is almost inherent in the nature of the doctrine of a right of Intervention in certain emergencies.

4. But, besides the efforts made by progressive States to bring their relations with other, and especially surrounding, States into harmony with their novel requirements, and the occasional acts of armed Intervention which at special junctures powerful States are, for one reason or another, induced to commit themselves to, there is another ground of War which is likely to show considerable persistence in the present condition of the States of Europe. This is the tendency on the part of leading States to form for themselves what are called "systems" of policy, which are designed to extend over a long period of time, and to which

Traditional systems of Foreign policy—

all temporary or partial objects are made to, subordinate themselves.

No doubt it is becoming increasingly difficult for statesmen to preserve an unwavering policy, and to hand it on intact to their successors. The constitutional changes which are rapidly passing over all the European States have for their immediate effect the diffusion of broad political interests over classes of society which have hitherto been forced to stand aloof from them, and have imparted a proportionate stimulus to general and popular political education. The result has been that popularly-constituted legislative Assemblies in the different countries have lately, for the first time, insisted on sharing in discussions on the conduct of International relations, and in assuming a large proportion of the responsibility attaching to International acts. These Assemblies are, of course, largely under the direct control, personal and constitutional, of the eminent statesmen who represent the Executive Authority of the day, and who are more or less deeply imbued — so far as party government admits of unity and consistency of purpose — with the spirit of a traditional national policy.

<small>modified by growing influence of popular assemblies.</small>

This increasingly familiar habit of publicly criticising and calling in question acts of International policy is conspicuous in the recently acquired attitude toward Foreign Affairs of the English House of Commons. Up to a few years ago it was the almost invariable practice in England for all momentous questions, in which diplomatic relations with other countries were involved, to be discussed mainly in the House of Lords, and there only at such times as the Government of the day deliberately selected, or the two party leaders, each well acquainted from experience with the reasons for caution and reserve, if not secrecy, concurred to approve. Nowadays, not only are the representatives of the Government in the House of Commons as

<small>The House of Commons now concerns itself with Foreign affairs.</small>

constantly plied with questions, and as pertinaciously pressed to expound their policy, at any critical stage of International complications, as in the House of Lords; but, even when no urgent occasion exists, debates on nearly abstract questions of International Law and Policy as frequently take place in one House as in the other. The multiplication of commercial treaties, following upon the prevalence of Free-trade doctrines, in the conclusion of which, as bearing on taxation, the popular chamber is held to have an almost exclusive concern, has done much to bring about this change of attitude toward Foreign Affairs; while the general spread of knowledge and education, as well as improved acquaintance with foreign countries, and greater appreciation of their institutions, have contributed to give an impetus to it.

The aggregate result is that the age of what is called secret diplomacy seems to be approaching an end.

Secrecy cannot be preserved in diplomacy.

Whenever a statesman pens a despatch, he knows full well that his every word will, sooner or later, become the subject-matter of vigilant and unsparing criticism at the hands of a crowd of censors. He may be able to support his policy by well-reasoned arguments, but he will not be relieved from the obligation of actually so supporting it. If his arguments fail to be understood, or to carry their due weight, or to rest on premises of expediency or justice which commend themselves to the common judgment of a thronged and promiscuous assembly, he risks, at the least, the loss of that amount of moral and financial support which his schemes demand, and, possibly, political defeat or ignominy.

This is, undoubtedly, the state of things to which the conduct of Foreign relations in the countries of Europe is steadily gravitating. But it has not yet been attained in all countries, and in some the approximation is far less complete than in others. Hence, it cannot be asserted that the era of systems of policy and abstruse traditional schemes of statesmanship has as yet passed away. On the contrary, there are sufficient symptoms that these systems and schemes still subsist in considerable vigor, and may possess a greater longevity in some quarters than is expected.

Systems of policy in the past. There have been curious historical instances of schemes of policy, which are said to have been persisted in by States for a great number of years, and which may serve as illustrations of the schemes here in view. Such were the recommendations said to have been bequeathed by the Emperor Augustus to his successors as to the inexpediency of further extending, in certain directions, the confines of the Roman Empire. A similar persistent scheme of policy, said to be still adhered to, is the programme of aggressive Russian policy contained in the somewhat apocryphal document entitled Peter the Great's Will. But, in fact, a great part of the history of mediæval Europe, on to the eighteenth century, is occupied with the development of very complex and yet decided and deliberately constructed schemes, in which, according to their several proclivities, most of the rising States of Europe took part.*

Origin of such schemes. These schemes were suggested by a variety of considerations, most of them of a kind which would command small sympathy at the present day, and some of them based on institutions which have passed away. Mere national prejudices, rivalries, and apprehensions, or still more coarse and barbarous self-seeking, also entered largely into their composition, or wholly directed their course. Out of such various elements as these proceeded the coalition of the Protestant States in the Thirty Years' War; the successive combinations, first against Spain and then against France; the habitual friendliness and alliance subsisting between States in proportion to their distance from each other, and their mutual jealousy and suspiciousness in proportion to their propinquity.

---

* See Lectures on Diplomacy, by the Rt. Hon. Mountague Bernard.

The special systems of policy which thus emerged blended at times with more general principles, such as the Balance of Power or Religious Uniformity; and at other times were temporarily lost in narrower principles, such as mere Dynastic interests and sympathies. The influence of such facts as common race, language, or traditions, or the recollection of mutual services in the past, for the most part combined to enforce such a systematic policy, though occasionally it conflicted with it.

Anyway, the general result is manifest in the field of modern European politics, in spite of the obstacles, which have been already alluded to, in the way of any far-seeing and consistently maintained scheme of political action. There are certain forces of attraction or repulsion which favor alliances, or easily engender hostile feeling, between different pairs of European States—which are at once the consequence of a long career of persistent policy, and the material which renders it possible. The very breaks, interruptions, or vacillations in such a policy only make the reality of it more conspicuous, by displaying the strength of the common sentiment which supports it.

<small>Systems of policy are still formed and maintained.</small>

It is only since the Crimean War that the abstract possibility of an intimate alliance between France and England for offensive purposes, and in prosecution of a European policy of great moment, has become a familiar idea. The same War witnessed the death-blow of one of the earliest and most enduring principles of policy professed by all Christian States—that of only combining against the infidel, and never with him against one of themselves. The same War further illustrated the acceptance or inauguration by England of a policy which seems likely to become the clew to most of her combinations, at least for offensive purposes, in the future. This policy is based on the resolution to maintain an undisturbed route overland to her Indian possessions, and to check at an early stage the advance of any competing European Power in the direction of those possessions. A policy which at some points presents a parallel to this is sometimes attributed to the United States, and was certainly advocated by President Monroe in his Message to Congress in 1823.* It may be briefly described as forbidding the further colonization by a European State of the American Continent, or the establishment there by such a State of monarchial institutions.

With respect to the actual systems of policy now being followed out by the different countries of Europe, any precise inquiry must be based on an aggregate of political indications, and would probably result, in most instances, in little better than conjecture. The present object is only to establish the general position that systems of policy actually exist, and are continually persevered in, and that these systems are to be reckoned among the causes of War. Nevertheless, the character of some of these systems is sufficiently patent to be obvious to all. The movements of Russia in Western Asia, and especially in the direction of British India, are certainly not unconnected with her action in Eastern Europe, and with her assiduous cultivation of friendly relations with the United States and France, the hereditary rivals and suspicious critics of England and Germany. The question need not be here mooted whether the ulterior object of Russia is aggrandizement in Asia or in Europe, the accomplishment of immediate designs in one quarter being only used as a means of distracting attention and force of an obstructive kind in another.

Among the more clearly distinguishable features of modern policy is that of maintaining the independence of Switzerland, of Belgium, and the Netherlands, partly for the sake of interposing physical barriers between the territories of such States as France and Germany,

Characteristics of modern policy.

---

* See as to the Monroe Doctrine, Wheaton's International Law. Dana's edition. Section 67 *seq.*, note 36.

which are notoriously disposed to irregular encroachment on each other's territory, and partly in order to prevent, by an absolute limit, the absorption of the smaller States of Europe by a few States of inordinate magnitude. The general disposition manifested on so many sides to advance the formation of the kingdom of Italy, and to maintain its integrity, is similarly based on a conscious or instinctive assurance that Italy, by its Alpine line of natural fortresses, and the opportunities for maritime warfare which its singular geographical position presents, would become an invaluable stronghold for any aspiring State which should succeed in occupying or annexing it. There has scarcely been a European War of moment in which some of the most decisive military operations have not been conducted on Italian soil.

These principles of policy have, indeed, some resemblance to the older one of the Balance of Power, differing from it, however, in the circumstances that no conscious attempt is made to maintain absolutely any existing *status quo;* nor is the mere fact of the aggrandizement of a State already influential, even to a portentous extent, held to be a legitimate ground of remonstrance or interference. The present policy is far more negative than the older historical one, and takes up its stand on only a few very general and somewhat indefinite notions, such as those above mentioned in reference to Switzerland, Belgium, Holland, and Italy.

Besides the more obvious tendencies here noted, there are, no doubt, at the present time other more or less distinct systems of policy, either actually operative on the minds of statesmen, or advocated by political speculators of various degrees of repute. Thus, there are many who speak of Germany being the "natural" ally of England; while others, such as the followers of Auguste Comte, believe that the true and only "natural" policy of England is to ally itself with France, and the Latin races generally, with the view of gradually founding a Republican community of Western States under the general supremacy of France.

As the general result of this examination, it appears that, apart from all considerations of passion, momentary self-interest, or indistinct national caprice, certain definite lines of action—sometimes very far-reaching and comprehensive, sometimes only prescribing certain negative ends, and adopted by the statesmen of each country in obedience to traditional habits, more or less consciously based on well-reasoned calculations of ultimate expediency—are found to emerge from the mingled tissue of what might seem, at first sight, to be nothing more than merely fortuitous and occasional freaks of policy.

The carrying out of these systems naturally involves chances of War, and therefore, in estimating the causes of War in modern times, a prominent place must be given to these systems. Many of them are, no doubt, themselves contrived for the express purpose of reducing the frequency and the probability of War; and it may turn out that it will be largely through the adoption of a truly wise, just, and expedient system of policy by each State that the State will do what it can in this direction toward the extinction of War. In the mean time it is obvious, even from the above glance at the actual systems of policy now in vogue, that these systems at present largely rest upon mutual suspiciousness and apprehensions, as well as, often enough, upon contracted and short-sighted views of national advantage. How far this state of things can be improved by direct political action, this is not the place to consider. How far it may be affected by moral agencies will be incidentally considered later on. How far improvements in International Law may have a beneficial influence will have to be discussed at length.

Schemes of policy frequently produce War.

5. Another cause of War, which includes many of the other causes, and co-operates usually with the others, though it may

exist independently of most of them, is the defective condition
of International Morality, and the false notions
of morality which commonly prevail. There is
no doubt that true moral ideas are of very slow growth, both
in the State and in individual persons. They are
the product of all the civilizing and humanizing
forces which have been in operation through the whole of past
time, or through the previous life. The systems of moral philosophers are, indeed, always some way ahead of the common morality of the time and place of their appearance; but they always reflect the best side of that common morality, and are never completely emancipated from it. Moral conceptions, again, have a most intimate relation with religious beliefs; and if these beliefs are various, conflicting, and tardy in their development, the current moral conceptions at each period are sure to exhibit a proportionate amount of uncertainty and vacillation.

It has thus come about that, in modern Europe, the moral ideas of duty, right, and wrong, and of the aim of life, so far as they only affect the individual human being in the smallest circle of domestic or social relationships, are tolerably precise and identical for different countries. So far as they affect persons in their relations to the State, and affect the State, or the Legislature, or the Executive Government, in their relations to private citizens, the primary moral ideas are blurred and uncertain, and differ widely from country to country.

As illustrations may be given the varying canons of right and wrong which prevail in different countries, and in different sections of society in the same country, as to the abstract right of revolution, or the duty of passive obedience; the wrongfulness of frauds on the revenue, of bribery at elections, of breaches of political engagements committed by statesmen, of neglecting pledges given at elections, of legislation for the regulation of vice or the punishment of certain moral offences, of public confiscations by the Legislature, or of excessive burdens in the shape of public debts cast upon posterity.

With respect to most of these matters, the elements of moral evaluation are numerous, subtle, and involved with each other, considerations of immediate and remote expediency interlacing at frequent points with notions of absolute right and wrong. It thus might be expected that moral philosophy would be at fault in keeping pace with the enormous strides of modern political and social movements, and in at once propounding a number of theses applicable to all cases submitted to it, which would generally be admitted to be incontrovertible when fairly stated. As a matter of fact, moral philosophy is, in reference to all *quasi*-political problems of the kind above stated, only proceeding after the most cautious and tentative fashion. And in default of the clear and decisive utterances of moral philosophy, self-interest, habit, ephemeral theories, or the purest conjecture, compete with each other for the solution of each difficulty as it presents itself.

If this is the case in the comparatively narrow field of national life, where common customs, language, traditions, and law weld the citizens together into a whole, penetrated with sentiments of patriotism, and working more or less harmoniously toward one and the same end, it might well be expected that the obstacles in the way of elaborating a scheme of morality applicable to the relations of States, as between themselves, would for a long period seem to be, and really be, insuperable. It is needless to draw attention to the facts which betray the miserably chaotic condition of moral philosophy as bearing on this wider subject. Beyond asserting generally that States are bound to abide by their treaties, not to make War inconsiderately, to abstain from needless cruelties in the conduct of War, and not to abuse a victory, moral philosophy is either wholly silent, or gives an uncertain sound, or is wholly divided against itself.

Problems of International Morality supremely difficult.

The gap has, indeed, been filled in some little degree by International Lawyers, who, from the time of Grotius, have been compelled to give practical answers to the actual questions which International relations in Peace and War have brought to the surface, and, in giving those answers, have done their utmost to conform to a moral Code, based on considerations of utility, justice, or actual usage, in such proportions as has seemed meet. But, in spite of the noble aspirations in which the writings of International Lawyers abound, and the lofty standard of justice they have generally upheld, it cannot be said that anything more than a fragmentary sketch of a true moral system, as applicable to the relations of States to each other, has as yet been composed. Such attempts, too, as have been made to construct some of the clauses of a moral Code have only dealt with negative morality, pointing out what injuries States ought not to inflict on each other, what engagements ought not to be broken, what rights ought not to be violated, what Rules of Law ought not to be broken or evaded. But for all that constitutes the essence of morality, as contrasted with Law, on the one hand, and the narrowest expediency or barest prudence on the other, International Lawyers have necessarily, and with better excuse than many others, held their peace.

Consequent incompleteness and uncertainty of its rules.

So far as the most authoritative utterances, either of professed jurists, or political speculators, or influential statesmen, have gone, it is a matter of entire uncertainty how far a State is bound to abide by a Treaty which, subsequently to making it, it believes to be seriously detrimental to its own interests or incompatible with its internal legislation;* or to have been imposed by force at the conclusion of

No distinct definition of Treaty obligations.

---

* As see the successful effort, in 1870, of Russia to escape some of the obligations of the Treaty of Paris of 1856; the refusal of England, in 1875, to abide by the provisions of the (Ashburton) Treaty of Washington of 1843, in the matter of extradition; and the effort made in England to disclaim some of the obligations arising under the Declaration of Paris of 1856.

a War, or to have been ratified without discussion in its own National Legislature, or to have been informally worded, so as to appear rather as an express understanding than a formal convention.

So, also, no canon of right or wrong is publicly avowed as to the circumstances under which it is held justifiable to go to War. The distinction has, indeed, been drawn from the times of Gro-

or of a just occasion for War. tius between a "just" and an "unjust" War; and Grotius himself seemed to consider the distinction to be one of practical moment, so as to carry with it certain qualifications of rights and duties. But, even if the distinction be a true one, and Wars may be just on one side and not on the other, and if it be further true that certain acts of warfare are more or less permissible, according as the original cause of the War was, on the side on which they are done, more or less urgent, yet when a real occasion is in view, with all its practical complications, the distinction, and the consequences following from it, are found to be either too large and sweeping, or not nearly large and comprehensive enough, for actual use. No practical test is afforded, capable of instant application, for determining whether it is, under given circumstances, morally justifiable, as distinguished from being prudentially advisable, or even seemingly necessary, for a particular State to go to War. The ordinary mode in which the question is handled is to merge all the considerations together, so as to erect what seems the only possible resource, or, at least, what is in itself a tempting enterprise, into a call of moral duty. It is, of course, quite possible that what is convenient and useful may be also conformable to the highest standard of morality, as existing at the day; and it is true that, in doubtful questions of morality, utility of a high order may supply the only index for a decisive course between competing courses of action. All that is here asserted is that, in the momentous matter of plunging two nations, and perhaps several nations, into War, no authoritative moral principles are wont to be cited by statesmen as relevant to the decision; and, so far as any principles at all are held relevant, and a substitute is not found for them in a feverish condition of the public mind, or in the inert condition which expresses itself in what is called "drifting" into War, the principles are mostly those of calculated gain or loss in the immediate present.

There are other matters, with respect to which the absence of a moral standard, or the imperfection of moral rules, is quite as conspicuous as in those just commented upon. For instance, in imposing conditions of Peace, though it is often vaguely hinted that the conquering State ought not to be too hard on the conquered, and that limits exist to the amount of compensation for the expenses of the War that may be exacted, and to the material guarantees for Peace that may be required, yet no clear and efficacious principles of action, in reference to these and the like matters, are anywhere laid down. If a State in the hour of victory abstains from exacting the utmost it can obtain, and imposing the most humiliating conditions, it is called merciful or far-sighted, as the case may be. In the opposite case it is called vindictive or short-sighted. But no guide or standard of a purely moral sort exists for the direction of a victorious State in such an emergency. Its own not too remote interests, and the rudely-formed and ambiguously-expressed public opinion in surrounding States, are the only practical limits to the most unrestricted abuse of a temporary physical advantage.

<small>Other instances of absence of clear moral rules.</small>

Other instances of the existing chaos of morality, as applicable to the relations of States, might be supplied from the numberless diplomatic advantages which a strong State holds itself entitled to assume in reference to weaker States; the evasion of one another's civil and criminal laws, which States habitually encourage or forbear to punish; and the uncertainty, already alluded to, that attaches to every stage of the question of Intervention— that is, when, where, how, how far, and how long to intervene.

Nevertheless, the foundations of a system of International Morality, as distinguished from mere International Law, are already sufficiently laid to make it clear that such a system is a possibility, and an admitted want, and may some day have its structure adequately completed. States recognize their own real and independent personality — as opposed to that of their ephemeral Governments, on the one hand, and to some or all of their citizen population, at any particular moment, on the other—by a variety of incontestable manifestations. They make Treaties which, it is at least professed, are binding upon them, it may be, for all future time, whatever internal changes the contracting States may undergo. By these Treaties they incur pecuniary obligations, acquire, transfer, or exchange territory, confer rights on each other's citizens, and undertake lasting national responsibilities. With respect to the more important classes of these Treaties, it is the better opinion that not even War can dissolve them. They continue valid when all else has changed, except the identity and integrity of the States which have concluded them. Certainly, corporate bodies which can, and do, perform acts in relation to each other of so solemn and enduring a character are thereby confessed to have a moral personality, which carries with it the same kind, though not the identical forms, of moral obligations which subsist between a State and its subjects, and between every human being and every other.

Indications that a system of International Morality is possible.

States are professedly bound by Treaties—

and recognize some moral responsibility.

This persuasion gathers force when it is recollected with what majestic issues for humanity, and what terrible alternatives of blessing or calamity, the adjustment of the relations between State and State is fraught. Wealth, Independence, a common contribution to great human ends, are on one side. On the other is Poverty, Isolation, Despotism, and War. It can scarcely be denied, then, that in every act which a State performs toward another State it is either conforming to or departing from a cogent moral principle, whether that principle has been as yet clearly ascertained or not. Conformity to this principle is doing right. Departing from it is doing wrong. It is obvious that the obscurity in which such principles at present rest, the absence of faith in the evidence of such principles, the passions, prejudices, and contracted interests which interfere with their complete supremacy, are a main cause of modern, as of all, Wars.

It is obvious, too, that it is through defective morality, and the absence of the self-restraint which only moral habits can engender, that, in the conduct of a dispute between two States, either State is so apt to believe that what it calls its "honor" forbids any further negotiation, and calls at once for the arbitrament of the sword. Sometimes, indeed, without so much as waiting for the result of negotiations, and putting the most unfavorable interpretation on acts of an equivocal kind, a State, believing its own honor concerned, suddenly commits itself to rash acts of the nature of reprisal, or, at any rate, of answering by fresh insult and provocation, which, of course, offends the susceptibilities on the point of honor of the other State. The only course for both States seems War, just as in parallel cases of late years in England, and even now in some European countries, the duel seemed the only creditable or possible resort in the event of private persons wounding each other's sentiment of honor.

<small>Morbid susceptibility on points of honor provokes War.</small>

But, as in the case of private persons, so in that of States, this sentiment of honor is often a most artificial one, and is rather the creation of a childish vanity and self-conceit, of which a really dignified State might well be ashamed, than the offspring of a genuine self-respect. The proof of this is, that when the sentiment is false, it is "sudden and quick in quarrel," rapidly becomes heated and exaggerated, spreads like wildfire throughout the whole community, and insures the popularity of any hostile proceedings which may be based upon it. Where the sentiment is true, the State which conceives itself to be offended is patient and forbearing, ready to appeal with confidence to public opinion, rather than precipitately to be judged in its own cause, sincerely eager to obtain an apology or redress, and cordially prompt in accepting the one or other.

It needs but a slight recollection of recent European history to show how far more often, when the honor of a State is said to be involved so far as to render War imperative, it is rather the shallow sensitiveness of the first kind than the deep consciousness of true claims of the second kind which is really concerned. It will especially be remembered that among the numerous causes which, either really or apparently, conduced to the breaking out of the Franco-German War of 1870, the treatment of the French Ambassador at the Court of Berlin, on what was, in fact, a mere matter of punctilious courtesy, was seriously included.* So also in the memorable "Trent"† case, in 1861, England was on the verge of a War with America, not only on the ground of a contested right—because the question of pure legal right was not decided, and has not yet been fully decided—but of injured feeling, to which, undoubtedly, both sides contributed. Nevertheless, War was undoubtedly imminent, and it would be difficult to say which side was most culpable in the matter. Further illustrations of the same temper may be found in the fanatical and wicked craze of the English people on the subjects of Chinese insults, and of French insult on the occasion of the Orsini conspiracy against Napoleon III., in 1857.

It would be interesting to consider—if this were the place for it—how far the increased publicity of diplomacy and the influence of popular institutions is likely to affect this morbid

Marginal note: Instances.

---

* See Annual Register, 1870.

† See Wheaton, Section 505, note 228; and Manning, p. 391 *seq.* Annual Register.

sensitiveness of States and their populations, in reference to the
presumed demands of the national honor. The
effect of telegraphic communications—brief, incessant,
and often mutilated—and of the Press in its
modern form, would also have to be taken into account. The
result of the inquiry would, probably, be to show that the immediate
tendency of the change is to precipitate quarrels between
States on insufficient grounds, through the disuse of confidential
methods of anticipating difficulties, and the inopportune
interference of badly informed, and as yet incompetent,
popular bodies. But the general tendency is likely to be wholly
beneficial, as popular assemblies learn to appreciate their true
functions in the management of International Relations, and at
once to control, to check, as well as to confide in and to stimulate,
the special persons to whom they may, from time to time,
directly intrust the management. The relations to each other
of the United States House of Representatives, the Senate, the
Committee of the Senate on Foreign Relations, and the President
may be taken as examples of a type which, in respect of
the conduct of their business with other States, the monarchial
States of Europe are but slowly approaching.

But it is not so much in a merely puerile or morbid sensibility
on points of honor that modern States exhibit
a deficient moral training and self-restraint,
as in disregard for the evils of War, when resort
to War is contemplated as the only satisfaction
for injured honor. To exhibit a want of concern for a vast
moral and physical calamity, and still more to act with indifference
as to whether it is brought about or not, is indisputably a
grave moral obliquity. In the case of so signal and far-reaching a
calamity as War, the practical indulgence of any sentiment, even
in itself honorable, which directly tends to precipitate the happening
of a calamity, is one of those peculiarly heinous offences
for which, in morals as in law, is reserved the name of *crime*.

It is true that, both in political discussion and in literature, War is beginning to be treated as presumedly and universally an evil, and, instead of War being welcomed as, *ipso facto*, "glorious," a public apology is generally held to be demanded of any State which is the first to enter upon it. Nevertheless, in crises of public excitement, arising out of a real or imagined affront, and when the national honor is largely and vaguely talked about, resort to War is almost greedily welcomed as a ready vent for the public enthusiasm, and nothing but visions of national *éclat*, political ascendency, and brilliant feats of heroism occupies the public imagination. The Statesmen and the writers of the Press, who are unofficial organs of the Government, partly share the common feeling, and partly feed it. The very expense— the least of the evils of War—is forgotten or neglected, and the whole nation, with a new-born zeal, attains a spurious consciousness of true unity of life and spirit in its resolve to strike at the foundations of national unity and strength in another State.

So far as this state of mind is not the result of mere igno-

A flagrant instance of political immorality.

rance and inexperience, it is, on the face of it, deeply immoral. In fact, it presents most of the features by which an immoral state of mind could be designated; and, most of all so, when it is not merely the less responsible and informed part of the population of the country which is involved, but the responsible Legislature and Government, which, for the moment, personate the State. Of these, at least, the utmost deliberation, circumspection, knowledge, diligence, and exact balancing of evils may be expected; and the want of these qualities and habits, and still more the presence of the opposite of them, furnish grounds for the gravest moral reprobation. It is plain, then, that in this aspect, too, among the causes of War the prevalent political immorality must be counted as one of the most conspicuous, and especially so when operating in connection with other causes.

6. There is another cause of War, which is, in fact, a product of War itself, and therefore the offspring of other causes of War; but it is now, and threatens to be hereafter, so important a cause in itself, that it demands an independent treatment. This cause is to be found in the organized preparations for War in time of Peace, and in certain social habits and institutions created by War itself, and which react in such a way as to predispose nations to War.

Standing Armies.

The institution of standing armies, in the developed and still developing form it wears among the modern nations of Europe, must be ranked among the most potent causes of War, and therefore it is not without reason that it is to the reduction of those armies that the best friends of Peace are directing their utmost endeavors. Not that this institution is free from the gravest objection on economical, constitutional, and moral grounds, as well as on the ground of it directly conducing to bring about War. But this is not the place to investigate those other grounds of objection.

It is obvious that the constant liability to which a State, belonging to the complex system of European States, is exposed of being, in virtue of some of the causes already examined, or of other causes, at a moment's notice plunged into War, must render a certain amount of preparation an indispensable necessity. The greater the liability, and the more incalculable the elements on which it depends, the more urgent is the need for being always in a condition of readiness for War at a few days', or even a few hours', notice. There is, perhaps, no problem which is pressing on the minds of statesmen at the present day with more urgency than how to maintain a sufficient amount of preparation for War, with the least sacrifice of the advantages of Peace.

Some preparation for War inevitable.

The solution of this problem is giving rise to a number of experiments, some of which have already been put to the proof. The general direction of these experiments is to avoid the harsh and unequal operation of the conscription by ballot, and yet to enlarge the army far beyond the limits which purely voluntary service would, in most countries, assign to it. The aims of military organizers are of the most ambitious kind, and the tendency of all the schemes is to embrace the whole male population in the national army—excluding only the very young and old, the infirm, and the holders of a few privileged offices—and to impart to every member of that army a military education.

Schemes for obtaining military efficiency with the least possible sacrifice.

Of these schemes the German is, as yet, the most complete, and has best established its military efficiency. It is well known that, according to this scheme, every able-bodied man in the Empire has his place in the list of the national forces, and for a certain period undergoes military discipline and drill. A distinction is made between those who wholly devote themselves to the profession of a soldier and those who belong to one or other of the branches of the reserve, and who, between the interval of actual service, or attendance on drill, pursue their ordinary civil occupations. The German scheme thus combines the advantage of a permanent Army, compactly organized, and devoted solely to keeping up military spirit and traditions and performing military exercises, and of a reserve army of almost unlimited size, sufficiently trained to be relied upon for service inside or outside the territory, as the case may be, and each individual man in which is a source for the diffusion of military zeal and ambition throughout the whole population.

The German military organization most complete.

The French are engaged in gradually transforming their military institutions after the same general type, and the same is true of the Russians. Other States which have enormous standing armies, as Austria and Italy, only differ from Germany in the degree of universality which attaches to the compulsory service prevailing among them. In Switzerland military service is universal and com-

Other States follow in the same direction.

pulsory, though available only for defensive purposes. In England the question of army reconstruction is recognized as of great urgency, and in some quarters the necessity of adopting the Continental system of universal service, or some species of conscription, is openly advocated. The Volunteer system has made great way in England, and recent changes in military organization, as carried into effect by Act of Parliament, must have the result of consolidating all the military resources of the country into a large standing military force, imbued with one spirit, and inheriting similar traditions.

<small>Proposals of army reconstruction in England.</small>

Inasmuch as the whole military forces of countries like Germany, Austria, Italy, and France, capable of being called into action on an emergency, and receiving a military training fitted to qualify them for service, are little short of half a million for each country, it is obvious that there are in Europe, in a time of profound Peace, several millions of men, the whole or a considerable part of whose profession is War. These men comprise the most robust, the most energetic, and the best trained and disciplined men to be found in the several States, England alone presenting for the time an exception, so long as military service here does not compete in attractions with other occupations, and recruiting is effected chiefly from the lowest class of the population.

<small>Enormous number of men trained to War in Europe.</small>

It has to be borne in mind, again, that there is much which is attractive and stimulating to the imagination in what may be called the outside of War. The active habits, and the exercise of physical capacity, which War presupposes; the inexorable routine, order, and punctilious regularity, which contrast so markedly with the troubles, confusion, or perplexity which the daily experience of home and civil life necessarily, at times, brings with it; the gorgeous pageantry of uniform, flags, bands, parades, and reviews, with which Governments never fail to entertain and se-

<small>External attractions of a military career.</small>

4*

duce the minds of their more illiterate subjects; the mutual reassurance and stimulus which each of those engaging in a common work, even when it is intrinsically disagreeable and repulsive, imparts to his fellow; the carefully cherished tales of all the heroic actions and of the indomitable endurance of which every War between civilized men cannot but contain memorable instances; and the instinctive suppression of all reference to the ferocity, brutality, and immorality of all sorts, which is the substantial material of which War ultimately consists; all these influences, taken together, and multiplied and magnified by the subtle agency of sympathy and active co-operation, extending over a field measuring millions of human beings, must create an inordinate predisposition to War, which must be constantly present in times of the greatest tranquillity, and when no other cause of War is manifest on the political horizon.

It is, again, to be remembered that War, in modern times, is

Numerous forms of activity directed toward War. Science and Art applied to military purposes.

becoming, to a rapidly increasing extent, a competition, not only in strength and in skill, but in the artistic appliance of the last results of physical discoveries. All the most precious products of an age of scientific research, and of engineering invention, are instantly pressed into the service of War, and Governments outstrip all other merchants and traders in offering premiums to discoverers and inventors. Thus, in this respect, as in a variety of others, War feeds the speculative and even the gambling tendencies of men—a single successful novelty bringing with it a reward which seems, in appearance at least, to make up for any number of wasted efforts, as a single victory is sufficient to feed the passion for War during any number of reverses.

The new phase on which War is now entering demands,

Development of military education.

again, at any rate for some branches of the military and naval service, a far superior order of military instruction than has been held requisite heretofore. It is now held that the commonest soldier does his work well or ill in proportion to his general mental education; and, of course, for officers in the strictly scientific departments, the highest order of mental attainment is indispensable; and in all these educational respects an active competition is proceeding as between different States. Military and Naval Colleges and Academies, special classes for military and naval instruction in universities and schools, and even, as many advocate, in the common national schools of the country, are arising, or about to arise, on every hand to supply the urgent demand. Literature lends its aid, and, partly by providing a new order of educational text-books, partly by dignifying, in fiction and poetry on the one hand, and in history and biography on the other, the art of War, and placing it on a platform equal to if not higher than that occupied by the occupations from which humanity profits the most, contributes its utmost to create a popular sentiment favorable, rather than unfavorable, to War.

All these institutions and practices, whether unavoidable or not, must have the effect of maintaining, among vast masses of persons directly, and among nearly all persons indirectly, a belief that the recurrence of War, at an earlier or later date, is as natural and certain an event as the recurrence of one of the seasons of the year; that the necessity of War, sooner or later, is the only explanation of some of the most striking and deeply-rooted institutions of society; that, but for the probability of War, millions of men would be without their current employment, and without such agreeably speculative chances of personal distinction as each rates so highly in his own favor; that, if War is deferred too long, the lives of millions may be passed without accomplishing the end to which an assemblage of strong personal and national impulses has mainly devoted those lives; and that if War be precipitated, the time is at hand to which the discipline and eager expectation of years have been directed; when, at last, each can know for himself, and demonstrate to his fel-

The numerous interests involved keep alive an expectation of War.

low, what he is worth, and when an expectant country, vitally concerned in the issue, will award the prize due to his bravery.

7. The cause of War which is often the most patent one, and therefore has attracted more attention than is, perhaps, really due to it, is the existing condition of International Law. This cause admits of more direct treatment than any of the causes above examined, and therefore it is natural that many persons, deeply persuaded that all War must come to an end sooner or later, have directed their main attention to what seems to them the only practicable remedy at present.

State of International Law, most commonly recognized cause of War.

It is well known that, owing to a number of historical and moral causes, the mutual relations to each other of the States of Europe, and of other States directly affiliated to them, have gradually evolved certain definite rules of action which, in public profession at least, have an obligatory force on the several States concerned. These rules are closely analogous to the rules of national law, and, in fact, largely trace their origin to the ideas, the structure, and the language of Roman Law. Nevertheless, in many obvious respects—as in the absence of a Legislature, of Courts of Justice, and of an Executive Authority—these rules noticeably contrast with national law. According to some writers (as the late Mr. Austin) these points of contrast are sufficiently serious to rob these rules of all title to the name *law*.

Nature of International Law.

This is a question, in a great measure, of terminology, and it is equally true that these rules have no greater title to the name which Mr. Austin is ready to concede to them, that of *morality*. Few people would, nowadays, deny that States have moral obligations toward each other of a far wider and deeper kind than any which could be contained in the sharply defined language of a formal rule. In fact, the relation of International Morality to these rules indi-

Not coextensive with International morality—

cates a fresh ground of analogy between these rules and national law. National law is never identical, or even coextensive, with morality, but it is the constant tendency of a progressive State to bring its law into harmony with the requirements of morality as understood at the day. Thus it is an intelli-

but related to morality as National Law is.

gible effort of terminology to designate the rules which, in the region of international society, bear a relation to international morality exactly corresponding to the relation which national law bears to national morality, by the same name of *law*. But, in spite of the real and undoubted efficacy of the rules of International Law, and their close parallelism with the rules of national law, it is none the less true that the

Vagueness of its rules.

rules of International Law are infected, at many points, with a peculiar measure of uncertainty; that, even where the form of the rule is certain, the interpretations that may be set upon it are numerous, conflicting, or ambiguous; and that, even when the meaning of the rules is clearly ascertained, the purport of them by no means, as yet, corresponds to the requirements of morality, expediency, or justice.

The rules of International Law, as explained by the most com-

Sources of International Law. Consent of States, and Law of Nature.

petent authorities, are said to be founded partly in the actual or implicit consent of States, and partly in the deductions which, it is said, are capable of being drawn from a so-called Law of Nature. Some writers are rather disposed to rely upon the former of these sources, and others rather on the latter. Perhaps a meeting-point of the writers who look mainly to the consent of States, as ascertained from their express conventions, or their tacit usages, and of those writers who are prone to refer mainly to the prescriptions of some abstract rule of right, however designated, may be found in the statement that the rules of International Law are such rules for the conduct of States, in their mutual relations, as they have sanctioned by express or tacit consent, and do not conflict with the requirements of International Morality, as those requirements are understood at the day. Thus an alleged rule of International Law must satisfy two conditions in order to maintain its validity. It must be the product of the actual or the tacit consent of States; that is, it must have been generally agreed to by treaty, or constantly observed in practice; and it must be in harmony with a scheme of International Morality, which is variously styled the Law of Nature, the Law of God, Abstract Justice, the Law of Right, Reason, and the like.

When it is remembered how comparatively rare, in past times, have been the points of contact of Eastern States otherwise than by War, in what a desultory way the intercourse between the States has been conducted, how fragmentary and imperfect is the evidence of that intercourse, and yet how indefinitely extended in some directions is the field from which the International Lawyer has to glean his proofs of usage and consent, it does not seem surprising that the whole region of International Law should be one of uncertainty and conjecture. But when to this are added the intricacy and depth of any problem which depends for its solution upon a true and exact view of Abstract Morality as binding on States, and the difficulties inherent in the interpretation of the documentary conventions which are alleged to afford evidence of consent, the uncertainty attaching to the most elementary rule of International Law begins to rise to a very high pitch. This sort of Law shares all the notorious uncertainty which cleaves to rules of national law, besides possessing a special uncertainty of its own, through the absence of express legislation, the paucity of the instances on which conclusions or analogies can be based, and the variety of the national languages, manners, and proclivities amidst which the Law has grown up.

Difficulty of forming distinct rules—

International Law is, however, not merely infected with an inherent uncertainty as to the purport and form of its general rules, but, when a rule is clearly ascertained, there are special difficulties in ascertaining whether or not it applies, or to what extent it applies, to a given condition of facts. Of course, this is simply a matter for a judicial tribunal, and great and beneficial efforts have been made by particular States to extemporize one, of the nature of a Court of Arbitration, for a special emergency, and the application of a rule of law has been practically settled as between those States. But, apart from such special and temporary arrangements, there is no permanent judicial machinery which is empowered and obliged to decide, authoritatively, the claims of suitor States to expound the bearing of a rule of law on a given state of facts, and to assess the amount of compensation which the invasion of a right equitably demands. In default of such a tribunal, each State is judge in its own cause, a long diplomatic altercation takes place on every occasion of a disputed right, the same learned authorities, treaties, and despatches are cited, with different intents, on both sides, the discussion grows more warm as it is more protracted, and, at last, it is either left undecided, or only decided by bitterly-felt concessions on one or both sides, thereby becoming a rankling sore ready to be opened afresh, it may be years after, and at the most inconvenient and unexpected of times.

And of determining when they are applicable.

No authoritative court of International Law.

Very recent history has supplied many painful instances of angry controversies, nearly resulting in War, which have taken their rise in nothing else than unsettled questions of International Law, and less recent history abounds in them.

Disputes upon unsettled points.

Any reader of Mr. Ward's "History of the Law of Nations" will remember his account of the endless disputes on the precedence of Ambassadors, which threatened to break up the most important negotiations, and were often an imminent occasion of War. These disputes have now been finally set at rest by the simple rules of precedence settled by the Protocol of Vienna of the 19th of March, 1815, and of Aix-la-Chapelle, of the 21st of November, 1818.* Many points of law relative to Ambassadors are, indeed, still unsettled, but it is to be hoped that European States have outlived the possibility of serious differences on such minute questions.

In time of War, when the passions even of Neutral States are apt to get inflamed, the uncertainty of International Law, and the want of an authoritative Court, are especially felt. The "Trent" case has been already alluded to. If in this case the question as to the right of a neutral to carry a belligerent's commissioners from one neutral port to another—and as to the duty of a belligerent captor to take a neutral ship, which he held to be carrying contraband, to the nearest prize court for judgment, instead of removing the contraband and letting the ship go free—could have been submitted at once to a competent Court of Justice, before which both England and the United States would appear as suitors, it is not conceivable that any of the strong feeling would have existed which so nearly gave rise to War. It was the sense of injury, coupled with the doubt as to getting the matter fairly investigated, and the law honestly laid down and applied, which stirred both nations, in an incredibly short time, up to fever heat. People feared that the uncertainty about some of the legal points would throw a veil over the whole injury, and their natural resource was to talk as loudly and fiercely about the matter as they could, in order to compel instant attention.

<small>Need for an International Court shown in the "Trent" case.</small>

A somewhat similar result followed in what is known as the "Alabama" case, from the uncertainty of the law relative to the obligations of Neutral States in the matter of their private citizens building and equipping ships of War for a belligerent, and from the difficulty of instantly bringing the question to a judicial issue. Though there is now little

<small>The "Alabama" case.</small>

---

* Manning, p. 107.

doubt that the English Government showed a dilatoriness in this case which was an infringement of neutrality, even according to the law as then clearly recognized, yet the measure of neutral duties, and the description of the amount of diligence which was incumbent on a Neutral State, was nowhere precisely laid down, was, from its nature, hard to lay down in unexceptionable language, and could, neither before the injury was committed, nor immediately after its commission, nor at any later time, be compulsorily submitted by either party to the adjudication of a competent Court. Thus time was allowed for all sorts of bitter sentiments, recriminating invectives, and exaggerated claims to gather head, and efforts at arbitration for a long time failed. Even the complete success of the Arbitration at Geneva, under the Treaty of Washington, has been a good deal marred by the national party feeling by which some of the Arbitrators were agitated, and from which a permanently constituted Court of Justice might (if it could be found at all) be expected to be moderately exempt.

The case of the "Virginius,"* which presented itself during the insurrectionary War in Cuba, and in which the Spanish Authorities arrested and detained a ship on the ground of its belonging to the insurgents, and put to death a considerable part of the crew by a summary judicial process—whereas the ship seems to have been, in fact, an American vessel—further illustrates the dangers to Peace, from the difficulty of, instantly and authoritatively, clearing up a doubtful point of mixed law and fact. The conduct of the Spanish Authorities was, on any interpretation of it, severe, and even cruel and vindictive, considering that the menial servants of the ship were comprehended in the sentence, and the American Government instantly demanded from the offenders satisfaction of a complete and even humiliating kind. The nationality of

Case of the "Virginius."

---

* See Manning, p. 470.

the ship was, nevertheless, extremely doubtful, as a matter of fact, and the rights and duties of an American vessel, really engaged in helping the insurgents, were by no means clear. If Spain had been a strong instead of a weak State, it would have been difficult to prevent War, because no strong State would allow itself to be dictated to, as was Spain by the United States, nor to have doubtful questions of fact and law peremptorily prejudged to its disadvantage.

Long controversy upon Canadian Fishery question. The Canadian Fishery question, which was settled by the last Treaty of Washington, had been pending for years, and was always liable to be reopened in a spirit of angry controversy whenever other inflammatory topics disturbed the political relations of England and the United States. Yet the whole matter bearing, as it did, partly on a question of territorial boundaries, partly on questions of customary usage, partly on the effect of an intervening War on the operation of Treaties made before it broke out, is one of exactly the same kind as those which are being daily adjudicated upon in the Courts of Justice of both countries, with tolerable satisfaction to suitors. Yet it was with the utmost difficulty that the matter could be finally referred to arbitration, and an arrangement of the nature of a compromise arrived at. The points of law are still left open for further controversy, or irritating dispute, whenever a fresh occasion presents itself.

Winslow Extradition case. The "Winslow extradition" case* is rather eminent for the conciliatory manner in which England and the United States conducted the controversy, than for the absence of grounds of mutual recrimination, which between any two other States, or even between those States at a different period, or under different circumstances, might have had disastrous consequences. The English Government were under-

---

* See Annual Register for 1876, and Lord Derby's Letter to Colonel Hoffmann, of June 30th, 1876.

stood, in some quarters, to uphold the anomalous principle that they are not bound to observe a Treaty which is of a kind which an English Statute no longer permits the Government to make, and even though the Statute, by a special clause, according to the obvious interpretation of it, specially excepts Treaties already in existence from being directly or indirectly affected by the Statute. Such a view of his conduct the Foreign Secretary wholly repudiated, and rested his position on a wholly diverse interpretation of the Treaty of Washington of 1842.

It was a question partly of law and custom, and partly of the interpretation of Treaties; and yet, apart from the constitution, by common consent of a special tribunal for the determination of all the questions involved, the judgment of which in the present case—as the prisoner Winslow was discharged—could have no retroactive effect, no formal and regular provision existed for ever bringing the matter to an issue, and still less for deciding it expeditiously as soon as the difficulty presented itself.

It will be remembered that the German Government recently brought considerable pressure to bear upon Belgium, in order to induce it to alter its criminal law dealing with political conspirators against Foreign States, just as Napoleon III. endeavored to do upon England in 1859. The pretence in both cases was presumedly based on the special conception of the legal duties of States toward each other. Belgium has admitted the duty by altering its law. England has apparently repudiated the duty by similarly refusing to alter its law. The point is thus left unsettled; and if hereafter raised, in conjunction with other grounds of dispute, may have serious consequences.

Laws relating to political conspirators against Foreign States.

The duties of a State to the citizens of other States are, at present, most imperfectly ascertained. It is quite unsettled how far special taxes or disabilities may be imposed on the alien citizens of a particular State, while obeying the laws of the country in which they reside, without incurring the charge, at the least, of a want of comity. Whether special conditions can be imposed on the travelling citizens of a particular State—as the possession of a *passe-port viséed* in a certain way—or whether rights of commerce can be refused altogether, or only to the citizens of some States, or only at ports not included in a special list; or whether, in time of War, the citizens of a Belligerent State, peaceably domiciled in the territory of the other belligerent, and conducting themselves inoffensively, can be made to leave the territory at a short notice, or at any notice, without a grave infraction of law—are all questions on which International Law, as now written, throws only a most flickering light, and yet which, within the last few years, have again and again excited heated controversies, which in some cases have been among the antecedents of War.

<small>Unsettled questions concerning citizens of Foreign States.</small>

The ex-territorial character of mercantile ships—and even, for some purposes, of ships of War—again, is a topic which recent experience proves to be most uncertainly ascertained and defined; and yet any day may discover two equally poised States, owing to a purely accidental course taken by a naval commander of one or other of them, vehemently supporting opposite doctrines, and yet having no opportunity of bringing their arguments to a conclusion sanctioned by a competent judicial authority. The consciousness of this helplessness, and the undefined sense of wrong it exaggerates and prolongs, is only too likely to co-operate with other potent impulses, if such should be present, in precipitating War.

<small>Frequency of maritime disputes.</small>

It appears from these illustrations, most of which have been selected from the experience of the last twenty years, that whereas International Law is an unmistakable reality, and, so far as its rules are precise and unquestionable, is one of the most effective guarantees of Peace, yet vast portions of the Law are, as yet,

<small>International Law a guarantee of Peace, but it is as yet incomplete.</small>

only dimly sketched out, and, in respect of all portions of it, the utmost inconvenience and risk is encountered, through the impossibility of obtaining a ready and immediate decision of questions of law and fact, which from time to time come into controversy.

<small>Great want of an authoritative tribunal.</small>

The effect on the frequency of Wars, and the permanence of War, of certain leading doctrines of International Law, especially as regards the mode of conducting War, and the rights and duties of neutrals in respect of trade, will more conveniently be considered later on, when the leading suggestions for the reform of the law on these topics have to be passed in review.

The causes of War which have been examined in the present chapter have been selected, partly, as being those which are often overlooked, or, at least, of which the importance, in modern times, is often underrated, and partly as admitting, more than other causes, of the application of direct remedial processes. It will have been obvious throughout the inquiry that no single one of these causes ever stands alone. Most usually several causes concur, and sometimes all these causes, and others in addition, are present at once. Thus, in the case of the Crimean war, the rapid political growth of Russia; the chronic revolutionary condition of the Turkish provinces, inviting the competitive intervention of Russia on the one side, and England and France on the other; the rival political schemes of Russia and England; indifference on all sides to the sufferings and losses to all concerned which War entails; the existence and *éclat* of fixed military institutions, especially in France and Russia; and the doubts attaching to the legal claims of the Christian subjects of Turkey, were all among the causes of War. To these causes might be added national and religious antipathies, and other still more vague political tendencies, in England and elsewhere, which cannot be usefully analyzed here.

<small>Various causes usually concur to produce a War, as in the Crimean War,</small>

So, in the case of the Franco-German War, the growth of Prussia and Germany has already been noted as the most direct of the causes. But to this cause must be added the alleged intervention of France, in nominating Hohenzollern as successor to the Spanish Crown, the real or imputed political schemes of the Emperor Napoleon, the antipathy existing between the French and German people, the territorial acquisitiveness on both sides, the enormously developed military institutions on both sides, and the alleged ill-treatment, or at least contemptuous treatment, of the French Ambassador at Berlin. Probably the first of these causes was the strongest, namely, the determination of Bismarck to secure a united Germany, under the military leadership of Prussia, and to put a final close, if it were possible, to the scarcely intermittent invasions by France of German territory. It may well be doubted whether the appropriation by the Treaty of Peace of territory so long attached to France will diminish, rather than increase, the probability of recurrent War.

and the Franco-German War.

There are some causes of War which, though they have figured conspicuously in past times, are now becoming extinct, at least among States enjoying an equal amount of civilization. Such are Wars of religion; Wars waged in order to extort commercial privileges; Wars waged in defence of colonies, or of the advantages of colonial trade; Wars of dynastic succession; and Wars proceeding from nothing else than chronic international hatred or jealousy, as were many of the Wars between England and France. That some of these causes of War are by no means obsolete when a civilized State has to deal with one less civilized, or at least with a State at once weak and physically remote from the operation of public opinion in Europe, the incessant Wars which England has waged with China, and which she is constantly waging with the Asiatic potentates whose

Some causes of War are becoming obsolete between European States.

territories border on her Eastern possessions, are sufficient proofs. But the principle of free trade, the modern policy of colonial independence, the general and steady advance of notions of religious toleration, and the lessened influence of dynastic families in political, and especially in international affairs, are quickly bringing to an end some of the most notorious causes of War in the past.

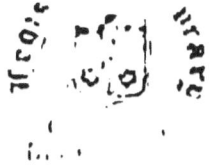

CHAPTER III.

OF SOME POLITICAL REMEDIES FOR WAR.

SECTION I.

OF THE NATURE AND POSSIBILITY OF POLITICAL AND OTHER REMEDIES FOR WAR.

IN the invention of remedies for the evils which beset the natural body, it is well known to be a source of fallacious treatment, and consequent disaster, to rely upon any single and definite medicament as always and everywhere applicable to a malady, the symptoms and causes of which are manifold, and differ widely for almost every individual case. This is equally true in devising remedies for special political evils; and is most conspicuously so when the evil to be grappled with is the product and expression of a vast variety of independent facts, each of which, in itself, is of a most complex kind, and connected with past events by a long chain of historical sequence. War is eminently an evil of this nature, and the complexity of the evil is sufficiently manifest from the brief review in the last chapter of some of the principal causes of modern European Wars. But each one of the causes there enumerated would admit of further analysis, the result of which would be to indicate that there is scarcely a human passion, or a folly, or a political error, and still less a political wrong, which has not contributed, in its measure and degree, to swell the great aggregate of causes of which War is

No one remedy of universal efficacy.

the inevitable effect. Hence, when it is purported to investigate remedies for War, it might be held that, in the strict sense of the word *remedy*, the enterprise would be not merely ambitious, but puerile. It is, then, matter for consideration in what sense of the word *remedy* the search for remedies for War can be held to be a reasonable and legitimate object of serious political inquiry.

<small>Is it reasonable to seek remedies for War?</small>

Though it is quite true that the grounds of War and of its perpetuation must be sought deep down in the nature of man, and in the general historical evolution of political society, yet it has been endeavored, in the last chapter, to establish that the consideration of the more general causes of War can, for modern times, and for the special circumstances of the civilized States of Europe and America, be reduced and narrowed to that of a limited number of groups of circumstances, which in part predispose States to War with each other, and in part directly originate Wars. These groups might, no doubt, be arranged in a variety of ways, and the groups themselves variously constructed; nor can any merit in the way of originality be claimed for one mode of classification as contrasted with another. All that has been here attempted has been to show that modern War between civilized States is an effect of a limited number of definite and clearly ascertainable antecedents; and that the antecedents are, each of them, to some extent at least, modifiable—always supposing there is a desire present to modify them.

<small>Causes of War can be ascertained and modified.</small>

For it must be assumed, in such an inquiry as this, that it is sincerely desired to get rid of War; an assumption which, however, very imperfectly corresponds with facts. The desire to get rid of War exists to a very different extent among different nations, though there is, probably, at the present moment, no one civilized nation that loves War for its own sake, or which would not encounter some sacrifice in order to keep it at a distance. Nevertheless, there

<small>A desire to abolish War must be assumed.</small>

are many States, and many persons in all States, to whom War seems by no means a considerable evil. To some persons and to some Governments occasional War seems, on the whole, to be more to be desired than the prospect of perpetual Peace, partly because of the coveted prizes which successful War may bring with it; and partly because of the enervating influences which unusually pacific pursuits are supposed, by some, to exercise on the national life.

It is not necessary to do more here than advert to these views as phases of current opinion, though the weight they carry in the conduct of international politics is immense. If it is held that War is all but the greatest of disasters, for the occurrence of which no mere positive gain can ever compensate, albeit the desire to avoid imminent loss might justify the encountering of it, then the sharers in such an opinion may lend an attentive ear to the suggestion of measures which aim at the abolition of War, as a proper object for the concentration of political effort. But if War is looked upon as only a moderate evil, of an equal magnitude with a number of others, and one which may properly be regarded as a ready instrument, ever at hand, for the achievement of ulterior designs, or the satisfaction of a finely wrought national sensibility, then the consideration of remedies for War must be a fruitless inquiry. It would imply nothing less than an exact calculation, repeated for each State in succession, of the value of the different objects which modern civilized States may now, or at any future time, set before themselves, and an indication of the general line of policy which each State must adopt, so that, by a reconciliation of all the various lines, conflicts and disputes may become infrequent or impossible. Such an inquiry would involve a complete scheme of general European policy, stretching into the far future; and though the preparation of such a scheme would not in itself be impracticable—as the majestic efforts of M. Auguste Comte and his Eng-

This desire not universally strong.

lish followers have demonstrated—and might not be without a value of its own, yet it must wait to be adopted *in toto* by all those States which are concerned, before the attainment of so much of its object as appertains to the abolition of War can be, even in a minute degree, reached.

Thus the first condition of engaging in a hopeful search for remedies for War, is that of believing it is an evil of so great and preponderant a magnitude as to justify the diversion of a vast amount of political activity to the solitary end of reducing the frequency of War. If such a course is resolved upon by any single State, the meaning of the word *remedy* is then plain for that State. There is not a single empirical device which, if adopted, can be a security against all War. There may be some settled plan of continuous policy, having divers branches, each of them addressed to one or more of the special group of circumstances which may be called in a peculiar sense causes of War, the adoption of which policy by any one State tends largely to reduce the chances of War, and the adoption of which by several or by all States tends, proportionately, to render the occurrence of War impossible.

Appreciation of the evils of War is essential in seeking remedies.

In prosecuting an inquiry, then, into remedies for War, it is, in the first place, assumed that War is looked upon as an evil of the first magnitude, and that any State which is sincerely in search of remedies for it is ready to make the abolition of War a distinct object of the most serious and unresting political concern, to the attainment of which object the conduct of its international relations, in all its departments, shall steadily and uniformly converge. In the second place, these remedies are numerous and often mutually inter-dependent, so that reliance cannot be placed on a resort to any one of them by itself, or even on a resort to any number of them, short of the whole. In the third place, these remedies

Abolition of War must be made a constant political aim.

The means to be employed many and various.

are often not solitary acts, or even lines, of action, so much as new attitudes, principles, tendencies, aspirations, all of a somewhat indefinite kind, and incapable of very precise description in language, though none the less real and potent in fact.

<small>Often incapable of precise definition.</small>

It is a misfortune that hitherto, instead of War being regarded as an evil, in itself demanding distinct remedies, it has rather ranked as the handmaid of politics, and has even borrowed from the realm of national law the dignity and consecrated garb appropriate to the administration of public justice. In International Law, War is spoken of as its ultimate sanction, in spite of the anomaly that War is resorted to at the arbitrary will of any State which conceives itself to be injured, or in peril of injury, and, in this respect, finds a fitter analogy in the lynch-law of the half-civilized community than in the calm and impartial justice administered by the tribunals of a European State. Nevertheless, this mode of thought has undoubtedly qualified public opinion as to the true character of War, and has disposed people rather to find in it generally an engine of justice, than to denounce it as presumedly rife with nothing else than injustice and cruelty. It is treated too much as a remedy for evils, and too little as one of the greatest of all evils, for which remedies are urgently demanded.

<small>War regarded as an instrument of justice, not as an evil to be abolished.</small>

Thus, the first step to be taken in finding a cure for War is to recognize it freely as a sign of bad health, and not of good; to make it a distinct object of public policy, not merely to avoid War for a time, but to hasten its extinction; to treat all international questions in the light of this urgent necessity; and to survey afresh the main points of customary contact with other nations, with a view of determining what beneficial changes of attitude and conduct can be introduced so as to bring about the desired end.

In the sections that follow, the main topics of international action will succcessively passed in review, in the hope that in the exact treatment of them such remedial processes, if any, as are applicable to the evil of War, will gradually disclose themselves. These processes, it has been already insisted, do not consist of a series of cleverly-contrived devices, but rather of the wisely and aptly directed adjustment of existing and familiar relationships, the end being always unswervingly kept in view, and all the courses of action denoted being, as opportunity occurs, simultaneously and persistently resorted to. The main point of difference between this inquiry and a wider inquiry into all the elements of international well-being is, that here it is held that the extinction of War is one of the first and paramount aims to which general international policy ought at present to be directed, and that to this aim it can be wisely and hopefully directed.

International relations will be here discussed with the purpose of discovering remedies for War.

SECTION II.

OF INTERVENTION AND NON-INTERVENTION.

The subject of intervention, as the word is usually understood, relates to two entirely distinct topics; one, the interference on the part of one State in the internal affairs of another State; the other, interposition on the part of any State in a dispute or War between two or more other States. It is, however, not always possible or even necessary to keep the treatment of the two sorts of Intervention quite distinct, because it usually happens that Intervention of the first kind immediately leads to Intervention of the second kind; the attempt to support any one political party or side in a conflict within the limits of a single State, usually leading to political complica-

Two kinds of Intervention—

the one often leading to the other.

tions, and probably to War, with the States which favor the other party or side. No better instance of this could be given than the anxious efforts which have been made by England, and other interested States, to abstain from giving open political support, either to the Turkish Government or to its insurrectionary subjects, for fear (among other reasons) of enlarging the area of conflict, and bringing about a War with Russia or Austria. In the same way, had any European power intervened in the late American Civil War, it is probable that similar results would have followed, and the War extended itself into Europe.

It would be of great service in the cause of maintaining European order if it could be definitely ascertained, and made a matter of general acquiescence, how far, at what times, and in what way, one State is entitled to intrude, for any purpose whatever, on the independence of another State. There are a variety of very different questions involved, which are often either wholly confused together, or only very imperfectly discriminated. There is, first (1), the strictly *legal* question, the answer to which ascertains under what conditions one State may encroach on the independence of another State without committing an actual breach of law. The ultimate limits of the *right* of Intervention being thus fixed; the next question (2) relates to how far a positive *legal duty* compels a State to intervene in the affairs of another State. A further question (3), of far greater difficulty than the former ones, relates to the *moral* right and duty, and the general political expediency, of Intervention, within the limits within which it, Intervention, is legally permissible.

Legal and moral questions relating to Intervention.

Thus, in any actual case which presents itself, it has first to be settled whether the circumstances are such as would render Intervention allowable, without a breach of law. Then it has to be determined whether a State is under any legal obligation to avail itself of its legal right to interpose. In default of any such legal obligation as a guide to political action, it remains to be considered whether it is morally obligatory, just, wise, or expedient for a State to avail itself of its legal right.

(1.) It is unfortunate that the topic of Intervention exhibits, in a peculiar degree, the inherent imperfection which at present clings to International Law, namely, the shadowy line which separates a *legal* from a *moral* right. It will be found that the writers on International Law are by no means explicit or agreed with one another as to what constitutes a legal justification for Intervention. They have fully recognized that the topic is closely bound up with that of the Sovereignty and Independence of States, and that the *onus* of proving a special justification rests upon any State which ventures to interfere with the internal constitution and administration, or with the external action, of another State.

Legal right of Intervention.

They have further investigated, often with much assiduity and conscientious spirit of research, the chief historical occasions on which Intervention has been actually resorted to, and they have collected and commented upon the best apologies which, in every case, have been alleged for the act. But, inasmuch as the story of the past, unhappily, rather presents a chronicle of lawlessness than a record of scrupulous conformity with legal rules and principles, and encroaching States have seldom failed to find a plausible legal plea for the most barefaced acts of aggression, history has not proved a very serviceable instructor, though in International Law its place, such as it is, must be the first and highest.

Teachings of history.

The result is, that this chapter of International Law is an extremely unsatisfactory one, the subject being, in fact, mostly relegated to the domain of morals and politics. The principles expressed in the now obsolete doctrine of the Balance of Power, in the claims of European order, in the claims of "humanity," and even in the arrogant pretensions of the Holy Alliance, and of what is sometimes known as the "Monroe Doctrine,"* partial as this last is in its application, will all be found to be sources in which writers on International Law have discovered legal limitations on the general principle of the absolute exemption of a truly independent State from any kind of interference from without. But the above principles, claims, and pretensions, by which the independence of States has been practically limited in the past, and is liable to be limited in the future, are either extremely vague and indeterminate in their nature, or only admit of being rendered precise and definite by reproducing an assemblage of by-gone historic circumstances and relationships, for which no true parallel could ever be found again.

Thus, when International Law attempts to lay down a broad principle that Intervention is never justifiable, or consistent with the doctrine of the independence of Sovereign States, it is instantly confronted with the facts that in almost every generation, since International Law attained any maturity, Sovereign States have forcibly and violently interposed in each other's affairs; that in many of these cases the Intervention has been countenanced by the impartial opinion of surrounding States, and approved by the judgment of posterity; and that, in the realm of practical politics, it is found that cases are almost daily presenting themselves in which, while all sorts of views are held as to the time and manner of Intervention, the legal right and moral justice of Intervention, in certain possible emergencies, is never a matter of controversy at all.

International Law only admits right of Intervention in exceptional cases.

Hence, the International Lawyer is compelled to recognize exceptions to the broad principle of exemption from interfer-

---

* See, for a full account of the scheme of the Holy Alliance, Manning's Law of Nations, Ed. 1875, p. 488; and of the Monroe Doctrine, Wheaton's Law of Nations, Dana's ed., Section 67 *seq.*, note 36.

ence. But it would seem that the time has not yet come for any general assent, sufficiently explicit to be the basis of law, as to the principles on which the exceptions are to be based. It is something that it is recognized, with increasing clearness, that These cases not clearly defined. Intervention must always specially justify itself on the ground of exceptional circumstances, and that the legal right of Intervention is, at best, only an exceptional right—being, as it is, in derogation of the primary and universal right of independence, which is essential to the very nature of a Sovereign State.

This is, undoubtedly, one of the topics on which it is desirable that the language of International Law should be made more clear and unmistakable. In this aspect, the subject may have to be referred to again. In the mean time it appears that International Law recognizes a legal right of Intervention, and indicates limits to this right, but affords a very dim and flickering light for the guidance of an honest and law-abiding Government, desirous of informing itself beforehand as to whether it will be legally justified or not in forcibly interposing in any case which presents itself.

(2.) There are cases, however, in which Intervention, either *Legal duty of Intervention.* in the internal affairs of a Foreign State or in a dispute between two States, is, or might be held to be, an inexorable legal duty, and, therefore, to include a legal right.

So far as a duty of Intervention in the internal affairs of a *Intervention in internal affairs of other States.* Foreign State goes, the circumstances in which such a duty could arise are becoming rarer every day. It is, indeed, difficult to conceive the existence of such circumstances, except in the cases which, in former times, and even up to the time of the Treaty of Vienna, constantly occurred, of two or more States combining together by Treaty to maintain a particular dynasty or form of Government, or special constitutional settlement, in one, or both, or all of the States. Thus the Parliamentary settlement of the Crown of England of 1688 was incorporated in the Treaty of Utrecht; the internal constitution of the Germanic Confederation was elaborated in minute detail in the Treaty of Vienna; and the States which formed the Holy Alliance reciprocally pledged each other jointly to support monarchical institutions, and to suppress insurrectionary movements in one another's territories.

Supposing Treaties or engagements of this sort to be really valid in point of law—which, in the case of such a one as that of the Holy Alliance, at least, is more than questionable—no doubt a legal duty to interpose might arise in the event of the *casus fœderis* actually presenting itself. But the rapid march of constitutional, not to say democratic, government in most of the States of Europe, is gradually rendering all notions of the propriety of guaranteeing any particular form of Government, or dynasty, or institutions of any sort, against the efforts of the people to change or destroy it, a daily-increasing anachronism. The inalienable moral right of the people of any State to choose and alter their own political institutions, and, if thwarted in their orderly constitutional action, to proceed to their end by any way which is open to them, is now hardly disputed anywhere, and is being even erected into a fashionable dogma, of which, by resort to so-called *plébiscites*, despotic rulers are not unwilling to avail themselves.

But, with respect to Intervention of the other sort, that is, interference in a subsisting quarrel or War between two or more other States, there are a variety of the most common and valuable Treaties, the execution of which must render it a cogent duty. To this class of Treaties belong all Treaties of general Alliance, whether only for defensive purposes, or both for offensive and defensive purposes; Treaties of guaranty and of neutralization of States, territory, seas, or canals; and Treaties

Intervention in Foreign disputes of other States.

Duty of enforcing Treaties.

of what may be called general settlement, of the kind of which specimens are found in Treaties of Peace at the close of a War, in which many leading States have been directly or incidentally concerned, such as (in recent times) the Treaty of Vienna of 1856, the Treaty of London of 1830, by which the kingdoms of Belgium and Holland were finally constituted, and the Treaty of Paris of 1856.

Treaties of general Alliance are becoming less and less com-

Treaties of general Alliance are becoming obsolete.

mon, as more comprehensive ideas of the relations of all civilized States to one another and to the whole are prevailing, and as the extreme inconvenience of making an engagement to fight in another's quarrel, without having any command of the diplomatic negotiations out of which quarrels emanate, if at all, is increasingly felt.

After the Crimean War, in which England and France were allies, a sentiment for some time continued to exist in both countries to the effect that those States were embarked in a common policy, were conscious of joint responsibilities, and were actuated by a perception of identical interests. As time wore on, and circumstances changed, this sentiment decreased in strength, and finally vanished. But, so long as it lasted, there was an indistinct feeling that England and France must have the same friends and enemies; and though there were no Treaty obligations to this effect, yet there was a strongly marked national disposition in that direction. It is probable that no two States will ever hereafter go farther than this in the direction of a general Alliance, unless there is a permanent confederacy of some sort between them, in which case other considerations come into view.

It is probable that Treaties of general settlement, by which

Treaties of general settlement ineffective; their probable disappearance.

it is vainly endeavored to crystallize forever, or for an indefinite time, the *status quo* at a particular epoch, and thereby to impose an iron barrier to the natural progress and development of States, restricting equally the most enterprising and the most stagnant, will become gradually discredited. The subject will be considered more fully under the section which deals with "Treaties;" but, in the mean time, it may be noticed that the most celebrated Treaties of this sort, commencing with those of Münster and Osnaburg, which followed on the Peace of Westphalia in 1648, and terminating with the Treaty of Paris of 1856, have either called for periodic revisions, usually at moments most favorable to the pretensions of powerful and arrogant States, or have had their provisions silently neglected—or have afforded an apology for mistimed encroachment, and thereby for aggressive War.

An engagement which contains complicated provisions, based on the assumption that the future will continue to be as the past, is made only to be broken; and the worst of it is, that if an engagement is not kept in the spirit, and, as far as possible, to the letter, the time and mode of breaking it will be selected by the strongest, while the engagement, in all its rigidity, will be enforced, as convenient, against the weakest. Thus it may be expected that Treaties of general settlement will shortly become obsolete, and the ground for the duty of Intervention be removed.

But the same is not likely to be the case with Treaties made *Treaties tend-* for the purpose of guaranteeing the performance *ing to Peace.* of other Treaties or engagements, and for the purpose of securing the Neutrality of States, territory, seas, rivers, and canals. Both these classes of Treaties have this advantage, that the direct object of them is either to prevent War or to limit its area. Treaties of guaranty can only impose the duty of Intervention when a clearly-ascertained and publicly admitted legal duty has already been grossly violated; and, therefore, the improbability of the *casus fœderis* arising is to be measured, first, by the antecedent improbability of any legal duty being ever so violated; and, secondly, by the superiority in force of a clearly-ascertained and confessed duty over an indefinite and doubtful one.

Treaties of Neutralization, again, are in many respects the most beneficial of all Treaties. They are, necessarily, made by a large number of States, some of them the most powerful and influential. They are dictated by a sense of general interest, and not of any special and narrow interest. Their direct tendency is to restrict the area of War, and thereby, in respect of certain places, to banish War altogether. If they are broken, the force which supports them is so overwhelming as to make Intervention, however decided, rather formal than belligerent.

It thus appears that, so far as the *legal duty* of Intervention is concerned, the occasions on which alone it might arise are, some of them, almost obsolete; others are becoming so; and the few remaining ones are of a nature directly to reduce the general area of War, and to make Intervention pacific rather than hostile.

(3.) It is, however, not with strictly legal questions, so far as these can be said to exist, but with what may be called moral and political questions, that the difficulties attaching to Intervention are really concerned. Assuming a State is legally entitled to intervene, either in the internal affairs of another State, or in a dispute between two States, and yet is not legally bound to intervene, the question is presented, whether Intervention morally *ought* to take place, or whether it is expedient it should take place.

Morality and expediency of Intervention.

The real issue at stake cannot be properly investigated without a preliminary inquiry into the mutual relations of States to each other, as members of a great corporate community, and the relations of each State to the community itself as a whole. It may be true that, as in the growth of a State, so in the gradual formation of a political community of States, the component members have been very imperfectly conscious of the social aim, to the attainment of which their best energies were directed, and which their very

Mutual relations of States.

vicissitudes and errors often as distinctly furthered as their conscious purposes and successes. The story of the past is, indeed, a chronicle of turbulent struggle, misconceived self-interest, and half-satisfied, half-blighted aspirations. The aspect of the present resembles that of a seething caldron, in which, from moment to moment, it seems uncertain which bubble will rise to the surface, will be the largest, will last the longest. The prospect of the future is veiled by a curtain, on which are inscribed only the guesses of statesmen, the visions of philosophers, the hopes of philanthropists. And yet a common human nature, common economical necessities, common sentiments of morality and religion, and increasingly assimilated institutions, are, and have long been, silently operating underneath all the more superficial influences, and tending to enforce at once the value of an independent national life and the equal value and moment of contribution and co-operation, through which each nation shall profit, and derive profit from the whole.

The notion of true and necessary relationships between State and State is steadily making way through a number of scarcely suspected avenues; and the attendant notion of moral rights and duties as existing between different States, independently as well of the will or caprice of their ephemeral Governments as of their populations, is recognized as the consequence and expression of those essential relationships.

Growing recognition of these relationships.

The very growth and structure of International Law—albeit, at its best, but a feeble image and counterpart of a moral system, is a testimony to the confessed belief in the existence of such relationships. From the inherent infirmity of that Law, it is obliged to lean on the strength of such sentiments as those of good faith, moral claim and obligation, equity and humanity. But these sentiments, whatever be the history of their evolution, if they are the bulwarks of Law, cannot be its products. They have rendered a legal system possible, and the legal system, in its turn, has done much to substantiate and protect them. But they subsist on an independent footing of their own, and imply that civilized States have toward each other, or (what for this purpose is the same) are generally believed to have, moral relationships, which are an exact reproduction of the relationships that every citizen of a State has to every other. In approaching, then, the question of the moral right and duty of Intervention, it must be assumed at the outset that moral relationships exist between State and State, which must be taken as the basis of interference, quite as much as the special and one-sided interest of a particular State, or particular States.

But, even with the help of this assumption, which regards *Points still undetermined.* civilized States, and pre-eminently those of Europe and America, as bound together by ties of moral right and obligation of the most enduring kind, the problem has yet to be solved as to when and how Intervention may properly take place. In all moral inquiries it is quite as perplexing an investigation to ascertain what is right and wrong, as to determine whether there is any right or wrong at all.

But the preliminary question, as to whether a State can be morally justified in wholly isolating itself, and in exhibiting no public concern whatever in transactions in which only other States seem to be concerned, even though these transactions may involve the most serious issues to the relative political situation of States, and even to humanity, must be answered first. England, in her history up to the last twenty years, has *Constant Intervention of England until recent years.* seemed to answer the question in the sense that Intervention is to be the rule, rather than the exception. But this opinion was due to circumstances peculiar to the position of England at different stages of her fortunes. First, her Feudal and Dynastical relations with France; then her Protestant sympathies as against Spain; then her implication in the Dutch policy in opposition to France; then her Hanoverian and German connections and alliances, hardly left England any choice as to whether she would, or would not, hold herself involved, for all purposes whatever, in the mesh of European politics.

The result was a sort of traditional diplomatic habit, on the part of English statesmen, of stepping forward in all emergencies, rather than holding back. This habit was, of course, a good deal exercised and stimulated by the actual military and naval successes of England, by her ever-widening Colonial Empire, and by her social and mercantile communications with all parts of the world. War and Peace meant, on the whole, perhaps, more for England of loss and gain than for any other country.

One result of these different tendencies and influences has been to generate a new party in England, which would directly reverse the whole previous policy of the country, and altogether forbid Intervention, either in the internal affairs of Foreign States, or in disputes and Wars between such States. The general principle of non-interference in the affairs of Foreign States was first practically asserted by Mr. Canning in 1826, especially as against the doctrines of the Holy Alliance. The Free-trade Movement, and his innate pacific disposition, stimulated Mr. Cobden to go still farther in the same direction, and to prepare the way for "Non-Intervention" being erected into a dogma, advocated by a distinct party, and having no inconsiderable influence in the domain of practical politics.
<small>Growth of Non-Intervention party.</small>

The tenets of this party have, no doubt, been expressed or represented in many exaggerated forms, which, if true, would have properly implicated the party in the charges of cruelty and inhuman avarice and selfishness, as well as of national disloyalty. But the utmost these tenets really mean, when carefully examined, as they appear in the language of their most competent supporters, is, that henceforward Intervention is to be the exception and not the rule; that
<small>Its true principles.</small>

all forcible Intervention in the purely internal affairs of Foreign States, whether by England or by other States, is to be strenuously discountenanced, and that England is only to intervene in disputes or conflicts between Foreign States when a sufficiently strong case seems to present itself—in weighing the merits of which case, not only the immediate and remote interests of England herself, but the interests of all other States, and the general establishment of permanent Peace and order, on the basis of free and independent national existence, must be taken into the estimate.

The following language of Lord Derby, in answer to a deputation on July 14th, 1876 (see *Times* for July 15th), probably expresses, fairly enough, the modern doctrine of Intervention, as held in England by practical statesmen, especially by way of limit to the extreme doctrine of Non-Intervention, in the form in which it is attributed to a certain party in England:

Lord Derby on Intervention.

"The doctrine of absolute indifference is not one which this country ever has professed, and I do not think it is one which would be popular with the nation at large. We have a great position in Europe; and with nations, as with individuals, a great position involves great responsibilities. We cannot absolutely decline to accept our responsibilities; for, if every nation that had reached a certain stage of civilization were to accept the principle of Non-Intervention in its absolute and extreme form, and say, 'we will never meddle in any international questions unless our own interests are touched,' the effect of that would be to leave the regulation of all international affairs to nations which have not reached that state of civilization. If the voice of England, in questions such as those we are now discussing, were to be silenced altogether, there would be one voice less heard on the side of Peace. No one is more strongly in favor of Non-Intervention, within reasonable limits, than I am; but we must push no doctrine to extremes; and an absolute declaration of Non-Intervention on all occasions would be a proclamation of international apathy, and I need not tell you that international apathy does not mean either Peace or progress."

This exposition of doctrine, even if it be valid as an expression of the current tendency of politics in England, is at best only negative, and leaves the question of the time, the occasion, and the manner of the Intervention of any sort to be settled in reference to some general principle, if such a principle, or such principles, could be found.

It may be considered that, so far as direct and forcible Intervention in the internal affairs of a Foreign State is concerned, the positive as well as the negative side of the doctrine is now pretty clearly established; that the mere strength, extent, or organization of an insurrectionary movement furnish no justification for interference either on one side or the other; the duration of an anarchical condition, coupled with the apparent improbability of order ever being restored, may justify interference on the ground of the interest which all States are presumed to have in the stability and integrity of each State; and gross acts of inhumanity persisted in on either side may, on grounds of humanity, properly precipitate Intervention.

Intervention in internal affairs. Rules now recognized.

But, even if this statement were admitted to be as fairly exact as any doctrine could be rendered in a few brief sentences, still, it is obvious that there are a number of indeterminate elements still left open, the arbitrary determination of which, by a single interested State in any given case, may lead to serious abuses. The hesitating reluctance of the United States to interfere in the struggle in Cuba,* and the grounds alleged by Servia for declaring War with Turkey—that is, the inhuman efforts made to suppress the insurrection in the neighboring Turkish provinces—exhibit

Cases for which they do not provide.

---

* See the extract from President Grant's speech, in Manning, p. 97.

the complication of private interest with public duty which perplex, or usually seem to perplex, the motives for Intervention. It is in the highest degree desirable that the element of private interest should be entirely removed—an object which can best be secured, in respect of such cases as these, by habits of combined policy among as great a number of States as possible, and those States especially who are above the suspicion of having an interested motive lower than that of promoting Peace, order, and general well-being. Thus, so far as this sort of Intervention is concerned, it is, above all, desirable that the purity of the motives should be conspicuous, and, for this end, the more States that join, the better the reputation for public honesty of the Government of those States; and the greater the publicity of the grounds of Intervention alleged, the less likely is the Intervention to be inexpedient, unjust, and provocative of general War.

Advantage of combined action.

The case of the other sort of Intervention, that of taking a public part on one side or the other in a dispute, or War, between two Foreign States, presents, at present, far greater difficulties than the former kind, because none but the roughest principles of action have as yet met with any general acceptance, and the interests at stake are usually of a far wider and more intricate kind.

Intervention in foreign disputes of other States.

Difficulty of the subject.

It is certainly not by mere abstinence from siding with one party or the other, any more than by precipitately meddling with the quarrels or feuds of other States, that a just and pacific State will always best promote the cause of Peace and order, or even succeed long in keeping War at a distance from its own borders. If it be true that the States of the civilized world, however various in character, magnitude, or temporary influence, together constitute a true political community, of which the component members owe moral duties, and have moral rights, in respect of one an-

Every War a matter of general concern.

other, then the breach of order and social continuity which War presupposes cannot but be a matter of the most urgent moment to every member of the community.

The bare fact that, as soon as War breaks out, every State not a party to the War acquires the rights, and is liable to the duties, of Neutrality, of itself makes the occurrence of War a matter of universal concern. But, apart from this change in legal position, and also apart from the social and commercial losses which War between any two States occasions in all directions, the imminent danger to the national existence of one or both the States concerned, and the open substitution of a reign of force for the current reign of law and right, is a deep moral injury and offence to every State which is a member of the great community of civilized States. The earnest diplomatic efforts which are often made, even as things are, in a truly unselfish spirit, to prevent the outbreak of a War, even between two remote States, are a token of this moral claim on the part of every State to pacific methods of settling differences at the hands of all other States.

If these efforts fail, and War breaks out, all the Neutral States have, in truth, a common cause. The object of a pacific policy should be to remove all occasions of divided and self-regarding interests from these States, so that, free from all prejudice, mutual suspiciousness, and vacillation of purpose, they may combine, either to keep clear of the struggle or to throw their weight into one scale or the other, or insist that the matter in dispute shall be settled by arbitration, at the risk of the recusant party being treated as the general enemy.

Duties and policy of Neutrals.

Though it is easy to point out the direction which policy should take in the matter of Intervention, the mutual distrust, not to say rivalries and animosities, which now prevail among European States, might well seem such as to render vaticinations of this sort chimerical. Nevertheless, it only needs two or three leading States to be united on the score of maintaining general Peace, to make any other War than a purely insurrectionary one almost impossible. Should France and Germany, for instance, forget the past, except for its instruction, and persist hereafter in desiring permanent Peace as sincerely as England does, European Peace might be almost absolutely secured. So with other possible combinations between States now accidentally estranged, as, for instance, Italy and Austria; the probability of such a combination seems, at present, so extremely small as, perhaps, to be hardly worth adverting to, even for the sake of pointing out that, if it were to occur, the variety of strong and otherwise opposed interests that would then be enlisted on the side of Peace would be able conclusively to insure it.

<small>Peace could be maintained by united action of leading States.</small>

SECTION III.

OF MEDIATION AND ARBITRATION.

AMONG political remedies for War, either apprehended or existing, the friendly Intervention or aid of States not directly concerned in the dispute properly occupies a high place. To many, indeed, this sort of remedy appears the most hopeful of all, and one of immediate applicability; and an enumeration of recently successful cases of friendly Intervention, or judicial aid, no doubt seems to give color to these hopes. But it has already been explained that War is the last expression of every other malady which disturbs the relations of States, and that it can only be removed by a series of remedial processes which address themselves to all these maladies at once. Nevertheless, the function of friendly service on the part of other States, whether taking a diplomatic form or not, deservedly ranks high among the agencies for keeping War at a distance, and finally, perhaps, providing a substitute for it.

It is not necessary, in this place, to say much about that form of friendly intervention which is known as Mediation. Its true character is well understood, from the close analogy presented in the circumstances of private life. Its success must always depend on the known integrity and disinterestedness of the mediating State, and the higher the reputation of a State for public honesty and impartiality, the more likely are its services to be put in requisition for this purpose. But the success of Mediation must depend upon the alleged grounds of dispute being the real grounds, and, therefore, upon the existence of a certain amount of genuineness and honesty of purpose in the Governments of the States which are verging on War, or already actually engaged in it. It thus appears that the province of Mediation will become larger and larger as national and international morality improves, and the desire of general Peace becomes everywhere more urgent and sincere. Any single State of conspicuous integrity, and still more, any group of two or three States, fortified by a strong, intelligent, and conscientious diplomatic service, may thus confer inestimable benefits in averting, at an early stage, the possibilities of War.

Mediation.

But the form of friendly intervention on which public attention has been especially fixed of late, is that known by the name of Arbitration. The essential elements of Arbitration consist in—(1) An agreement on the part of States having a matter, or several matters, in dispute, to refer the decision of them to a tribunal believed to be impartial, and constituted in such a way as the terms of the agreement specify, and to abide by its judgment; and in—(2) Consent on the part of the person, persons, or States, nominated for the tribunal, to conduct the inquiry and to deliver judgment.

Arbitration.

On the mere face of this description, it is obvious that there are certain conditions which must be satisfied in order to render Arbitration even so much as possible. In the first place, the matter in dispute must in itself admit of being formulated in such a way as to be made a matter of judicial decision, as distinguished from an equitable arrangement or adjustment of political claims. Of course, the terms of the reference may be large and indefinite, and considerable powers may be given to the Arbitrators of adjusting claims, even of an indeterminate kind, and making compensatory settlements of a variety of sorts. But the claims, however indeterminate, must be included in precise language, and the limits of the capacity of the Arbitrators must be strictly defined. This condition points to the obvious suitability of Arbitration to all cases in which the dispute relates to a matter of unsettled law, or to controverted matters of fact, or to the correct interpretation to be placed on a Treaty or other legal document, or to the fixing of a boundary line, or to the amount and kind of compensation due for an admitted wrong, or to monetary claims on the part of a State against another State, or of a citizen of one State against another State. In all such matters as these, in which the mere statement of the ground of dispute indicates a readiness to accept a conciliatory solution of it, if such can be found compatible with national self-respect, the field for the friendly offices of other States in forming, or assisting to form, tribunals of Arbitration, is almost illimitable; and it is likely enough increased recourse will be had to this mode of reducing international difficulties, as its value becomes better recognized, and the greater complication of the relations between State and State multiplies occasions of possible disagreement.

Precise definition of points in dispute essential to Arbitration.

Cases obviously suitable for Arbitration.

But there are other cases of dispute which are far more formidable than those just alluded to, and yet which involve elements of such a refined or incalculable kind that, on the face of it, the settlement often seems to set at defiance the capacity of the best constituted tribunal exercising powers of the most elastic and equitably adjustive kind. These cases of dispute are, as often as not, kept secret by means of a plausible insistence on other more palpable grounds—which are, however, constantly shifted, as a fresh turn in the course of diplomatic negotiation seems to suggest.

The abnormal cases which, on the face of them, seem, for one *Difficulty of fulfilling the necessary conditions in other cases.* reason or other, far less adapted for a tribunal of Arbitration than those previously mentioned, belong usually to one or other of the following classes. Either a State believes that the action, or menaced action, of another State is such as seriously to menace its own independence, or even its national existence; or it believes such action is hostile or fatal to some scheme of policy which it has, for reasons sufficient to itself, deliberately adopted and long perseveringly adhered to; or it believes some act of another State, or some imputation cast on itself, to be injurious to what it designates as its own "national honor," and to call not only for instant repudiation, but, possibly, for condign punishment. The question is, whether cases of dispute belonging to these several classes can be looked upon as fulfilling the conditions which the possibility of reference to Arbitration demands.

As to the first class of cases, in which the independence or existence of a State is believed to be menaced, it is evident that the terms here used are so wide and indefinite as to afford, in almost any conceivable case, a ready excuse for declining Arbitration to a State indisposed to settle promptly a pending dispute; and as much might be said of the third class of cases here denoted, in which the "national honor" is said to be involved. In respect of both the first and third class of cases, it is often alleged that when once it is believed that existence, independence, or honor are really involved, no State could ever be expected to submit to the judgment of any tribunal, however constituted; and, even if it were, the matters in dispute are usually of too delicate and intangible a kind to be made matters of judicial reference.

This jealousy—certainly, at present, not a wholly irrational one
—of all tribunals of Arbitration in respect of questions believed to be vital, is due to the struggling rivalries, the selfish assumptions, and the sinuous and unfathomable policy which at present characterize European States. A deep political distrust, easily stirred into active hatred, and generally allied with an overreaching covetousness, is keeping the nations apart, almost as forcibly and constantly as a crowd of moral, social, and economic influences, over which Statesmen have only an indirect control, are drawing them together. The notion, which is banished from the economic world, still survives in the political world, that nations profit, on the whole, from one another's weakness and misfortune, rather than from one another's strength and prosperity. There are innumerable influences at work which are combating this persuasion; but, so long as it continues widely prevalent, no true political equality can exist among States, of a kind to enable any one State to trust itself implicitly to the integrity and justice of all the rest.

Mutual distrust of States: its gradual decrease.

Thus, though the field of Arbitration is undoubtedly limited at the present moment, there are two directions in which it is now undergoing, and may be made to undergo much more rapidly, further extension. In the first place, the sensitiveness of States as to what touches their existence, independence, or honor, is already being greatly reduced, and may be reduced still further, especially when a true view is taken of the terrible alternative presented by War, and of the superior concern which all States have in the welfare, rather than in the misfortunes, of other States.

Reasons for anticipating a more general resort to Arbitration in the future.

Injurious and wrongful, too, as any contumelious treatment of one State by another is, the remedy is sought by a mutual massacre of the peaceably-disposed citizens of both States, and an enormous destruction of wealth on both sides is by no means satisfactory, either to the States concerned, or to the rest of the world. If the injured State proves to be

Appreciation of the evils of War.

the stronger in a military sense, a fresh career of injuries from the other side does little to re-establish permanently peaceful relationships. If it proves to be the weaker, the original injury remains, without so much as the shadow of redress, and a fresh crop of injuries, of the most embittering kind, succeeds to it. The final result is a rough and hasty settlement, under circumstances of impassioned hostility, and usually not without the friendly services of those very States whose appearance on a Tribunal of Arbitration would have been, at the outset, indignantly repudiated.

In the second place, it is probable that a greater confidence in the disinterested integrity of Foreign Governments will lead to a disposition, on the part of single States, to trust even their most vital interests to the general voice of the European community, rather than to the chances of War. This time seems very remote; but in respect of all neutralized States, and even of all very small States, this end is already practically attained. Even in respect of the largest States, it would hardly be publicly professed that their claim to continued existence is to be exactly proportioned to the military preparations and ability available, from moment to moment, for their protection. The whole tendency of civilization in International, as in National, society, is the other way, and is directed to ridding the individual members of the community of the necessity of self-defence, and to saving the waste of private effort which the necessity for constant readiness occasions.

Growth of confidence in the community of States.

As to the second class of cases, in respect of which it may seem impossible that a State will consent to refer to any tribunal whatever matters which seem to touch a scheme of policy to which it is (in its own eyes) irretrievably committed, this class of cases can only become reduced by a general simplification in such schemes, accompanied by greater diplomatic publicity. This subject will be discussed lower down in a distinct section.

There are a variety of schemes which have been devised, and

Schemes for constituting Courts of Arbitration.

some of which have been put in practice, for the constitution of Arbitration. Some of these schemes are very elaborate and ingenious, and are only wanting in regard for the true political difficulties which, at present, have to be overcome. It has become the fashion of late years to include in Treaties provisions for Courts of Arbitration, variously constituted, to which may be referred the decision of pending questions, or of matters of dispute which may hereafter present themselves, or the interpretation of the language of the Treaty itself. The value of such provisions is very considerable, as the experience of the use of Arbitration, and familiarity with its practice, are likely to help much in extending its scope. But it would be a great gain if any tribunal

Desirability of a permanent Court.

could be constituted in advance, to which questions might be referred from time to time as they arose. The permanence of such a tribunal, and the continuity of its acts, would impart some credit for indifference in respect of any special matter submitted to it. Even if, for a time, very few questions were, in fact, submitted to it, its very existence would be a type and pledge of an institution which the community of States must inevitably hereafter develop, and must facilitate the way to its formation.

SECTION IV.

OF TREATIES, AND ESPECIALLY TREATIES OF PEACE.

The formally-written conventions by which States ascertain

Importance of Treaties in forming International Law.

their legal relations to each other, have, naturally, considerable influence in determining not only those relations, but also their moral relations. A Treaty, testifying, as it does in the most explicit manner, the deliberate assent and consent of two States at least, has a far wider operation in International Society than a legal contract has in National Society. International legal relations are, at present, almost exclusively built upon the express or presumed acquiescence of States which share in them; and, therefore, a formal document which purports to register the nature and extent of that acquiescence on the part of two or more States, and in reference to a more or less limited subject-matter, properly carries with it enormous weight. A series or assemblage of such documents, in which a great variety of States take part, is equivalent to a legislative act, or the last decision of a supreme Court of Appeal. Even a single Treaty, in which a number of States take part, may, in connection with other circumstances, introduce, and go far to substantiate, a wholly new principle of law, which will shortly be held binding on all States. In the case of an ambiguous or long-disputed point of law, even a single Treaty between not more than two States may, by adopting or excluding a particular interpretation, go far to terminate all controversy on the subject, or, at least, to prepare the question for exact logical treatment.

Treaties differ from the legal contracts which are made within the limits of a single State in the following (among other) particulars. In the first place, they are never negotiated by the true and sole parties to them—that is, by a State with a State, but by the mediation of what is, usually, a double agency. That is, the Executive Government of the day, in greater or less dependence on the Legislature, operates as the organ of the permanent State, and deputes its own envoys or delegates to arrange the terms of the engagement—reserving, of course, the right of giving constantly fresh directions, and of finally ratifying, or of not ratifying, the Treaty in its completed form.

Points of difference between Treaties and civil contracts.

In the second place, the only form of conveyance of territory known to International Law is that by Treaty. It is true that, in national law, the same document often contains both a contract and a conveyance; and some Courts of Law even place upon terms apparently designed only to effect a contract, an interpretation by which a conveyance is actually effected quite as much as a contract. But in International Law a conveyance, whether by way of gift, sale, partition, or exchange, can be effected in no other way than by Treaty; that is, territory can only pass by the force of the assent of the two States which are interested in the transaction, and it is a Treaty which registers this assent and engages both States, under the obligations of public honor and good faith, to adhere to and in every way support the arrangement, at any rate as between one another.

In the third place, as has been already noticed, Treaties go far to construct the law itself as binding on the parties to them, and afford most important testimony to the condition of the law as binding upon all States. This is, of course, not the case with ordinary contracts, which are, from first to last, under the control of rules of law, the application of which they can only modify within very sharply-defined limits.

It is important to point out these differences, because it is so common, in handling the subject of Treaties, to follow servilely the analogy of the contracts of civil life, and thereby to lose sight of certain precautions which Treaties, in so far as they differ from those contracts, peculiarly demand.

Treaties are made by States; and States, as was explained in an earlier part of this treatise, are in a condition of incessant flux and change, of a kind which can be very imperfectly calculated or predicted. Nevertheless, Treaties which include conveyances of territory, and affect to establish a permanent settlement in the political relations of States, have been often enough—and even in recent times—made in all the excitement, irritation, or exhaustion which attend the close of a War.

Defects of Treaties.

The difficult circumstances in which they are drawn up.

Such Treaties, again, though held to be forever binding on

States, under all their vicissitudes of Governments and constitutions, are often made by a party in the State temporarily paramount in influence, without concert with their rivals, without pledging the whole Legislature to their views, and without encountering public discussion in the country. The Treaties, too, are necessarily made by envoys, adjusted from moment to moment, according to the changing phases of the negotiation, with very incomplete facilities of communication between the Government and their representatives, and under circumstances, usually, of great pressure and haste.

Political hesitation, again, about their own future conduct, and the lurking propensity to reserve themselves the right of profiting by new emergencies which may present themselves, generally induce States to introduce vague and indeterminate stipulations into their Treaties, of a kind which no two contractors in civil life would ever consent to in drawing an ordinary written agreement. Treaties, or provisions in Treaties, for guaranteeing the independence of a small State, for neutralizing States or territories, or for supporting a dynastic settlement in a newly-constituted or reformed State, are proverbially vague and large in their language, leaving it quite uncertain what is to be the exact moment and occasion of Intervention under the Treaty; whether the engagement is only a joint or only a several one; whether Intervention is optional or obligatory; what is the kind and amount of Intervention which is contemplated. Many recent cases illustrate the extreme danger and inconvenience of leaving all these points open, to be settled by every State at a juncture of great public excitement, in accordance with the caprice either of its Government or of a partially informed majority of its population, which may succeed in making themselves heard.

Indefiniteness of their provisions.

The same hesitation or indefiniteness of purpose, as well as the necessities of the case, lead to the language of Treaties being usually couched in a form peculiarly liable to generate difficulties and doubts in the matter of interpretation. The mere fact that two contracting States commonly use different languages, and therefore, in composing a Treaty, are obliged either to resort to a third language, habitually used by neither of them, or to have a separate copy of the Treaty in each language, of itself prepares the way for much uncertainty in interpretation. But in the composition of every important legal document destined to have an enduring existence a choice has to be made between resorting to purely technical verbiage, the true significance of which can only be understood by professional students, and by them handed on from one age to another, or employing ordinary speech and words, in their common colloquial meaning at the day; or employing partly the one class of words and speech, and partly the other.

Need for precise legal phraseology—

It is the misfortune of Treaties, and of the States which make them, that the last of these modes is that most familiarly resorted to in the composition of them. They are the joint product of statesmen, professional diplomatists, and professional lawyers. Immediate expediency, deliberate policy, diplomatic routine, and tradition, courtesy, and a polite desire to abstain from rough and hard pressing in clear and explicit terms of a claim or advantage, all compete with the lawyer's demand for inexorable minuteness and logical precision.

It will be remembered that when a controversy arose as to the admission of what were called the "indirect claims" of the American Government among the matters of reference to Arbitration, under the Treaty of Washington of 1870, the expression "'Alabama' claims" was found to have been vaguely used in the Treaty to embody a vast quantity of indistinct grounds of alleged injury and demands for compensation, which had been made at various times, and were nowhere precisely specified in the Treaty. As it happened, the Arbitrators at Geneva, at the very outset of the

shown in the Geneva Arbitration.

proceedings, had the good sense to put a clear and narrow interpretation upon the expression "'Alabama' claims." But the looseness of the wording had already led to bitter charges and recriminations between the people of England and the United States, and had very nearly rendered the Arbitration proceedings impossible. Had the question not been one of Arbitration, the inexact language might well have prepared the way for War. It appeared that one of the negotiators of the Treaty, at least (Mr. Mountague Bernard), was throughout in favor of drawing the document in precise legal phraseology, but the professional diplomatists and British Government discouraged such a course. The general consequence of so fluctuating and inexact a form being imparted to documents so lasting and weighty is, that Governments have been able to avail themselves of a strict or lax interpretation of the Treaty as suited their convenience, the legal part of the phraseology seeming to favor the former, and the colloquial part the latter.

The above general considerations seem to suggest certain improvements in the making of Treaties, which may be expected to have a most beneficial influence in diminishing the causes of War. In the first place, (1) it would be well if Treaties could be made perfectly definite in respect of the matters which are really agreed to by the contracting parties, so that, as soon as ever the event occurs upon which action is to be taken by one or other party under the Treaty, there may be no doubt as to which party is to act, and as to how the party is to act, and that there be as little option left in the matter as possible, whether action at all shall be taken or not. In the second place, (2) Treaties might with advantage be made more definite and exact in their language. The progress and gradual codification of International Law will have the effect of evolving a juridical language, and the concert of professional students of abstract law in different countries will call into existence a juridical school, both of which together may have, and

Remedies for these defects.

must be made to have, a weighty influence in the composition and exact interpretation of Treaties.

No doubt statesmen shrink from Treaties being interpreted with the rigorous and too often pettifogging particularity which is familiar in Courts of Justice in the case of ordinary contracts. But this is only saying that, though States are styled "juridical" or "artificial" persons, they are not human beings, and political relations are to be determined by reference to principles which are not applicable to the relations between man and man. But, admitting this to the full, accuracy and certainty, where attainable, are obviously better than shiftiness and ambiguity of meaning; and the best way of securing an undeviating fixity in the signification of terms and sentences is to promote, in every way possible, the growth of juridical science, and to bring into the closest communication the jurists of all countries. When once the intent of statesmen is ascertained, it is to professional jurists, sensitively acquainted with the amount and kind of accuracy which the occasion really demands, that the formal composition of Treaties alone belongs.

In the third place, (3) there is an obvious inconvenience in

General settlements should be negotiated in time of Peace, not at the close of a War.

taking the occasion, as was eminently done in some of the most celebrated Treaties, of a Treaty of Peace to make a general settlement of a number of long disputed questions. There are no Treaties which are, from their very inception, so brittle as Treaties of Peace. There is always an element of force and violence in the imposition of them which is wholly alien to the deliberate voluntariness which a true mental engagement presupposes, and which, in the case of any ordinary legal contract, must be present as of course.

Apart, too, from force, such a Treaty is always made under circumstances of irritation and animosity, as well as of haste, at a moment when the interests of the contracting parties seem to be violently opposed, and when the latent object of the

Treaty on both sides must be, not to further the common advantage of both, but to further the separate ends of each at the expense of the other. It is impossible to picture an occasion less suited to that impartial survey of a number of conflicting and complex interests, and that calm appreciation of the merits of competing advantages, near and remote, present and future, certain and contingent, which a hopeful settlement of long disputed questions between a variety of States eminently demands.

The later history of the Treaties of Münster, of Utrecht, of Vienna (1815), and of Paris (1856), is full of illustrations of the truth of these remarks, and has done much to bring Treaties into disrepute, and to make the obligation which attaches to them almost proverbially synonymous with open bad faith or fraudulent evasion. This imputation on the actual validity of subsisting Treaties is by no means just, inasmuch as all civilized States are parties to a vast multiplicity of Treaties on all sorts of subjects which are habitually and rigidly observed, even in their minutest provisions. But the complex political settlements and territorial conveyances which have been contained in some of the most celebrated Treaties of Peace have been, undoubtedly, followed by acts of disruption and reconstruction, which have done much to bring all Treaties into discredit, and to occasion War.

Assuming that those settlements and conveyances were, in themselves, recommended by considerations of general expediency and justice, any time would seem to be more propitious for effecting them than that of the close of a War, and any document more suitable than the same document which contains the hard terms of Peace imposed by the conqueror on the conquered. It would seem advisable that matters of general settlement and conveyance, when not forming essential terms on which Peace is concluded, should always be arranged during Peace, and at some distance of time from the closing of a War.

No doubt, at present, the susceptibility of many European

Governments is so finely strung that there is a general fear of suggesting questions of readjustment, however obviously desirable in the interests of all parties, for fear of awaking hopes and fears which cannot be quieted, and thereby precipitating the very disputes which it is designed to avoid. But as mutual confidence between State and State grows, and as it subsists between the United States of America and most European States, the anticipation of disputes by friendly settlements in time of Peace becomes increasingly possible, and the most laudable object of an enlightened diplomacy.

Akin to this topic is another one, to which the late Mr. John Stuart Mill drew attention, that Treaties are too frequently made without any provision for the circumstances under which they are made undergoing a complete change, and, therefore, an alternative being presented, either of their being violently infringed, or of a pressing request for their revision being tendered by one of the parties at a moment when the other party may find it peculiarly inconvenient to resist. It will be remembered that Russia selected the moment of France being occupied with the German War of 1870 to demand from England and France, and the other signatories to the Treaty of Paris of 1856, a revision of an important clause in the Treaty, and the demand was necessarily, though reluctantly, acceded to.

Advantage of providing for the revision of Treaties.

Mr. Mill proposed that no Treaty should endure for longer than a definite time without revision; but this could not be made to apply to Treaties which are in the nature of conveyances, which must be permanent. The better rule would be that, for all Treaties not of the nature of conveyances, the arrangement be made for a short and definite time, at the end of which time any party to the Treaty should be entitled to convoke a congress of the signatory States for the purpose of revising the Treaty. If, at the time for revision, one of the signatory States should be at War with another, the time should be deferred till a year had elapsed after the conclusion of Peace.

There is another question, in respect of improvements in the mode of making Treaties, which has to be answered, that is, the amount of public discussion, in popularly constituted legislative Assemblies, which it is expedient they should undergo. In all the States of Europe, and in the United States of America, it is the Executive Government which alone is charged with the task of negotiating, concluding, and ratifying Treaties with other States; though sometimes, as in the case of the concurrence of the Senate with the President of the United States, the Executive Government has a peculiar constitution imparted to it for this purpose.

Share of popular Assemblies in making Treaties.

The increasing dependence in modern States, and especially in England, of the Executive Government of the day on the popular branch of the Legislature, both for its existence and for the pecuniary supplies needed to enable it to carry out its political projects, enforces the general importance of freely communicating to the public all information on Foreign Affairs, and inviting popular sympathy and aid at every stage in the conduct of lengthened negotiations. Nevertheless, the necessity for instant action, the privacy inherent in the notion of confidential instructions and suggestions to foreign agents, the claims of Foreign Governments to have the secrecy of their own communications, within certain limits, respected, as well as the vast amount of special knowledge which the conduct of relations with a complex network of foreign States demands, must always seclude a large part of diplomatic action from the public eye.

Some amount of secrecy a necessary evil.

It should be remembered, however, that this privacy is an evil, even though it be a necessity; and is to be acquiesced in only to the extent to which it is proved to be a necessity. As the whole State is permanently responsible for the discharge of its Treaty obligations, it is of the utmost importance that these obligations should be, as far as possible, thoroughly understood and deliberately undertaken by the people as a whole; and it may be fairly taken for granted that those fine stipulations, and neatly-adjusted arrangements, which are most commonly removed from the broad area of public discussion, often grow into the most potent causes of dispute and War.

There is another remark which must be made on the subject of Treaties. It is, that when a clear case presents itself of a State breaking its Treaty, the punishment, of whatever kind it be, should come from the hands of all civilized States at once, and not only from the hands of the other signatory or signatories. The offence is far more of the nature of a crime than a mere breach of contract or civil injury; and it is a crime which strikes at the root of the moral and legal relationships on which the community of civilized States is based. Mr. Mountague Bernard* has shown how impotent were all the cumbrous oaths contained in the Treaties of the Middle Ages, and how they have been superseded by the simplest language. But a truer appreciation of the nature of the offence contained in a national breach of faith will lead to a sentiment of such general indignation being aroused by it, that the vindication of the broken law may be as safe in the hands of those least directly interested as of those most so.

All States should combine to punish a breach of Treaty.

SECTION V.

OF GREAT AND SMALL STATES, AND OF THE EQUILIBRIUM OF STATES.

THE question as to what is the most suitable magnitude for States to attain, in order best to promote the interests of Peace and of general prosperity, is too purely abstract to be matter of

---

* See Obligation of Treaties, p. 190 of Lectures on Diplomacy.

profitable speculation. Some political theorists, indeed, have endeavored to answer it, and it is well known that M. Comte mapped out the whole world into 120 Republics, only some of them roughly corresponding to existing States. These inquiries are not without their value, as they tend to disclose principles which may be useful guides in solving the narrower and more immediate problems of practical politics. These problems spring out of directly historical causes, and it is only by glancing at these causes that the true purport of modern problems can be so much as understood.

In reverting to the later history of Modern Europe, from the time, say, of the Peace of Westphalia, in 1649, it will be seen that two distinct political tendencies have constantly manifested themselves as bearing on the distribution of Europe into separate States. One of these tendencies has been that of compounding large States out of small ones; the other, that of disintegrating States and making small States out of large ones. Both of these tendencies have been beneficial, and the combination of both tendencies together more beneficial than either of them alone. The recent consolidation of Germany, Italy, and Austria expresses quite as manifest an inclination of forces in the modern political world as does the separation of Belgium and Holland, the creation of the Kingdom of Greece, the establishment of the Principalities of Servia and Roumania, and the persistent recognition and support of the independence of the Netherlands, of the Swiss Confederation in its successive forms, of Portugal, of Denmark, and of Sweden and Norway.

Consolidation and disintegration of States in Modern Europe.

Different principles have been alleged in favor of the several political modifications which have produced these results, and these principles have often been alleged in favor of carrying the movements still further. Sometimes geographical limits have been assigned as a sort of natural mark of the territory of a State. Sometimes community

Alleged reasons for these changes.

of race, religion, or language has been assigned as ground for political distribution or redistribution.

Still more frequently has a still vaguer principle of political cohesion been found in alleged nationality, which seems to imply a reference to a unity of political traditions in the past— possibly a very remote past. One or other of these grounds for extending an old, or forming a new political aggregate, have been familiarly alleged by aggressive despots and revolutionary leaders. The truth is, that in considering any special case in which the propriety of extending the limits of a State, of adjusting the frontiers of two bordering States, or of forming a new State, comes into question, all the circumstances must be taken into consideration together; and though the condition of the population, in respect of race, language, religion, and nationality, is essential to the inquiry, yet no one of these characteristics can, by itself, be admitted to dominate over the reasoning; and not even all of them together can afford a certain clew to a decision.

Nevertheless, the general consequences which attend the formation of great and of small States respectively, and especially of the combination of the two in certain proportions, can be approximately assigned as a guide to general political action.

The relative value of great and of small States is capable of being fairly estimated by referring to the recent changes which have been made in the constitution of certain States with a Federal organization, such as Switzerland, Germany, and the United States. In all these countries the purely Federal constitution has been rapidly giving way to a strict republican or parliamentary form of Government, and this change has not only been promoted through a conscious experience of the inferiority of the earlier stage, but seems to have been abundantly justified by the subsequent results. In all three cases, external strength and influence, internal harmony, fiscal convenience, and invigoration of the national

Relative advantages of large and small States.

spirit, have taken the place of weakness abroad and disunion at home.

But this is no argument in favor of the indefinite aggregation of small States into larger ones. If pushed beyond a certain limit of extension, a State may include an amount of territory, and a sort of population which, under its existing constitution, its Government cannot control; and its constitution may not easily admit of the only radical changes which would enable it to extend its dominion. Beyond a certain point, again, an extension of the frontier may bring the State face to face with new rivals, or with new occasions of difference or dispute. This is especially true when the new territory of a State enters, as a wedge, into the territory of another State, or is enclosed, on the land side, wholly by the territory of another State, or borders the territory of several States. In this way a natural limit would seem to be imposed to the indefinite territorial expansion of States, and this limit ought to be observed in making Treaties of Peace.

But, even apart from any question of further expansion, a State in which the territory and population are both large has always strong inducements to convert a large proportion of its resources to purely military purposes. Its strongly centralized institutions favor this disposition, while the *éclat* which attaches to military display on a great scale further stimulates it. The importance of internal repose and external security seem further to justify it. Thus, looking merely to the interests of Peace, it is not without reason that large States are, in proportion to their dimensions, regarded as dangerous to those interests.

Large States dangerous to Peace.

Small States, on the other hand, can only subsist by the practical toleration, or the express guarantees, of the larger States. In some cases it may be the generally recognized interest of all the larger States that the small States should be maintained in their integrity,

Small States dependent upon the observance of Public Law.

rather than swallowed up by any one of themselves, and general guarantees are, in such a case, easily obtained. But in other cases, where no such guarantees exist or could be obtained, these small States rest upon no other foundation than that of Public Law. Their existence is a standing testimony to the validity of that law; and in no more distinct and concrete form can the notion of law, as determining the relations of States, be maintained in its unmutilated integrity than by promoting the creation, and defending the independence, of small States.

The relation of small States to large States has usually been discussed in connection with the doctrine of the Balance of Power—a doctrine which has, perhaps, since the beginning of the sixteenth century, exercised more influence than any other single doctrine over practical European politics. It is worth while examining how far this doctrine is really obsolete, as is commonly alleged, in the present day, or what transformation it has undergone. The following are the chief instances in which the notion of an equilibrium of States as an object of European policy appears, in the present century, on the face of public documents.

Principle of the Balance of Power.

The Preamble of the Treaty of Paris of the 30th of May, 1814, recites, among the purposes of the Treaty, the desire of the parties to it to terminate the long agitations of Europe, and the sufferings of mankind, by a permanent Peace, *founded upon a just repartition of force* between its States, and containing in its stipulations the pledge of its durability. The Treaty was signed by the representatives of Austria, Great Britain, France, Portugal, Prussia, Russia, Spain, and Sweden. "Separate and Secret" Articles were signed at the same time between what may be considered as the Great Powers—that is, all the parties to the main body of the Treaty, except Portugal, Spain, and Sweden.

References to it during the present century.

The first of these Articles is as follows: "The disposal of the territories given up by His most Christian Majesty, under the third Article of the Public Treaty, and the relations from whence a system of real and permanent Balance of Power in Europe is to be derived, shall be regulated at the Congress upon the principles determined upon by the Allied Powers among themselves, and according to the general provisions contained in the following Articles." Thereupon follow a series of three Articles dealing severally with the boundaries of the Austrian and Sardinian Territories in Italy and the guarantee of Switzerland, with the territory of Holland, and with the aggrandizement of Holland by the acquisition of the "German Territories upon the left bank of the Rhine, which have been united to France since 1792." The third Article expressly recites that the "establishment of a just *Balance of Power* in Europe requires that Holland should be so constituted as to be enabled to support her Independence through her own resources."

At a Conference held at Vienna on the 14th of June, in which Austria, Great Britain, Prussia, and Russia took part, a protocol stated the principles from which the Powers started, relative to the Union of Belgium with Holland. The first clause of this protocol stated that "the Union was decided upon by virtue of the political principles adopted by them for the establishment of *a state of equilibrium* in Europe."

The establishment of a "just equilibrium in Europe" was again referred to as among the general objects of the Treaty of 31st May, 1815, between Austria, Great Britain, Prussia, Russia, and the Netherlands, for determining the boundaries of the Kingdom of the Netherlands, and ascertaining the basis of the Union of the Belgic Provinces. This Treaty subsequently formed Annex X. of the Vienna Congress Treaty of the 9th of June, 1815.

In the Treaty between Prussia and Russia of the 3d of May, 1815, by which the claims of Prussia and Russia in the Polish Duchies created by Bonaparte were adjusted, and the Polish Constitution, under the Czar as King, was created, the Preamble recites, as among the objects of the Treaty, that of settling the state of affairs "by combined negotiations founded upon the principles of a just *Balance of Power* and division, discussed and agreed upon at the Congress of Vienna."

In 1850 a Conference was held at London relative to the integrity of the Danish Monarchy, in which the Plenipotentiaries of Austria, Great Britain, Denmark, France, Russia, Sweden, and Norway adopted a protocol on the 4th of July, which recited that the several Powers, "considering that the maintenance or integrity of the Danish Monarchy, *bound* to the general *interests of European equilibrium*, is of great importance for the preservation of Peace, have resolved, at the invitation of His Majesty the King of Denmark, to establish the perfect accord which exists between the Cabinets relative to the maintenance of that principle."

Again, the Treaty of the 21st of November, 1855, signed at Stockholm by the Representatives of Great Britain, France, and Sweden and Norway, recites that these several Powers, "being anxious to avert any complication which might disturb the existing *Balance of Power* in Europe, have resolved to come to an understanding with a view to secure the integrity of the United Kingdoms of Sweden and Norway."

In the Treaty of the 12th of March, 1854, by which Great Britain, France, and Turkey agreed on the principles of their alliance against Russia, the Preamble recited that the Parties to the Treaty were fully persuaded "that the existence of the Ottoman Empire in its present limits was essential to the maintenance of the *Balance of Power* among the States of Europe."

The same principle was appealed to in the Austrian Manifesto of War with Prussia and Italy, on the 17th of July, 1866; in the French Manifesto of 19th of July, 1870, alleging the causes of War with Prussia; and in the Russian Note of the 31st of October, 1870, denouncing the Stipulations of the Treaty of Paris of 1856, and inviting a revision of some of them. Numberless other references to the same principle have been contained in the preambles of conventions and the protocols of conferences, in reference to the various settlements of the affairs of the Ottoman Empire, which have been made or attempted to be made.

It will thus be seen that the principle of what is variously styled the *Balance of Power* and the *Equilibrium of States*, was openly announced as the ground of the resettlement of Europe, broadly delineated in the Treaty of Paris of the 30th of May, 1814, and carried out by the Vienna Congress Treaty of the 9th of June, 1815. The same principle has been since incessantly appealed to in the language of Treaties, Conventions, and Protocols, by which the independence of the smaller or weaker States, as Holland, Denmark, Sweden, Norway, and Turkey was guaranteed. The principle has also occasionally been appealed to in disputes between the larger States, even when the interests of the smaller States have been only remotely and indirectly concerned. These observations, as illustrated by reference to the actual circumstances in which the principle of a "Balance of Power" has been, on each occasion, appealed to, lead to the following conclusions:

<small>Conception of the Balance of Power in the past.</small>

The notion of a Balance of Power is not obsolete in European politics, though it wears a very different shape now from what it once wore. The older conception wavered between two principles; one, that of supporting an existing *status quo*, and resenting any redistribution of power—however otherwise equitable and generally beneficial—which might seem to assail it; the other, that of bringing general pressure to bear—whether diplomatic or belligerent—against any single State which, by acquisitions of territory, or political annexations in Europe, seemed likely to be able to set at defiance the restraints of public law. Each principle was effective for preventing War, or for determining alliances at the commencement of a War, or during a War; and was, in fact, the basis of the political combinations against Spain in the sixteenth century, and against France in the seventeenth century.

But if a War had lasted some time, and territory had been occupied and conquests made on both sides, there could no longer be any thought of maintaining an absolute *status quo*. The best hope, then, was to supervise the provisions of the Treaty of Peace, and readjust the map of Europe in such a way as might carry into effect the second of the above-mentioned principles. The Treaty of Münster, in 1649, by which, at the close of the Thirty Years' War, among a vast number of territorial and political rearrangements, the independence of Switzerland and the United Provinces was formally acknowledged; and the Treaty of Utrecht, in 1713, by which it was provided that the Crowns of France and Spain should never be united, afford the most signal instances of the true purport and practical application of the doctrine of the Balance of Power in one of its forms.

There can be no doubt that the prevalence of the Doctrine
Its tendency to promote Peace. did, on the whole, tend to preserve the existence of the smaller States, and, in the end, to promote the Peace of Europe. Of course the principle, when it was professed most loudly, mingled with, and was often subordinated to very different considerations, such as those due to the chances of successful War, elaborate diplomatic contrivances, and traditional systems of policy. But the principle was undoubtedly a real, as well as an apparent, influence of the greatest moment, and the habit of recognizing and deferring to it kept the States of Europe in close relations of intimacy with one another, and made the Wars that were actually waged of a less purely selfish kind, and more profitable in their results, than they might otherwise have been.

It is usually said that the doctrine of the Balance of Power was first publicly proved to have lost its efficacy on the first division of Poland in 1772; and the progress of Napoleon's conquests, as well as the nature and grounds of the opposition to him, certainly showed that the doctrine of the Balance of Power could, at the commencement of the present century, no longer be relied upon as a principle of cohesion among the States of Europe, nor trusted as an instrument for securing Peace and order. The doctrine was still customarily adverted to in public documents, but rather as a euphonious supplement to more potent considerations than as possessing any inherent vitality of its own. It is, in fact, now little more than a convertible expression for the policy of maintaining the territorial integrity and independence of the smaller States.

Present Inefficacy of the doctrine.

If it be asked how this weakening of the doctrine of the Balance of Power has been brought about, the answer must be found in the gradual disintegration of the society of European States, which has been long operating—and, recently, at a rapid rate—through an assemblage of causes—political, religious, and commercial—which are mostly of a novel kind. States no longer are bound together in large groups by widespread dynastic ties, or even by uniformity of political constitutions. They can no longer be broadly classed as Protestant or Catholic States. The doctrine of Free-trade, though in a very true sense it promotes the sense of national inter-dependence, does none the less also tend to isolate States from one another, and make them indifferent to the value of accidental alliances or casual ties. Thus, a period is now intervening during which the old traditional connections between States are being broken up, and new and, it is hoped, more extended and permanent, relationships are forming themselves.

Causes of its waning influence.

In the mean time it cannot be a matter of surprise if a doctrine such as that of the Balance of Power, which, for its general application, demanded an habitual and intimate co-operation of all the States of Europe, should have fallen into desuetude. This is, no doubt, what has happened, and the exaggerated form which the English principle of "Non-Intervention" at one time took, is an exhibition of the change. But there is good reason to believe that effective substitutes for that which has passed away are discovering themselves, and that ambitious schemes will be effectually repressed, and small States protected in the name of large principles—less timid, selfish, and provocative of War than that of the Balance of Power.

SECTION VI.

OF THE NEUTRALIZATION OF STATES, SEAS, AND CANALS.

THE practice of insulating certain of the smaller States, as well as territories, navigable rivers, and inland seas, and giving a guarantee of their Neutrality in time of War, has been one much resorted to during the present century. The meaning, the value, and the true use of this practice, as a means of preventing War, must here be examined, and the most convenient mode of conducting the examination will be by recurring to the leading instances of actual or suggested Neutralization in modern times.

The main purpose of Neutralization is the rescuing from the field of possible conflict some State or place which, from its situation or peculiar advantages, is likely either to be a perpetual object of competitive struggle on the part of covetous, strong, and military States, and therefore to generate Wars, or to be incidentally drawn into any War which may occur, thereby extending its area and complicating its issues.

Object of Neutralization.

There is no doubt that a collective guarantee of Neutrality of itself affords some novel occasions for War; as a breach, or apprehended breach, of the Neutrality by any single party to the engagement not only is a *casus belli* which imparts to each of the other States the

It may become an occasion of War.

right of going to War, but also may be held to impose, in some sense, on each of them, the duty of doing so. In estimating, therefore, the pacific value of any given Treaty of Neutralization, a balance must be struck between the probability that the subject of the Treaty would have occasioned new Wars, or widened the areas of existing Wars, had the Treaty not been made, and the probability of the Treaty itself, if made, becoming itself the occasion of War.

Thus, everything depends on the circumstances of the particular case, and the principles which can be laid down for the successful use of Neutralization are only of a very broad and general kind. Most of all depends on the strength of the guarantee, which will be due partly to the number, the political influence, and the territorial situation of the guaranteeing States, and partly to the prevailing sense of obligation, which lies on every one of those States, to combine with the rest to defend the Neutrality, when invaded or seriously menaced.

The actual advantage of confining the area of War, and there-*Benefits of Neu-* by not only rescuing an increasing quantity of *tralization.* territory from its calamitous effects, but restricting the extension of those feelings of national animosity which become the most fruitful source of future Wars, ought not to be disputable, though it is, in fact, disputed. Both in respect to this question, and to the kindred topics of the strengthening *Its efficacy in* of Neutral Rights in time of War and the miti-*promoting Peace has been* gating of the ferocity of War, a controversy exists *questioned.* as to whether permanent Peace is really promoted by interposing obstacles, which may be called artificial, in the way of belligerents prosecuting the War to the utmost, and in any modes which seem to suit them at the moment. It is said that the only way to discourage War effectually is to assist belligerents in fighting out their quarrel with as little interference as possible from without, whether by general rules of warfare, by premature efforts at mediation, or by arbitrary localization, of the kind now being considered. This whole argument must be considered more fully when the general topic of Neutral Rights comes under treatment.

In the mean time it must be borne in mind that interest and strong national sentiments have far more to do with the origin of Wars than a mere recollection of the general suffering they cause; that where the real or apprehended interests are equal in favor of Peace and of War, the vehemence of a personal hostility, widely diffused, is a far stronger incentive to War than a cold calculation or reminiscence of its miseries is a deterrent; and, therefore, it should be a general policy to reduce and narrow at every point that bitterness and international enmity out of which Wars not only grow, but necessarily recur. Neutralization is one mode of effecting this.

Neutralization of Seas, Rivers, etc.

In the cases of rivers passing through the territories of several States, of inland seas bordering on the territory of several States, and of certain artificial constructions sharing in the nature both of rivers and of straits of the sea, as the Isthmus of Suez, and the proposed Isthmus of Panama, which are of great importance as international highways, there are other considerations present in favor of their Neutralization beside those of preventing War, or of merely restricting its area. In these cases, not only an actual War, but the menace of a War, and even the enduring possibility of a War, which might involve any one of the bordering States, or any part of the continuous stream, causes an aggregate amount of diffused mischief and loss, which is wholly disproportionate to the belligerent advantages which are reaped by either or both of the hostile parties to the War.

The Rhine.

The Treaty of Vienna, of 1815, provided in the following Article (the 26th) for the Neutralization of the Rhine: "If it should happen (which God forbid) that War should break out among the States of the Rhine, the collection of the customs shall continue uninterrupted, without

7

any obstacle being thrown in the way of either party. The vessels and persons employed by the custom-houses shall enjoy all the rights of Neutrality. A guard shall be placed over the offices and chests belonging to the customs."

By the 9th Article of the Treaty of Paris, of 1856, the Black Sea was Neutralized in the following terms: "The Black Sea is Neutralized; its waters and its ports, thrown open to the Mercantile Marine of every nation, are formally and in perpetuity interdicted to the flag of War, either of the Powers possessing its coasts, or of any other Power, with the exceptions mentioned in Articles XIV. and XIX. of the present Treaty." By a separate convention, bearing the same date as the Treaty, and embodied in its 10th Article, the "Sultan declared he was firmly resolved to maintain for the future the principle invariably established as the ancient rule of his Empire, and in virtue of which it has, at all times, been prohibited for the ships of War of Foreign Powers to enter the Straits of the Dardanelles and of the Bosphorus; and that, so long as the Porte is at Peace, His Majesty will admit no Foreign ship of War into the said straits." The six other Powers who were parties to the Treaty, on their part "engaged to respect this determination of the Sultan, and to conform themselves to the principle above declared."

The Black Sea.

The 11th Article of this Treaty, declaring the Neutralization of the Black Sea, was abrogated by the 1st Article of the Treaty of London, of the 13th March; but the general principle of closing the Dardanelles and the Bosphorus to ships of War was maintained—power, however, being reserved to the Sultan of "opening them in time of Peace to the vessels of War of friendly and allied Powers, in case the Sublime Porte should judge it necessary, in order to secure the execution of the stipulations of the Treaty of Paris, of the 30th March, 1856."

It is to be noticed that the principle of the partial Neutralization of the Dardanelles and of the Bosphorus had been explicitly affirmed some years before by a Convention of the 13th of July, 1841, at London, between Great Britain, Austria, Prussia, Russia, and the Ottoman Empire, "for the purpose of maintaining the principle that the passage of the Straits of Dardanelles and of the Bosphorus shall remain always closed against foreign ships of War while the Porte is at peace."* It is worth noticing, in reference to this subject and the remarks which follow, that in the Treaty of Adrianople, of 1829, the Bosphorus is called "*le canal de Constantinople.*"

With respect to artificial communications between the territories of different States, or through the territory of one State, but connecting public international highways, the celebrated "Clayton-Bulwer Convention" indicated a course and method of Neutralization which have already been fruitful in results, and are likely to be still more so in times to come.

<small>Canals, Railways, etc.</small>

This convention was entered into at Washington, on the 19th of April, 1850, between Great Britain and the United States. It recites the desire of the contracting parties "to set forth, by a convention, their views and intentions with reference to any means of communication by ship-canal, which may be constructed between the Atlantic and Pacific Oceans, by the way of the river St. Juan de Nicaragua, and either or both of the Capes of Nicaragua or Managua, to any port or place on the Pacific Ocean." By Article V. the parties engage "that when the said Canal shall have been completed, they will protect it from interruption, seizure, or unjust confiscation, and that they will guarantee the Neutrality thereof, so that the said Canal may forever be open and free, and the capital invested therein secure." The Neutrality and security were guaranteed conditionally on the managers making regulations "not contrary to the spirit and intention of the Con-

<small>Agreements relating to the Isthmus of Panama.</small>

---

* Murhard, vol. xxxv. p. 128.

vention," and six months' notice of withdrawal from the guarantee was to be given.

The following passage is important, as noting the public and truly international character which it was attempted, from the first, to impress upon these undertakings. By Article VIII. the contracting parties "having not only desired, in entering into this Convention, to accomplish a particular object, but to establish a general principle," agreed to "extend their protection, by Treaty stipulations, to any other practicable communications, whether by canal or railway, across the isthmus which connects North and South America, and especially to the interoceanic communications, should the same prove to be practicable, whether by canal or railway, which are now proposed to be established by the way of Tehuantepec or Panama." The communication was to be freely open to all States willing to join in the guarantee.

The spirit and letter of some parts of this engagement were carried out in a Treaty made in London on the 27th of August, 1856, between Great Britain and the Republic of Honduras.* The second clause of an "Additional Article" to this Treaty is as follows: "In consideration of the concessions previously named, and in order to secure the construction and permanence of the route or road herein contemplated, and also to secure for the benefit of mankind the uninterrupted advantages of such communication from sea to sea, Her Britannic Majesty recognizes the rights of sovereignty and property of Honduras in and over the line of the said road, and for the same reason guarantees positively and efficaciously the entire Neutrality of the same so long as Great Britain shall enjoy the privileges conceded in the preceding sections. And when the said road shall have been completed, Her Britannic Majesty equally engages, in conjunction with the Republic of Honduras, to protect the same

---

* Samwer Contin. tom. xvi. part 1, p. 549.

from interruption, seizure, and unjust confiscation, from whatsoever quarters the attempt may proceed. The guarantee may be withdrawn if the managers act contrary to the spirit and intention of it."

These engagements, no doubt, furnished a precedent for the Treaty of 1869 between the United States of America and those of Colombia, giving the former exclusive right to construct an International Canal across the Isthmus of Darien, at any point which might be selected by the American Government, the Canal to be under the control of that Government, and navigation to be open to all nations in time of peace, but closed to "belligerents."

The subject of the Neutralization of artificial canals has been
<small>The Suez Canal;</small> brought into some prominence of late through the peculiar circumstances of the Suez Canal, particularly in connection with the large pecuniary interest which the British Government has recently acquired in it. The situation
<small>Its Importance.</small> of this Canal, on the main highway between England and her Indian possessions, and as the best route for European commerce with the East, claims for the subject a special amount of attention in promoting the cause of Peace.

It has been held in some quarters, though with little show of reason, that an artificial Canal of this sort, joining two ocean highways, shares *ipso facto* in the properties of a natural strait, and cannot be closed against the ships of War of any nation, at all events in times of general Peace. It is not necessary to discuss this abstract question, inasmuch as the international use of this Canal is sure to be settled at an early date by Treaty. There are, however, some difficulties in the construction of such
<small>Complications of the case.</small> a Treaty which are peculiar to this case. It might be vital to England to transport ships of War, soldiers, and ammunition, through this Canal, while engaged in an Asiatic War; and, therefore, any Treaty which excluded the use of the Canal for belligerent purposes must draw a line, never

yet attempted, between Wars of this kind and ordinary European Wars. It certainly is in the interest of European Peace that the largest amount of use be obtained from the Canal for all purposes of Peace, and the least amount of use for any purposes of European War. The mere guarantee of the abstract Neutrality of the Canal, without detailed provisions for defending it, would at once disclose a number of questions to which the Treaty would supply no answer.

M. de Lesseps, on the 28th of February, 1856, enclosed to M. Barthelemy de St. Hilaire the following draft-clauses, the result of notes from M. Thiers's dictation in the previous June, for incorporation in the Treaty of Paris:

"The Signatory Powers guarantee the Neutrality of the Suez Marine Canal forever.

"No vessel shall at any time be seized, either in the Canal or within four leagues of the entrance from the two seas.

"No foreign troops shall be stationed on the banks of the Canal without the consent of the Territorial Government."

At the present moment the subject is greatly complicated by the unprecedented mercantile position which England occupies in reference to an enterprise conducted within the territorial limits of another State. The circumstances of the Ottoman Empire, subject, as it is, even in times of Peace, to political pressure on so many sides, are such as further to complicate the question. This is manifestly one of the cases in which as many States as possible must be induced to co-operate and to facilitate the adoption of measures by which no belligerent, or intending belligerent, shall turn the Canal to account for the purpose of advancing his ends, either at the expense of his enemy or at the expense of Neutral States using the Canal in the only appropriate way. It is obvious that a Treaty sufficient to carry out these ends will differ in many respects from any previous Treaties of the same kind, but would be by no means arduous to devise or impossible to execute.

Switzerland and Belgium afford signal and very illustrative instances of the application of the principle of Neutralization in the general interests of Peace, and it is worth while examining, in some detail, the successive arrangements by which this end has been secured in each case.

The first Treaty of Paris, of the 30th of May, 1814, simply Neutralization of Switzerland. declared by its 6th Article, that "Switzerland, independent, should continue to govern herself." The eight Powers which signed this Treaty—Austria, Great Britain, France, Portugal, Prussia, Russia, Spain, and Sweden—signed a Declaration at Vienna, on the 20th of March, 1815, which formed Annex XI. A. to the Vienna Congress Treaty of the 9th of June, 1815. The following is the preamble of this Declaration:

"The Powers called upon to mediate in the arrangement of the affairs of Switzerland, in order to carry into effect Article VI. of the Treaty of Paris, of the 30th of May, 1814, having acknowledged that the general interest demands that the Helvetic States should enjoy the benefit of a perpetual Neutrality; and wishing, by territorial restitutions and cessions, to enable it to secure its independence and maintain its Neutrality; after having obtained every information relative to the interests of the different Cantons, and taking into consideration the claims submitted to them by the Helvetic Legation; Declare, that as soon as the Helvetic Diet shall have duly and formally acceded to the stipulations contained in the present instrument, an Act shall be prepared containing the acknowledgment and the guarantee, on the part of all the Powers, of the perpetual Neutrality of Switzerland, in her new frontiers; which Act shall form part of that which, in the execution of Article XXXII. of the Treaty of Paris, of the 30th of May, was to complete the arrangements of that Treaty."

On the 27th of May, of the same year, the Swiss Confederation signed, at Zurich, an Act of Acceptance of this Declaration.

The Diet, in the course of this Instrument, " expressed the eternal gratitude of the Swiss nation toward the High Powers who, by the above Declaration, assigned to them, with a boundary far more advantageous, its ancient important frontiers; united three new Cantons to the Confederation; and promised solemnly to acknowledge and guarantee the perpetual neutrality of the Helvetic body, as being necessary to the general interest of Europe."

By the 84th Article of the Vienna Congress Treaty, of the 9th June, 1815, the above-cited Declaration of the 20th March " was confirmed in the whole of its tenor; and it was declared that the principles established, as also the arrangements agreed upon, in the said Declaration, should be invariably maintained." By Article XCII. of the same Treaty, "the provinces of Chablais and Faucigny, and the whole of the territory of Savoy to the north of Ugine, belonging to His Majesty the King of Sardinia, were to form a part of the Neutrality of Switzerland, as it was recognized and guaranteed by the Powers."

The concluding part of this Article is interesting, as illustrative of the interpretation placed upon Neutrality by the Treaty, and the mode designed for making it efficacious. " Whenever, therefore, the neighboring Powers to Switzerland are in a state of open or impending hostility, the troops of His Majesty the King of Sardinia, which may be in those provinces, shall retire, and may, for that purpose, pass through the Valais, if necessary. No other armed troops of any other Power shall have the privilege of passing through, or remaining in, the said territories and provinces, excepting those which the Swiss Confederation shall think proper to place there; it being well understood that this state of things shall not in any manner interrupt the administration of these countries, in which the civil agents of His Majesty the King of Sardinia may likewise employ the municipal guard for the preservation of good order."

By a later Treaty of the same year, signed at Paris, on the 20th of November, in which Austria, Great Britain, France,

Prussia, and Russia took part, the Neutrality was still further extended into the territory of Savoy.

The Neutrality of Belgium dates from the Treaty of London, of the 15th of November, 1831, between Austria, Belgium, Great Britain, France, Prussia, and Russia, relative to the separation of Belgium from Holland. The 7th Article of this Treaty declares that "Belgium, within the limits specified in Articles I., II., and IV., shall form an independent and perpetually Neutral State. It shall be bound to observe such Neutrality toward all other States."

Neutrality of Belgium recognized, though not guaranteed, 1831.

An Article (the 8th of the Annex incorporated in the Treaty) identical with the above was inserted in the Treaty of London, of the 19th of April, 1839, between the Netherlands and the same Powers, exclusive of Belgium. A Treaty, of the same date, was also signed, at London, between Belgium, Austria, Great Britain, France, Prussia, and Russia, cancelling the earlier Treaty of the 15th of November, 1831, and re-enacting, word for word, the Article respecting the independence and perpetual Neutrality of Belgium. By a Treaty of the same date, and signed at the same place, the King of the Netherlands, in conformity with his Treaty engagement, simultaneously entered into with the Five Great Powers, made a Treaty with the King of the Belgians "agreeing to" the Articles included in the Treaty with the other Powers.

Again in 1839.

Thus the Neutrality of Belgium was recognized afresh on the 19th of April, 1839, by Austria, Great Britain, France, Prussia, and Russia, and was also made the subject (among other subjects) of a special Treaty engagement between Belgium and the Netherlands. The Netherlands again were specially bound to protect the Neutrality by their independent Treaty with the Powers, and Belgium to perform the duties of Neutrality by its independent Treaty with the same Powers. But it cannot be said that the Neutrality of Belgium was actually guaranteed, or that provisions for insuring it were anticipated.

At the time of the War of 1870, between France and the North German Confederation, this infirmity in the securities for the Neutrality of Belgium—which, from its situation, was so peculiarly exposed to violations of its Neutrality on the sides of both of the Belligerents—attracted the attention of the British Government, and two Treaties were concluded at London, on the 9th and 11th of August, between Great Britain and Prussia, and Great Britain and France, respectively, the language of the two Treaties being almost identical, and the purpose of each of them being to provide that if either of the Belligerents violated the Neutrality of Belgium, Great Britain and the other Belligerent would co-operate jointly "in taking measures separately, or in common, to secure the Neutrality and Independence of Belgium." The Treaties were to be in force during the War, and for twelve months after the ratification of any Treaty of Peace.

Two Treaties, securing the Neutrality of Belgium, 1870.

Luxemburg is another small State which has played rather a conspicuous part in the recent history of Neutralization, and which, therefore, throws light on its true nature and possible uses in the future.

On the 11th May, 1867, a Treaty was concluded at London between Austria, Great Britain, Belgium, France, Italy, the Netherlands, Prussia, and Russia, for the purpose of "maintaining the ties which attach the Grand Duchy of Luxemburg to the House of Orange-Nassau, Neutralizing the Duchy," and making such provisions for the evacuation and demolition of its fortresses as its new position of permanent Neutrality seemed to demand.

Luxemburg Neutralized, 1867.

The 2d Article of this Treaty is as follows: "The Grand Duchy of Luxemburg, within the limits determined by the Act annexed to the Treaties of the 19th of April, 1839, under the Guarantee of the Courts of Great Britain, Austria, France, Prussia, and Russia, shall henceforth form a perpetually Neutral State. It shall be bound to observe the same Neutrality toward all other States. The High Contracting Parties engage to respect the principle of Neutrality stipulated by the present Article. That principle is, and remains, placed under the sanction of the collective guarantee of the Powers signing the present Treaty, excepting Belgium, which is itself a Neutral State."

In the 3d Article it is declared that "the Grand Duchy of Luxemburg being Neutralized, according to the terms of the preceding Article, the maintenance or establishment of fortresses upon its territory becomes without necessity as well as without object. In consequence, it is agreed, by common consent, that the City of Luxemburg, considered in time past, in a military point, as a Federal fortress, shall cease to be a fortified city."

The above Treaty of Neutralization is unusually precise and explicit in its terms, and yet, at the commencement of the Franco-German War of 1870, it was thought expedient for the French and North German Governments severally to notify, in July, 1870, their intention to respect the Neutrality of the Grand Duchy as long as it was likewise respected by the other Belligerent.*

A question subsequently arose as to whether the Neutrality of Luxemburg was not violated in a variety of ways by the French, and a circular on the subject was issued by Count Bismarck on December 3d, 1870; the previous notification was referred to, and such acts of violation of Neutrality were alleged as the provisioning of railway trains at night from Luxemburg for the use of a French fortress; the transit of French soldiers and officers in masses through the Grand Duchy for the purpose of evading the German posts; and the official furtherance of these acts by the French Vice-Consul residing in Luxemburg. Count Bismarck announces, at the close of his despatch, that his "Government can no longer

Alleged violation of the territory by the French, 1870.

---

* See Lord A. Loftus's Despatch in Herlslet, p. 1877, and Count Bismarck's Circular, Herlslet, p. 1901.

consider itself bound to any consideration of the Neutrality of the Grand Duchy in the military operations of the German Army, and in the measures for the security of the German troops against the injuries inflicted on them from Luxemburg."

The obvious import of this circular was explained and limited by a communication of Count Bernstoff to Earl Granville on the 8th of February, 1871, in which he stated that he had been instructed by Count Bismarck to express the satisfaction with which he had learned that Her Majesty's Government were convinced that it was not his intention, in his Circular of the 3d of December, 1870, to denounce the Treaty of 1867, by which the position of Luxemburg was defined and secured, but that he had been actuated by the desire to take precautionary measures of defence, necessitated by the military position, against military injury to the Prussian cause from violation of the territory of Luxemburg.*

Other instances of Neutralization are supplied by the case of Cracow, and of the Ionian Islands.

Neutralization of Cracow, 1815. The Neutrality of Cracow was guaranteed by the Vienna Congress Treaty of June 9th, 1815. By the 6th Article of this Treaty, "the Town of Cracow, with its territory, is declared to be, forever, a Free, Independent, and strictly Neutral City, under the protection of Austria, Prussia, and Russia." In the course of the 8th Article, it is declared that "no military establishment shall be formed that can menace the Neutrality of Cracow, or obstruct the liberty of Commerce, which His Imperial and Royal Apostolic Majesty grants to the town and district of Podgorze." By the 9th Article, "the Courts of Russia, Austria, and Prussia engage to respect, and to cause to be always respected, the Neutrality of the Free Town of Cracow and its territory. No armed force shall be introduced upon any pretence whatever."

---

* See Herlslet, p. 1903.

The Neutrality of the Ionian Islands is secured by two Treaties, of which the first was concluded between Austria, Great Britain, France, Prussia, and Russia, at
London, on the 14th of November, 1863; and the
second between Great Britain, France, Russia, and Greece, on
the 29th of March, 1864. The 2d Article of the first of these
Treaties declares that "the Ionian Islands, after their union to
the Kingdom of Greece, shall enjoy the advantages of a perpetual Neutrality; consequently, no armed force, either naval or
military, shall at any time be assembled or stationed upon the
territory or in the waters of those Islands, beyond the number
that may be strictly necessary for the maintenance of public order, and to secure the collection of the public revenue. The
High Contracting Parties engage to respect the principle of
Neutrality stipulated by the present Article." By the 3d Article of the same Treaty, it is agreed that " as a necessary consequence of the Neutrality to be thus enjoyed by the United
States of the Ionian Islands, the fortifications constructed in the
Island of Corfu and its immediate dependencies, having no longer any object, should be demolished."

The Treaty of 1864 was concluded in pursuance of Article VI. of the Treaty of 1863, just cited, by which
the "Courts of France, Great Britain, and Russia,
in their character of Guaranteeing Powers of the Kingdom of
Greece," reserved to themselves to conclude a "Treaty with the
Hellenic Government with regard to the arrangements which
may be necessary by the union of the Ionian Islands to Greece."
By the 2d Article of the consequent Treaty of 1864, " the
Courts of Great Britain, France, and Russia, in their character
of Guaranteeing Powers of Greece, declared, with the assent of
the Courts of Austria and Prussia, that the Islands of Corfu
and Paxo, as well as their dependencies, should, after their union
to the Hellenic Kingdom, enjoy the advantages of perpetual
Neutrality."

From the instances which have been above given, it will be seen what are the usual circumstances under which Neutralization is resorted to in modern times, and what are the conditions which are favorable to its success. Like many other arrangements accomplished by Treaty, Neutralization essentially consists in converting indefinite into definite causes of War, and the pacific value of the arrangement in any particular case will depend on the degree in which indefinite causes of War really exist, and on the nature of the substitution which is devised for them. Thus, in the case of Belgium, the situation of its territory in respect of Germany, France, and the Netherlands, and its assailability from the sea, present a variety of incentives to warlike aggression, especially when the relations of adjoining States have become temporarily disturbed. The Treaty of 1839, by which Austria, Great Britain, France, Prussia, and Russia guarantee the Neutrality of Belgium, exposes an ambitious or reckless State violating Belgian territory, not only to the certain resistance of Belgium itself, and a casual resistance on the part of any chance allies of Belgium, but to the separate or joint resistance of the most potent States of Europe. Thus, while a new cause of War is introduced for each of the Guaranteeing States, the probabilities of a War with Belgium, or of the extension of a War into Belgian territory, are reduced in proportion to the validity of the guarantee. At the time of the Franco-German War, it was felt that the guarantee in this case was scarcely strong enough, and England made temporary arrangements with each of the Belligerents to fortify it.

Neutralization substitutes definite for indefinite causes of War.

It promotes Peace in proportion to the effectiveness of the guarantee.

This is, indeed, the difficulty which besets all these far-sighted arrangements. When the time comes for actively vindicating a guaranteed Neutrality, each Guaranteeing State by itself is apt to feel its own interests too remotely affected to justify its going to War in defence of them, and the sense of public obligation to maintain a bare right is generally too infirm to step in where selfish interests fail. Nevertheless, there is more than a probability that two or more of the Guaranteeing States will, first diplomatically and then forcibly, interfere on the occasion of an outrage on the guaranteed Neutrality, and, therefore, the aggregate consequences are more decidedly in favor of Peace than of War.

The incidental advantages of Neutralization, where favorable conditions exist for it, are very great. This is plainly obvious in the case of inland seas, navigable rivers, straits, and artificial canals. All circumstances which favor uninterrupted locomotion and international intercourse, and which prevent the possibility of casual breaches in one or the other, through events not capable of being foreseen, distinctly tend to promote commerce, international harmony, and permanent Peace. Circumstances of the reverse kind similarly promote and sustain Wars.

<small>Neutralization facilitates pacific intercourse;</small>

But, further, as in the case of such territories as those of Belgium, Switzerland, and Luxemburg, it is of the highest importance to interpose vast barriers to the march and operations of opposing armies, by which not only are hostile acts checked and impeded on both sides, but a standing protest is made, in some quarters at least, in favor of Peace. This prevents what might, otherwise, not be an impossibility—the unrestricted sweeping of armies over the whole of Europe, and a general substitution of a reign of War for one of Peace.

<small>and impedes military movements.</small>

SECTION VII.

OF STANDING ARMIES.

As though in anticipation of the present War between Russia and Turkey, and since the date of the War between France and Germany, the constitution and organization of the armies of all the leading European States have, of late, undergone a decisive change. The modes of warfare, especially as dependent on scientific inventions and economical applications, have been submitted to innovating alterations, which are closely parallel with each stride in the march of industrial progress. Even the laws of War are being subjected to a novel process of systematic revision, and are being taught to conform to the demands of a better calculated utility, if not of an advancing morality. It could not have been expected that facts so sudden and so universal would elude general attention, and, as a matter of fact, they have not. Military writers, politicians, economists, and social philosophers have based all sorts of auguries for the future on the character and magnitude of the new European armies, and, no doubt, many of these speculations are sound, and will have a fruitful bearing on practice. But there is one aspect of these changes which has either wholly escaped attention, or has met with far less attention than it has deserved— that is, the bearing of all these changes on the reduction of the frequency of Wars, or on the total abolition of War.

Recent changes in military methods.

Their bearing on the frequency, or the extinction, of War.

It is impossible to conceive that changes so vast, so widely ramified, and so vital as those now affecting the preparations for War, and the actual conduct of Wars, can be without any influence in generally predisposing nations for War or Peace; and, even if there are those who regard all hopes for a time of permanent Peace as utopian, it is not denied in any quarter that there are general causes which produce both Peace and War, and that these causes can, to some extent, be controlled so as to foster the one and not the other. With a view, then, partly to prognosticate the increasing tendencies in Europe toward Peace or War, and partly to direct sympathy and guide practical action in some directions rather than in others, it is worth while accurately to estimate the real nature of the extensive military changes which have been accomplished, and to trace their probable influence on the reduction of the frequency of Wars.

The changes in the constitution and organization of armies are still going forward, and in some countries, as England, have only just commenced. It is, however, well recognized in constitutional countries that the modes of filling and of controlling the army belong as much to the field of general public discussion as to that of military experience, and that even distinct and immediate military advantages must not be sought at too heavy a price to public liberty, or to the permanent interests of Peace.

In solving the problems of new organization which may yet be presented, it may thus be a highly relevant consideration to reflect how far the changes which have recently been brought about have increased or diminished the chance of recurrent Wars. There are, probably, few persons nowadays who would have the hardihood to deny that, other things being equal, that course is to be preferred which, on the whole, is likely to promote, and not to endanger, general Peace.

It may, too, prove a matter of consolation that even those institutions and practices which are most disastrous in the present, and ought least to be maintained or copied, do, nevertheless, in some respects, operate in a way which must finally bring about their own annihilation. Thus, even some of the most alarming phases of modern national life may, when strictly scrutinized, be found rife with hopefulness for a not very distant future. Where the prospect is, for the present, the most gloomy, and the only lesson to be learned from looking around is what to avoid, there may, on a closer view, be presented the vision of a stable and pacific future, of which the longest interval of Peace in past history is only a flickering image.

It will be convenient to distribute the subject under the following four heads: (1) Modes of recruiting for the army; (2) The size of armies in Peace and in War; (3) The organization and internal constitution of armies; (4) Modes and instruments of warfare.

1. *Modes of Recruiting for the Army.*—There are three generic modes which are possible for replenishing the ranks of the army, though each mode admits of numerous variations. There is, first, the mode of depending on the ordinary laws of supply and demand, and of trusting to the competition of the army with other branches of remunerative industry. This mode is still pursued in England, though much fault has been found with its operation, and proposals of one kind and another have been made to alter it.

Methods of Army Recruiting.

It has been said that the class of soldiers supplied belongs to the dregs of the population; that the number of deserters is enormous; and that, depending as the supply does on the general conditions of trade, voluntary enlistment is too precarious for a nation to rely upon at all times.

Voluntary enlistment in England.

Proposals have been made in the House of Commons, especially by Mr. John Holms, M.P. for Hackney, to meet the objections to voluntary recruiting by shortening the terms of service, raising the soldier's pay, facilitating marriage in the army, and generally ameliorating the conditions of the service. Though

Mr. Holms's comprehensive scheme has not been yet carried out, it marks the directions in which improvements are already being spontaneously made by the authorities. Shorter terms of service have been introduced, deferred pay has been granted, and the pay of non-commissioned officers increased. The result during the past year (1876) seems to have been satisfactory. According to the report of the Inspector-General of Recruiting for 1876, all the requisite recruits have been obtained with such facility that the standard of requirements, which had in some points been lowered, is to be raised again. The number of recruits for the year is 29,370, as against 18,494 in 1875.

<small>Conscription by ballot.</small> The second mode of recruiting is that of determining how many men are required for the army, either each year, or at a special crisis, and then forcibly levying them throughout the country by a process of balloting. This was the practice which the first Napoleon's Wars rendered so familiar to Europe, and which still has a peculiar connection with his name.

<small>Universal service in force in continental countries.</small> The third mode is that which has only within the last few years been put in practice by all the chief European States, and may be described as that of universal service, modified by the ballot. Every male citizen, within certain limits, and when not within classes specially exempted, is not only liable to active service for a certain number of years, but, owing to the way in which the magnitude of the army is, in practice, adjusted to the population, is pretty sure to be actually compelled to serve. The ballot is used to <small>Modified by the ballot.</small> determine, either who shall compose the narrow margin between the numbers of recruits needed and the number of citizens available for the draft, or (as in France) who shall serve for five years, and who for six months, or a year.

In Germany, the ballot, in some districts, is never resorted to at all, and the authorities generally discountenance its use, as letting in an element of chance which is not conducive to the good of the service. Thus, in 1862, the number of male citizens coming of age was 227,000, of which 69,000 were found available for service. Sixty-three thousand was the required contingent, and thus only 6000 would be saved from active service by the ballot. In 1867, 262,000 male citizens came of age, of which 110,000 passed as fit for service. One hundred thousand of these were taken. About a margin of ten per cent. on the available population is allowed to remain outside the demands of the army for active service of three years' duration.

In Germany.

In France, the contingent needed each year is divided into two classes, of which the first is to serve for a full period of five years, and the second for six months or (in certain cases) for one year. Somewhere about 300,000 male citizens annually come of age, of whom 150,000 are found to be exempted. Of the remainder, 75,000 fall into the first class, and 75,000 into the second. This would give about 450,000 men in the standing active army. The *Almanach de Gotha*, however, estimates, as the result of the reorganization now proceeding, that the active army will consist of 704,714 men.

France.

In Austria, the ballot divides the annual contingent into three classes, of which the first, consisting of 95,000, serve at once for three years in the line, the second form a reserve for recruiting the standing army, and the third pass into the *landwehr*, or reserve force, which can only be called into active service in certain emergencies. It will be conjectured that the size of the second and third classes must be very small compared with that of the first, for which so large a portion of the available population is already drawn.

Austria.

In Italy, the ballot similarly distributes the available citizens into two classes, with liabilities of service like those in France.

Italy.

In all the countries mentioned, as well as in Russia, military service is, by an express law, made "obligatory on all citizens." Substitutions and exemptions by payment are expressly forbidden, though it is said that in Russia a purchase of exemption is permitted, in practice, for the sum of 800 roubles, or £120. Certain grounds of exemption are allowed in all countries, which may be either permanent or temporary, total or partial, absolute or conditional. These grounds are much alike everywhere, but they are specially numerous and precise in France.

<small>Exemptions from service in France.</small> The following are exempted from service in France:

1. Eldest of orphans (having neither father nor mother alive); 2. Only son, or oldest son or grandson, or oldest grandson of widow, or of wife separated from her husband, or of a father upward of seventy; 3. Eldest of two brothers liable for service at the same time; 4. Younger of two brothers whose older brother is serving in the active army; 5. Younger son of a family whose elder brother had died in the service, or been discharged for wounds or illness contracted in the field. Moreover, certain pupils, teachers, professors, artists, members of religious associations, and ecclesiastics are exempted, and partial or additional exemptions can be granted by municipal councils and local authorities to young men contributing to support their families, or engaged in studies or avocations that would suffer from interruption; but these latter exemptions are subject to revision at the hands of military councils. It is also the general practice to afford opportunities to young men of education to complete their term of active service in a year, on passing certain examinations.

Before commenting on the bearings of this system of enlistment, it is necessary to refer to another main characteristic of the new method of replenishing armies—that is, the distribution of the army into those engaged on active service with the colors ("*bei den Fahnen*," "*sous les drapeaux*"), and those who (as the German *landwehr*),

<small>Divisions into active army and reserves.</small>

though undergoing periodical discipline, are only liable to be called upon to engage in active service in case of urgent need, as in that of actual or threatened invasion. A further subdivision is also made between those who are serving in the regular army throughout the year, and those who form the reserve of the regular army, and, though actually under arms for a few weeks only in the year, are always ready to fill up the ranks of the active army as occasion demands. Yet another class, again, has been created in most countries, as, for instance, in Germany and Russia (*Landsturm* and *Reichswehr*), including all persons between certain ages not included in any other part of the army, and otherwise exempted. This class can only be called out for service in extreme emergencies. Thus all those available for active service who are saved by the fortune of the lot from having instantly to serve in the active army, are placed either in the reserve of that army, or in the *landwehr*, or second reserve; while all men, whether available for active service or not, and between certain wide limits of age, are included in the ultimate reserve.

The system of recruiting here explained is practically identical for the countries of France, Germany, Austria, Italy, and Russia. The differences are only in matters of detail, such as in the number of years of active service, varying from the customary number of three years to the number of six years (as in Russia); in the limits of age (usually from the age of twenty to that of thirty or forty) for active service; in the length of the periods spent in the successive reserve forces; and in the machinery by which the ballot ascertains whether a recruit enters on active service, or only into one or other class of the reserve forces.

The same system adopted by leading continental States.

Slight variations.

The above system was originated in Prussia on the proved failure of the Prussian organization in 1859, when Prussia mobilized her army on the Rhenish frontier, at the time of the successful campaign of the French in Italy, which terminated in the battle of Solferino. In

The method originated by Prussia, 1860.

the following year the executive Government, supported by the aristocracy, and in the teeth of persistent popular opposition in the Chamber of Deputies, introduced the first elements of the modern German system. Between 1860 and 1866, the yearly supply of recruits was raised from 40,000 to 63,000. The fruits of the reconstruction were reaped by the victory over Austria in 1866.

In 1868, Austria adopted the Prussian system, and the war-footing of the land army and the marine was fixed for ten years at 800,000 men. In the same year, the French system of recruiting was recast by a law of the 1st of February, which was the basis of the existing practice, as provided for by laws passed in 1872, 1873, and 1875. The existing German practice rests on a series of laws passed in 1874 and 1875; the Italian, on laws passed in 1873; and the Russian, on a law of 1874.

It appears, then, that the comprehensive recruiting system above described may be treated as one and the same for five of the most powerful and populous States of Europe; that in almost all of them it is of such very recent growth that its full effects could not be yet seen, nor scarcely conjectured; and that the introduction of the system in each country synchronizes with political changes, if not convulsions, unprecedented for their breadth, depth, and social significance.

It is not necessary, for the present purpose, to dwell upon the obvious evils which are incident to this system of universal compulsory service. It is not denied in any quarter that to withdraw nearly all the best young men of a country, as soon as they come of age, for a period of three years at the least, from every sort of industrial, professional, and intellectual occupation, and to apprentice them to idleness and inanity, if not to worse, is, in itself, neither good for the men themselves, nor for the country to which they belong. Nor is it denied that both in Peace and in War incidental evils follow of no ordinary magnitude. The effects on family life, on mar-

Evils of universal service.

riage, on industrial education, even on individual happiness, are such as need no statistics to establish, and of an amount which no prudent statesman can leave out of account. The only counterbalancing argument which can be alleged is, that a choice must be made between two evils, and that the new system of universal service is the only alternative to national extinction.

The position of affairs, then, is this: There are five States, each one of which is submitting its population to a calamity of the first magnitude, owing to a necessity which is imposed upon it by some or all of the rest. Were all these States independent human beings, it is obvious that in a very short time they would find it to be the interest of all to provide in such a way for the security of each that all the losses, risks, and miseries in-
<small>It is necessitated by—</small> curred by individual efforts (often unsuccessful) at self-protection, might be forever escaped. But the States in question cannot do this; but only for reasons which are transient and accidental in their character. These reasons are of the following kind:

In the first place, the internal constitution of four of these
<small>Internal unsettlement—</small> States is, to a great extent, weak and fragile, and the product either of recent revolutions, or of tentative combinations of imperfectly cohesive elements. The Russian constitution alone is the product of traditional despotism, official routine, and modern popular aspirations. Thus the Government of each State depends, though in different degrees, for its existence and stability far more on the actual exertion of executive authority—that is, on the possession for the time being of pre-eminent physical force—than on an unbroken custom of loyalty on the part of the governed. The result is twofold: first, a certain diffidence as to its situation and its capacities, which hampers it in its relations with other States; and, secondly, an habitual reliance on military force, and an indisposition to part with an undisputed manipulation of it in its most concentrated forms.

In the second place, the existing territorial, political, and diplomatic relations of these several States to one another are the product of so many past Wars and accidents, that no single State can be persuaded to treat those relations as final. Thus, each State is tempted to feel it has more to lose than to gain by a lasting Peace. The original conditions of any mutual accord, for the purpose of merely protecting each against the violence of the rest, are wholly wanting. Each State has a hidden consciousness that itself may be the one concerned in exerting violence against one of the rest.

and external mistrust.

This, then, explains the generation of an unparalleled system of universal enlistment, and of the tribute of honor which is paid to it on so many sides. It is the direct offspring of internal unsettlement and external mistrust.

But there are influences steadily at work which must counteract this system of converting a nation into an army, and must finally destroy it. In Italy, Germany, Austria, and France the new military institutions are closely connected in their history with critical paroxysms in the national history, with vast revolutionary movements, with new political combinations, and with powerful executive governments. In Russia, the new army is the outcome of an age of slumbering revolutions and aspirations.

But in all these countries the tyrannical strength of the government is only the cloak, and, perhaps, the support, of internal social movements which are ceaseless and unmistakable. These movements are in the direction of individual liberty, local self-government, effective parliamentary institutions, a free press, a free right of public meeting, and a popular control of the acts of the executive, and of public expenditure. As these movements progress, the voices opposed to the current military institutions will be multiplied and become louder. The conscripts themselves, those liable to service, and all connected with them, will not be

The growth of liberty must prove destructive of this system.

silent. The employers of labor who suffer from the raising of wages, the farmer, and the manufacturer, who are exposed to an incessant change of hands, will clearly know their own minds and make others know them. The general tax-payers will resent an expenditure for War in successive years of profound Peace.

An organized public opinion must find clearer and ever clearer utterance, to the effect that the existing military institutions are evils scarcely second to those of internal revolution and external defeat. When once this opinion is boldly formulated, it needs but the new range of liberal institutions to convert it into a determinate policy. The state has been acquiring stability and cohesion, and the executive government has been slowly becoming the effective instrument of an ascertained popular will. The jealousies of diplomacy have become softened or removed by assiduous international contact and concert. A common sense of evil, and a common desire of good, runs like a lightning-flash from nation to nation, and by a common policy, industry, commerce, knowledge, humanity, and all that is meant by Peace, reassert their sway.

2. *The Size of Armies in Peace and in War.*—The consideration of the size of modern armies is, of course, involved, to some extent, in that of the modern system of recruiting, but the former has some further aspects in reference to the prospects of Peace, which will be more conveniently treated by themselves.

In estimating the actual size of the armies of what may be

<small>Difference in size of armies in War and in Peace.</small>

called the leading military states — that is, Germany, Austria, France, Italy, and Russia — a distinction has to be drawn between the footing of the several national armies in time of Peace and in time of War. It is the policy of the new method of organization, in time of Peace, to keep as small an army as possible in active service; to have a successive series of reserve forces ready in time of War to supply the breaches and increase the strength of that army, while provision is made for the whole male population being ready to take the field in certain extreme emergencies. Thus, in estimating the size of one of these national armies, for some purposes it would be proper only to count the forces actually under arms; for other purposes, besides these, all the reserve forces ready to be called out at the moment of War breaking out, or being apprehended; for other purposes, the whole male population, say between twenty and sixty years of age, not totally invalided.

But the number of soldiers constituting the active army, even in times of Peace, is, for all the above-mentioned States, far larger than at any previous epoch, and in most of them is rapidly increasing from year to year. Indeed, it has already been seen that usually the limits of the active army are only assigned by the rate of progress of the population, only about ten per cent. of the available population being excepted from the annual draft for active service. In Germany the number of the forces, and the yearly sum appropriated for its support, were fixed by legal enactment, in 1874, for a period of seven years, though the duration of any one Parliament is limited to three years. The number of the standing army in time of Peace was fixed at 438,831 men. The War footing of the army, which, from the nature of the case, must be a variable quantity, including all classes of reserves, seems to approach somewhere about 1,700,000 men.

German army.

In France the reorganization which is still proceeding seems to promise even more striking results. The estimate of the Minister of War for 1874, for the active army, was 540,000 men. The *Almanach de Gotha* calculates that the present changes will produce for the active army 704,714 men; for the reserve of this army, 510,294 men; for the "Territorial" army, 582,523 men; for the reserve of the Territorial army, 625,633; making the whole forces available in the utmost emergency up to 2,423,164.

French army.

In Russia, by the time the present changes are accomplished, the field army will consist of 955,000 men, and her whole forces, first and second reserves, and 180,000 Cossacks, will amount to 1,945,000 men.

Russian army.

In Italy, the Peace footing is nearly 200,000 men, and the War footing 450,000. In Austria, the Peace footing is about 480,000, and the War footing 840,000.

Italian and Austrian armies.

It will be instructive to add together in a tabular form the results here given:

	Peace Footing.	War Footing.
Germany................................	438,831	1,700,000
France ("Active" Army)............	704,714	2,423,164
Russia...................................	755,000	1,945,000
Austria..................................	480,000	840,000
Italy......................................	200,000	450,000
Total............................	2,578,545	7,358,164

Thus, excluding the cases of England and the smaller or Neutralized States, it appears that five great States of Europe at present retain, even during a time of profound Peace, 2,500,000 men constantly under arms, and that, over and above these, they train in habits of warfare, and submit to some degree of military discipline, in view of possible service at some time or other, between seven and eight millions of men. These patent facts give rise to several reflections, having a direct bearing on the present subject.

Total results.

The inordinate size of European armies under the new system aggravates enormously the obvious evils of War, especially in times of Peace; makes these evils of universal concern to all nations, even to those which are the most habitually pacific; and projects the tableau of these evils in such striking colors and glaring relief that they must sooner or later invoke a radical remedy.

The expense which the maintenance in one of the great military States of an enormous army in time of Peace involves, must be measured, first by the actual cost of feeding, clothing, equipping, and managing some half million of men, and secondly by the loss entailed in a variety of ways, by withdrawing for some years from the fields of directly productive industry the best men in the nation at the most precious period of their lives.

<small>Great armies involve a waste which affects the whole community of nations.</small>

This cost and loss is not encountered by the nation alone which raises and maintains the army, but, in the present circumstances of Free-trade and growing international intercourse, by every other civilized nation; and the aggregate cost and loss which is entailed on any single nation through this cause is the sum of the expenses of the army in every other nation with which it has commercial or social relations. Thus, as things now are, no nation, by ever so pacific a policy, and considerate and just a treatment of other nations, can avoid paying a considerable part of the price of the military institutions of other nations. This is a fact to which peaceably disposed nations cannot but become increasingly awake; and as the number of such nations grows, a public opinion must gradually be formed throughout Europe wholly adverse to enormous military preparations in times of Peace, and the advent of liberal political institutions in States now overawed by an omnipotent executive authority must favor the conversion of this opinion into practical action.

Another notable consequence of the enormous size of European armies is the breadth of the operations in times of War, the increased expensiveness of War, and the vastly aggravated loss and suffering occasioned by War. This expensiveness of loss and suffering is not compensated, as has been sometimes supposed, by any necessary shortening of the duration of a War. This happened, indeed, at first, when the vast scale of modern armies was yet an untried

<small>Great armies extend the area of War:</small>

experiment, to which Prussia, Austria, and France were committing themselves for the first time. The wholly incalculable effect of a new and imperfect organization, and other special circumstances, conspired to render the campaigns of Solferino and Sadowa marvellously brief, considering the magnitude of the results. But in the Franco-German War it was not the size of the armies which shortened the War, but the wholly unexpected collapse of the French organization. At many periods during the War there seemed every prospect of it being indefinitely prolonged; and had the French been able to draw (as they will be able in the next War, and as the Germans did) on successive series of wholly unused reserves, the War would have been incessantly recommenced at different points. Thus, there is no compensation whatever for the evils following in the wake of the exaggerated size of modern armies. It only means more War, worse War, and longer Wars.

do not necessarily shorten its duration.

But there are other consequences which follow from the size of modern armies to which attention must yet be drawn. In the first place, it is obviously the present policy, of some at least of the leading military States, to urge their military preparations, even in time of peace, to the utmost limits fixed by the population and by the national resources. But these preparations always and rapidly become an inveterate institution, ever growing and never lessening, and from time to time drawing renewed life and energy from popular panic or passion, or from a fresh influx of administrative zeal. But all the true and natural elements of national well-being, as marked by the growth or steady maintenance of the population, and by the general resources, must be ever fluctuating to and fro. The pressure of the army is, however constant, always on the verge of being overwhelming, and at recurrent intervals actually so. Quite independently of the mere influence of public opinion, no nation can long stand

The strain of a vast military organization cannot be long borne.

this incessant strain. Either the State must be sacrificed to the army, as in the middle period of Imperial Rome, or the army must be curtailed in accordance with the exigencies of the State. The present magnitude of army preparations and expenditure can, then, be only regarded as marking a transient phase of European history. It is predestined either to undergo conspicuous transformations, or to fail in the attainment of its chief and worthiest objects.

In the second place, the fact that the magnitude of military preparations seems in some States to have no other limits than the calculable resources of the nation for the time being, has at least this advantage, that War and its results must increasingly bear a ponderable relation to all the statistical elements by which national progress is ascertained. Thus the events of War must, to a growing extent, cease to be speculative, and become matter of exact prevision. The more this is the case, the less likely is it that actual War will be resorted to. The relative strength of nations will be generally acknowledged, and will express itself in ways less costly and disastrous to the strong as well as to the weak. The long suspension of actual War must be accompanied by an expansion of international trade, a freedom of general intercourse, and a development of credit, which will make the recurrence of War widely unpopular among all classes of society to an extent scarcely imagined at present. The burdens of War will be less and less patiently endured in times of Peace; and here, again, by help of the diffusion of liberal parliamentary institutions, the very copiousness of modern military institutions will work their destruction.

marginal note: As the result of War becomes calculable, resort to it will be less frequent.

3. *The Organization and Internal Constitution of Modern Armies.*—Besides the changes in the military institutions of modern States which have been already adverted to, there are some others deserving note here which are either direct conse-

quences of the other changes, or are a further embodiment of the policy which led to them.

There are two competing principles in modern army organization which are each admitted to be independently important, and which it is the object of reformers, as far as possible, to reconcile, without an undue compromise of the claims of either. One is that of what is called "localization," the other "mobilization." According to modern ideas, the merits of a military system would be mainly tested by the success with which the burden and maintenance of every part of the national forces could be evenly distributed throughout the national territory in time of Peace, and be none the less instantly available in the most centralized form for convergent action anywhere in time of War.

Localization and mobilization in modern armies:

The present German organization is the most complete exhibition of the modern method, and is no doubt the type which other States are, so far as peculiar national conditions permit, keeping in view. The whole infantry of the German Empire, in active service, consists of four army corps, making seventy-four brigades and one hundred and forty-eight regiments. To every one of these regiments of the line is attached a *landwehr* regiment, bearing the same number as the regiment of the line, and having with it a common provincial name. Each *landwehr* regiment consists of two battalions, and each of these battalions is complete and independent in all its parts, is wholly raised in a particular geographical district, and is permanently connected with this district. The recruiting for the line regiment to which the *landwehr* regiment is attached proceeds, as was above described, simultaneously for both; the arrangements for men on leave, for invalids, and for putting the forces in motion, are managed for both regiments by one and the same machinery. Thus there is, from first to last, and at every stage of their fortunes, the intimate relation maintained between the line and *landwehr*

exemplified in the German system.

regiment on the one hand, and a definite geographical district on the other.*

In France the whole forces are divided into the active and the territorial army, each of which has its own reserve. In Italy the forces were, by a law of September 3d, 1873, distributed under the two heads, the permanent army and the movable militia. But the conditions of the Italian territory are peculiar, the character of the population in north and south being of a very different type. For this reason the whole country is divided into five zones, and each regiment is composed of men drawn from all of these zones. In this way the territorial principle is recognized so far as it is believed to be compatible with military efficiency. The military meaning and purpose of this novel method of organization will be understood from the following extract from General Trochu's treatise on "The French Army in 1867:"

<small>The territorial principle in Italy.</small>

"In Prussia and in Russia, the active army, in time of Peace as in time of War, is formed into several parts, each composed of divisions, brigades, regiments, staff, depots, with their own officers and their own *matériel*, all constantly and permanently acting together, with the proper re-enforcements in reserve, so that from one day to another the whole body is ready for action. This species of military organization may have some inconveniences, as what has not? But it would be superfluous to enlarge on its incalculable advantages for purposes of War, when it has penetrated the habits of nations and of armies; the advantage of keeping alive the military spirit, by the ties thus formed in all ranks, between those who command and those who obey; the advantage of a condensation of moral force and of experimental knowledge of every

<small>Its working described by General Trochu.</small>

---

* See Organisation und Dienst der Kriegsmacht des deutschen Reichs. Achte Auflage. Von Baron v. Wolff, neu bearbeitet durch Alfred Baron v. Eberstein. Berlin, 1876.

detail of a complicated mechanism; the advantage of rapidity of concentration, and concert and energy in execution, when the hour of action is come; advantages of all kinds in the preparation of War, which can thus be carried on without putting a whole country and a whole army into agitation by violent and multifarious movements, which have the serious evil of disclosing long beforehand the efforts made."*

Its proposed adoption in England.
Even in England, where all the military conditions are well recognized as differing from those on the Continent, the territorial principle was deferred to in the Army Regulation Act carried by Lord Cardwell under Mr. Gladstone's Government in 1871, and it seems that it will shortly be still further carried out. The full conception of Lord Cardwell's reconstructive measures included the linking of the line battalions into pairs, one of each pair being at home and the other upon foreign service; the closer connection of the line with the militia of each locality; and the formation of depots common both to the militia and the line of the locality, for the purpose of recruiting, training, and ultimate organization in the reserves.

Lord Cardwell retired from office in 1874, and the changes were not completely matured, though Parliament spent £3,500,000 in carrying them out. A committee, composed of most influential and authoritative persons, was appointed by the War-office to report on the operation of the changes so far as they had yet been carried out. This committee has only just reported. In answer to the question, "Are battalions of brigade to be looked upon as being merely united for administrative purposes, or are they to be viewed as constituent parts of one body?" the committee answer, "We have no hesitation in replying that they should be constituent parts of one body; and al-

---

* See Lieutenant-colonel Chesney's Military Resources of Prussia and France. London: Longmans, 1870.

though we are not unaware of the very grave considerations which are involved, we are constrained to record our opinion that full advantage cannot be obtained for the money spent by the country until the connection be more closely drawn than at present between the line battalions of each brigade, and between them and the militia battalions of the sub-district." They consider this is best to be effected by their being treated as one regiment, under eight territorial designations, the line battalions contributing the first and second, the depot being common to all and contributing the last, and the militia battalions contributing the rest. The existing numerical designations, dear as they are to military memories, are to be obliterated.

The changes here recommended are radical enough, and are all in two directions—one, that of combining, in the most compact manner possible, all the parts of an army into easily manageable groups; and the other, that of permanently connecting each group with a definite territorial district. This is, in fact, identical, in spirit at least, with the German system of localization.

The direct and indirect influences of this new mode of organization are not hard to trace. The army can no longer, in any country, be a remote fact and institution, only thought of in time of War, or, at the most, only brought to mind at the period of recruiting, or at seasons of occasional debate in legislative assemblies. The new policy is to merge the military institutions with the civil and social life of the country, and the civil and social life with them. Of course, those institutions are likely, for the moment, to draw energy and sustenance from the bracing association. But if they are ever recognized as being excessive, and to a constantly growing extent needless, the popular insurrection against them will be decided, widespread, and irresistible, just in proportion to their territorial distribution. No misunderstanding of the existence, the nature, and the extent of the evil will hamper the agitation

Military institutions thus interwoven with the whole national life.

The pressure will, therefore, be universally recognized.

for its removal or restriction. The newly-discovered forces of effective local self-government will fan and feed the flame. Every year of Peace, every season of impoverished national resources, will accumulate arguments for reducing armies and promoting an international policy of Peace. A common and exactly distributed pressure will be the best preparation possible for a united and universal reaction.

(4) *Modes and Instruments of Warfare.*—It needs a very superficial glance backward at recent battle-fields, or around at the military preparations assiduously at work in all the leading countries of Europe, to note the decisive changes which are in course of accomplishment in the modes of warfare. Chemical, mechanical, electrical, aeronautical, and mathematical inventions and discoveries are pressed into the service of War. Civil education is forced to contribute, and whole nations are drilled in the school-room, if not in the nursery. The railroad, the steamship, the telegraph, each new industrial appliance and convenience, are eagerly laid hold of so as to render War more widely and infallibly disastrous. It were a gain, indeed, if War could be fought out by machinery and not by living men. But, unfortunately, it is not so. The elaborate mechanism only serves to prepare and clear the field for an exorbitantly enlarged number of living combatants—these, too, no longer unimpassioned, professional soldiers, but peaceful citizens, carrying back to their homes—if they reach them—the coarse and bitter memories and hostile passions of the battle-field.

<small>Rapid adaptation of new inventions to military purposes.</small>

So far as the purely military nature and products of these incessant and comprehensive changes go, they seem to be as follows: The exclusive possession of any single scientific advantage of a signal kind might hereafter decide the fortunes of a campaign; but then, in the present circumstances of international intercourse, and of unresting military competition, proceeding even in times of

<small>Expense involved by their adoption.</small>

Peace, it is increasingly unlikely that any single State will succeed in maintaining any such exclusive advantage. The use of the new military implements and machinery will call for a better trained and educated soldiery, and the novel method of recruiting, as practised on the Continent, harmonizes with this demand.

The general result is likely to be favorable to the private soldier's condition, education, and general training, and his opinion and feelings must become a serious element of political consideration. Some of the new improvements are directed to multiplying the action of explosive shells, balls, and bullets, thereby occasioning suffering and not death; others have in view the "demoralizing" the enemy's front at a greater distance, so as to precipitate the "decision," and afford an earlier opportunity for an advance. Other improvements, again, are addressed to facilitating commissariat arrangements, as by employing in War ordinary trading companies for the purpose, or to rendering engineering operations more easily disposable and effective, or to determining the exact proportions and circumstances in which cavalry, heavy and light infantry, and artillery ought severally to be employed.

There can be no doubt that by the time a sufficient amount of intellectual energy, guided by adequate experimentation, has been devoted in different countries to the problem of how the new improvements can be turned to the best account, War will reproduce all the last achievements of civilization. But it will do this at an almost inconceivable cost for each country both in Peace and in War; and there is no reason, except one grounded on economy or poverty, which need cause any one country to lag behind the rest. Thus the question of success in War must become increasingly one as to whether a nation can pay for it, or will prefer to pay for it, in the place of paying for other things. When each nation is firmly assured of this, the speculative hilar-

This waste a further reason for anticipating that War will become unpopular.

ity which now belongs to War will have vanished, and it cannot be long before the nations, under liberal and constitutional governments, combine to adopt some scheme of mutual assurance less extravagant, calamitous, and inhuman than that of self-protection.

SECTION VIII.

OF INTERNATIONAL CONFERENCES AND CONGRESSES.

Objects of Conferences during the present century.

ONE of the most obvious methods that suggests itself of settling existing disputes without armed conflict, and making political arrangements which may prevent the reappearance of such disputes in time to come, is that of summoning Conferences or Congresses in which all the States immediately, or even remotely, interested are represented.

This method has been largely resorted to during the present century with very varying degrees of success. The purposes of resorting to it have been manifold. Among these purposes may be mentioned (1) the making detailed territorial, financial, or political arrangements, contemplated by the general provisions of a Treaty, especially a Treaty of Peace; (2) the interpretation or modification of the terms of a Treaty; (3) the consideration of the conditions on which a temporary truce may be converted into a Treaty of Peace; (4) the consideration of the basis on which questions relating to the boundaries and new settlement or Neutralization of States should be determined by Treaty; (5) the establishment of new rules, or the republication in an improved form of existing rules, of International Law; (6) the acceptance of some novel principle of general international action or policy.

It is worth while illustrating these several purposes for which Conferences have been, or may be, held, by a review of the subjects of the chief Conferences which have been held in Europe since the Peace of Paris in 1814. The Treaty of Paris of the 30th of May in that year provided, in its 32d Article, that "All the Powers engaged on either side in the present War should, within the space of two months, send Plenipotentiaries to Vienna, for the purpose of regulating, in General Congress, the arrangements which were to complete the provisions of the present Treaty."

Vienna Congress, 1814–'15.

The Plenipotentiaries met in Congress at Vienna on the 22d of September, 1814, and closed their labors on the 19th of June, 1815. The result was the Treaty of Vienna, of 9th of June, 1815, which contained no less than seventeen "Annexes," that is, declarations, engagements, or special Treaties of particular States, and comprehended a general settlement of the international relations, and in some cases of the internal constitution, of the chief States of Continental Europe.

By the 15th Annex, the Plenipotentiaries of all the eight Powers which signed the Treaty of Vienna (that is, Great Britain, Austria, France, Portugal, Prussia, Russia, Spain, and Sweden), solemnly denounced the slave-trade, proclaimed their wish to put an end to "a scourge which had so long desolated Africa, degraded Europe, and afflicted humanity;" and declared in "the face of Europe that, considering the abolition of the slave-trade as a measure particularly worthy of their attention, conformable to the spirit of the times and to the generous principles of their august sovereigns, they were animated with the sincere desire of concurring in the most prompt and effectual execution of this measure by all the means at their disposal."

Denunciation of slavery.

Seven years later—in November, 1822—a Congress, composed of the Powers which were represented at the Vienna Congress, with the exception of Portugal, Spain, and Sweden, met at Verona, and after reciting that the commerce in slaves, solemnly proscribed, still continued, had

Congress at Verona, 1822.

gained in activity, and even taken a still more odious character, declared that their respective sovereigns continued firm in the principles and sentiments contained in the Declaration of 1815, and that their respective cabinets "would eagerly enter into the examination of any measure, compatible with the rights and the interests of their subjects, to produce a result that may prove to the world the sincerity of their wishes, and of their efforts in favor of a cause worthy of their common solicitude."

As illustrating the principles by which the usefulness of Conferences, as expedients for the prevention of War, may be tested, the Conferences of Troppau, in 1820, in which Austria, Prussia, and Russia took part, in reference to the revolutionary movements in Spain, Portugal, and Naples, may be aptly cited.

Conferences of Troppau, 1820.

A circular despatch of the Austrian, Prussian, and Russian Sovereigns to their respective missions at Foreign Courts, purported to contain a narrative of the first results of the Conferences. It recited the principles of the Holy Alliance which it was sought distinctly to revive, and asserted that "the Powers had exercised an undeniable right in concerting together upon means of safety against those States in which the overthrow of a Government caused by revolution could only be considered as a dangerous example, which could only result in a hostile attitude against constitutional and legitimate Governments." It was further alleged that "the ministers who could be furnished at Troppau with positive instructions from their Courts, concerted together on the principles of the conduct which they were to follow toward those States whose form of Government had received violent shocks, and on the peaceful or coercive measures which, in cases where important effects of a salutary influence could be obtained, might recall those States within the bosom of the Alliance."

The answer to this despatch, thus inviting co-operation, written by Lord Castlereagh on January 19th, 1821, and circulated among the British Missions at Foreign Courts, is instructive, as pointing out the dangers to which Conferences may pave the way, if they are not sufficiently representative in their constitution, and do not restrict their action within the limits prescribed by International Law. After saying that some of the measures proposed would be in direct repugnance to the laws of England, Lord Castlereagh goes on to assert that "even if this decisive objection did not exist, the British Government would nevertheless regard the principles on which the measures rested to be such as could not be safely admitted as a system of International Law. They were of opinion that their adoption would inevitably sanction, and, in the hands of less beneficent monarchs, might hereafter lead to, a much more frequent and extensive interference in the internal transactions of States than, they are persuaded, is intended by the august Parties from whom they proceed, or can be reconcilable either with the general interest, or with the efficient authority and dignity, of independent sovereigns. They do not regard the Alliance as entitled, under existing Treaties, to assume, in their character as Allies, any such general powers, nor do they conceive that such extraordinary powers could be assumed, in virtue of any fresh Diplomatic Transaction among the allied Courts, without their either attributing to themselves a supremacy incompatible with the rights of other States, or, if to be acquired through the special accession of such States, without introducing a federative system in Europe, not only unwieldy and ineffectual to its object, but leading to many most serious inconveniences."

Protest of Lord Castlereagh.

The most frequently recurring subject of Conferences between States falls under the fourth of the above-mentioned heads, that of the consideration of the basis on which questions relating to the boundaries, fresh settlement, or Neutralization of States have to be determined by Treaty.

Thus the Conference of December, 1828, at Poros, on the affairs of Greece, in which the representatives of Great Britain, France, and Russia took part, contemplated both this general object, and also that of arriving at a "definitive opinion" upon several points of the Treaty of London, of the 6th July, 1827. The purport and limits of the subject-matter of the Conference is thus precisely stated in the opening paragraph of the protocol: "Acknowledging, on the one hand, the impossibility of obtaining perfectly accurate details respecting the statistics of Greece, where ruin, the result of the War, has succeeded to the arbitrary dominion of the Pachas; and, admitting, on the other, that the information which has been acquired is, notwithstanding these difficulties, sufficient to furnish useful data and approximate estimates; religiously adhering to the principles and object of the Treaty of London, the aim of which is the pacification of the Levant by means of a mediation, if that be still possible; and, in the last place, confining themselves to seeking for Greece guarantees for tranquillity and facilities for defence, the Representatives have come to the following conclusions relative to the four questions specified in their instructions, namely: Boundaries, Tribute, Indemnity, and the relations of Suzerainty to be established between the Ottoman Porte and the Greek Government.

<small>Conference on Greek affairs, 1828.</small>

A similar Conference between the same Powers was held in London, in March, 1829. In the protocol of a similar Conference, again held in London, in February of the following year, a clause was contained declaring that "Greece should form an Independent State, and should enjoy all the rights, political, administrative, and commercial, attached to complete Independence."

Greece again became the subject of Conferences in 1852, in London, between the Plenipotentiaries of Great Britain, France, Russia, Bavaria, and Greece, on the subject of the succession to the Throne of Greece.

<small>More recent Conferences on the affairs of Greece.</small>

A Conference was again held in London in May, 1863, between

the Plenipotentiaries of Great Britain, France, and Russia, also relative to the Greek Succession; another was held in London on the 5th June of the same year, between the Plenipotentiaries of Great Britain, France, Russia, and Denmark, the subject being the succession to the Throne of Greece, and the Annexation of the Ionian Islands to that kingdom; another was held between the Plenipotentiaries of the same Powers, excepting Denmark, on the 26th of the same month, respecting a guarantee of the "Political existence and of the Frontiers of the kingdom," the union of the Ionian Islands to Greece, and the Greek loan; and others, in August and November of the same year, between the Plenipotentiaries of the same Powers respecting the title of the Sovereign of Greece.

Conferences relating to various other countries. Conferences have been held on the affairs of Holland in 1830, of Italy in 1843, of Denmark in 1850, of Denmark and Germany in 1864, of Luxemburg in 1867, and very numerous Conferences since 1853, on what is called the "Eastern Question," on the Neutral relations of the Ottoman Empire and its subject provinces, and on the integrity of that Empire.

Besides the instance already adduced of the circular despatch of Lord Castlereagh's, in which, on the part of the British Government, he refuses to take part in a Conference which seems to menace the independence of States not represented in it, there are two other notable instances in which Great Britain has refused to take part in a general Conference, on the ground that she might thereby put it out of her power adequately to guard either her own interests or the interests of others.

Conference on European Peace proposed by France, 1863. In the year 1863, the Emperor of the French, Napoleon III., addressed to the Queen of England a proposal for an "International Congress for the preservation of the Peace of Europe." The general grounds of the proposal, as broadly stated in the first note, are that "it is impossible not to admit that on almost all points the Treaties of

Vienna are destroyed, modified, disregarded, or menaced. Hence there are duties without rule, rights without title, pretensions without restraint. A peril the more formidable, since the improvements produced by civilization, which has united peoples together by an identity of material interests, would render War still more destructive." Some further correspondence ensued, conducted by Earl Russell on the one hand, and M. Drouyn de Lhuys on the other, the points being closely argued whether the changes which had taken place in Europe since 1815 amounted to a general rupture of the Treaty of Vienna, and whether the existing claims, somewhat menacingly avowed by Russia, Poland, Austria, Italy, Germany, and Denmark, were of a nature to be surrendered or modified at the bidding of a Congress, supposing other modes of obtaining the same ends proved, or might prove, ineffectual.

The only passages here relevant, as illustrating the limits to the usefulness of Conferences and the view of those limits taken at the time by the British Government, are contained in the following extracts from Lord Russell's two despatches:

Objections of British Government expressed by Earl Russell.
"When the Sovereigns or Ministers of Austria, France, Prussia, Russia, and Great Britain met at Verona, in 1823, upon the affairs of Spain, the first four of these Powers carried into effect their resolutions by means of armed forces, in spite of the protest of Great Britain. Is this example to be followed at the present Congress in case of disagreement? Upon all these points Her Majesty's Government must obtain satisfactory explanations before they can come to any decision upon the proposal made by the Emperor. Her Majesty's Government would be ready to discuss with France and other Powers, by diplomatic correspondence, any specified questions upon which a solution might be attained, and European Peace thereby more securely established. But they would feel more apprehension than confidence from the meeting of a Congress of Sovereigns and Ministers without fixed

objects, ranging over the map of Europe, and exciting hopes and aspirations which they might find themselves unable to gratify or to quiet. * * *

"If the mere expression of opinions and wishes would accomplish no positive results, it appears certain that the deliberations of a Congress would consist of demands and pretensions put forward by some and resisted by others; and, there being no supreme authority in such an Assembly to enforce the decisions of the majority, the Congress would probably separate, leaving many of its members on worse terms with each other than they were when they met. But if this would be the probable result, it follows that no decrease of armaments is likely to be effected by the proposed Congress."

The Brussels Conference of 1874, in reference to proposed amendments in the rules of Military Warfare, will afford material for discussion in a later chapter, when the bearing of the Laws of War on the prevention of War is under consideration. But this celebrated Conference must be here alluded to, in order to explain, by illustration, the nature of Conferences in general, and to prepare the way for some general discussion of the whole subject lower down.

Brussels Conference, 1874.

A circular despatch was issued on the 17th of April, 1873, by Prince Gortchakow, the Russian Minister, and addressed to the Russian Embassies at the several European Courts. It recited a proposal which had been made by the "Society for the Amelioration of the Condition of Prisoners of War," and referred to a previously announced intention of the Russian Government to lay before the different Cabinets "a draft for an International Code with the object of determining the laws and usages of Warfare." The draft Code was transmitted therewith. The despatch went on to say, that it seemed "indispensable to establish by common accord, upon a basis of complete reciprocity, rules which might be binding on all Governments and their armies." The Russian Government

Proposed by Russia.

believed this to be both the duty and the interest of every State. The draft submitted to the examination of the Cabinets was only a starting-point for ulterior deliberations, which, it was trusted, would prepare the way for a general understanding. To this end the Government was of opinion that a Conference of special Plenipotentiaries might be convoked to discuss these questions, and to decide upon a definite Code, which might thenceforth be clothed with an international character. The city of Brussels seemed to be particularly appropriate for such a Congress, on account of the neutral position of Belgium.

Nearly all the Powers to which invitations were sent agreed to be represented at the Conference. But England, in the person of Lord Derby, took up such a peculiar and exceptional position, that it must be examined in some detail in reference to its bearing on the general subject.

In Lord Derby's letter to the British representative at St. Petersburg, Lord A. Loftus, dated the 4th of July, 1874, he says: "Her Majesty's Government are not convinced of the practical necessity for such a scheme for the guidance of military commanders in the field, and cannot but fear that, unless the discussion is conducted in the most guarded manner, the examination of any such project in a Conference at the present juncture may reopen causes of difference, and lead to recrimination between some of the delegates appointed to take part in it. Nor do Her Majesty's Government fully understand the scope which it is intended to be given to the deliberations of the delegates. * * * Her Majesty's Government are firmly determined not to enter into any discussion of the rules of International Law by which the relations of belligerents are guided, or to undertake any new obligations or engagements of any kind in regard to general principles. * * * I have accordingly to request your Excellency to state to the Russian Government that, before agreeing to send a delegate to the Conference, Her Majesty's Government must request the most

Opposed by England.

positive and distinct assurance from that Government, as well as from the Governments of all the Powers invited to take part in the Conference, that their delegates at the Conference shall be instructed to confine themselves to the consideration of details of military operations of the nature of those dealt with in the project of the Russian Government, and shall not entertain, in any shape, directly or indirectly, anything relating to maritime operations or warfare."

A somewhat copious account has been above given of the leading Conferences and Congresses which, in the present century, have either actually been held or have been suggested at special crises for the solution of pending problems. The real meaning and purport of such assemblies of the diplomatic representatives of States, as well as the limits of their usefulness, will probably be better understood from actual illustrations than from general reasonings and anticipations.

The last two illustrations, indeed, exhibit England in the somewhat ungracious attitude of declining to co-operate, or, at least, to co-operate fully and heartily, in schemes for European Congresses which were ostensibly projected in the cause of Peace and humanity. The answer of Lord Castlereagh to the circular despatch of 1820, inviting co-operation with the Conferences at Troppau and Laybach, also presents England occupying a somewhat similar position. On the other hand, in some of the most celebrated Congresses, as those of Vienna in 1815, and of Verona in 1822, in reference to the general affairs of Europe and to the Slave-trade, and in the series of Conferences, held in different times and places, in reference to the political circumstances of special States—as Greece, Belgium, Denmark, and Turkey—England has taken a prominent and often the leading part.

England has sometimes co-operated in Congresses, sometimes held aloof.

Of course, it would be vain to contend that England, or any other State, has been really consistent in her policy throughout, and has only varied in her action in view of the difference in the circumstances presented. Modern States, and especially those which are the most constitutionally governed, are far too much subjected to the influence of passing waves of political opinion to be steady and uniform in their international action through more than half a century. Nevertheless, a reference to the grounds on which England has freely taken part in numerous important Conferences, and has, especially in the persons of Lord Castlereagh, Lord Russell, and Lord Derby, shown herself notably averse to sharing in others of most plausible pretensions, will assist the examination of the conditions on which the usefulness of Conferences depends.

Grounds of her policy.

There are two obvious cases in which a Conference must be wholly unprofitable, and therefore, probably, mischievous, and under one or other, or both, of these cases most of the objections alleged by the above-named English statesmen will be found to range themselves. One case is where influential States taking part in the Conference have not yet arrived at a determination of the general policy they intend to advocate, and do not wish or intend that policy to be determined by discussion outside, or by the casual events or mutual concessions to which the Conference may casually give occasion. The other case is where influential States are so far determined on their general policy, that no such events or concessions will ever induce them to change or modify it.

Conditions essential to the usefulness of Conferences.

Excluding these two cases, of uncertainty and of absolute fixity of policy, the only cases in which Conferences are likely to prove productive of useful results at once present themselves to view. There must be found, in all the influential States which take part in the Conference, a firmly fixed resolution as to the general policy they intend to advocate, and also an exact apprehension of the limits of the variations in matters of detail

A distinct policy.

Concession on points of detail.

which will be held admissible should the result of the discussions at the Conference seem to recommend them. The efficiency of these conditions involves the presence of several others, as, for instance, that the general policy pursued by the several States taking part in the Conference is harmonious, if not identical, and that within the limits of admissible variation from the general policy, the representatives of the States are free, and personally disposed, to follow the dictates of reason, prudence, and a spirit of mutual concession.

Unanimity of purpose.

On applying these remarks to the instances already cited of successful, of partially successful, and of abortive Conferences, it will be seen that they have been successful in proportion to the clearness of view, and general unanimity of purpose, with which the States have entered into them; and that these favorable circumstances have chiefly presented themselves where either a previous Treaty has established all the main lines along which alone disputation may take place, or some general principle of humanity is believed to be involved, which it is the concern of all States equally to support, and the permanent interest of no single influential State to controvert.

The Congress of Vienna, and the various Conferences which succeeded it during the next half-century for the settlement of some of the minor States of Europe, fall under the first of these heads. The Congresses which related to the suppression of the Slave-trade fall under the second head. The Conferences at Troppau and Laybach, which Lord Castlereagh refused to join, could only have succeeded if a sufficient number of influential States had been willing to revive the policy of the Holy Alliance, and find a spurious substitute for the cause of humanity in the cause of the Monarchical institutions then existing in Europe. The Congress suggested by the Emperor of the French, in 1863, contemplated the discussion of a variety of matters, in which the several States rep-

Application of these rules.

resented had very different proportions of interest, some of them interests of the most potent kind, some of them no apparent interests at all. Whatever issues of humanity and of Peace were involved were of a kind far too indefinite and discursive to become matters of profitable, or even possible, debate.

In the case of the Brussels Conference of 1874, the cause of humanity, as distinguishable from that of the interests of special States, was the only ostensible matter involved. There was no reason to doubt the *bonâ fide* generous intentions of the Czar of Russia, who issued the invitations to the Congress, and the conduct of the Russian representative throughout the proceedings was above suspicion. It did indeed appear, in the course of the discussions, that the smaller and larger States had, or thought they had, opposing interests involved, and therefore unanimity was purchased at times at the expense of unsatisfactory compromises or evasions. The refusal of England to take part in the Conference unless maritime warfare was excluded from the discussion, was a necessary course, assuming it is the fixed policy of this country to commit herself to no changes in her modes of maritime warfare, even at the price of diminishing the evils of warfare on land. It is this policy which is rather to be regretted, than England's refusal to take part in discussion in which her only attitude could have been that of persistent obstinacy.

It remains to be considered how far Conferences and Congresses may be regarded as hopeful instruments for the prevention of War in the future. It must be remembered that Conferences may often serve useful purposes, even though they do not attain the complete result which is expected of them. It is true, for instance, that the Brussels Congress of 1874 discovered differences of interest and opinion between some of the smaller and larger States in reference to the Laws of War which were not wholly anticipated. But if such differences really existed, it was a great service to bring

Utility of Conferences.

them to the surface, with a view to their nature and extent being carefully measured, and their causes scrutinized to the foundation. It does not seem that any process less solemn and inquisitorial than a formal debate, conducted in the presence of Europe, would have had exactly the same effect.

Conferences, then, must be treated at once as the token of growing political agreement, and important means of bringing it about. Whenever occasions present themselves in which the interests of all States are clearly subordinated to directly moral and humanitarian ends, or where the difficulties lie rather in the adjustment of a complex mechanism of States to a distinctly perceived and jointly pursued end, the usefulness of Conferences seems almost limitless. But, as has been seen, Conferences may be made, in dishonest, unwise, or ambitious hands, a means of enforcing the interests of a few States on a number of others which are ostentatiously invited to co-operate, and are yet too weak to do more than protest.

CHAPTER IV.

OF LEGAL REMEDIES FOR WAR.

BESIDES the obvious advantage of making the rules of International Law more certain, and, so far as is possible, systematizing and codifying them, so as to prevent disputes at the outset, and of providing effective judicial machinery for the settlement of purely legal difficulties and misunderstandings, there are two classes of legal reforms which imperatively call for immediate attention in the interests of Peace. One of these classes concerns the operation of War on the trade of Belligerents and Neutrals. The other concerns the Laws of War, in reference to the limitation of the severities with which War is conducted. These subjects must be treated in turn.

Reforms in International Law.

SECTION I.

OF THE LEGAL OPERATION OF WAR ON TRADE, AND MORE ESPECIALLY OF THE PROPOSED EXEMPTION OF PRIVATE PERSONS AND PROPERTY FROM MARITIME CAPTURE.

THERE are some subjects of international importance which it seems to be almost impossible to discuss from any other than a purely national, or even spuriously patriotic, point of view. The subject of the exemption of private persons and property from capture at sea is eminently one of these. The interests of different States seem, on the surface, to be so conflicting in the matter, that, on whatever side

Maritime capture:

of the controversy a writer ranges himself, he finds himself exposed to the charge of prejudice on the one hand, or of affectation and eccentricity on the other. Credit for honest impartiality seems to be absolutely refused to writers on both sides.

<small>commonly treated from a national stand-point.</small>

There is no doubt that some color is given to suspicions of unfairness by the actual course adopted in the past by writers on International Law. Instead of setting an example of rigid Neutrality, and confining themselves to a statement of the law as it is, they have too often written in the spirit of violent and unscrupulous partisans; and they have more frequently condescended to appear as the professional apologists for the policy of their own Governments, than acted as the unbiassed critics of the illegal or unjust conduct of all Governments, including their own.

It is with good reason that England is regarded as the stronghold of the doctrine which admits of the capture of private persons and property at sea, while disallowing it on land. Every considerable European State, as well as the United States of America, has, at one time or another, either publicly advocated the expediency of introducing the opposite doctrine; or (as in the case of Italy and France) has adopted the principle of reciprocity; or has already actually afforded a precedent of exempting private property at sea from capture, as in the case of the War of 1866, between Austria and Prussia, in alliance with Italy, and in that of the War of France and England with China, in 1860.

<small>England alone has perseveringly opposed the exemption of private property from maritime capture.</small>

The only State which has, when unhampered by alliances, adhered with tolerable, though by no means complete, consistency to the severer doctrine, is England. The most notable expression of the English view of the doctrine is that given by Lord Palmerston, on the 3d of February, 1860, when he announced that, in his opinion, the existence of England depended upon the maintenance of her empire over the sea, and the capture of the merchant-ships and seamen of States with which she was at War was essential to this end. It is interesting to notice, for a purely biographical purpose, that at Liverpool, on the 10th of November, 1856, when Lord Palmerston was interested in defending the recently-made "Declaration of Paris," he said that he could not but believe that the amenities of warfare lately introduced and practised must be extended farther, and that, in the course of time, the principles applied to land warfare must be applied likewise to warfare by sea, and private property be no longer subject to aggression in either case. He further noticed that, looking to ancient precedents, we should not find any country vanquished by the private losses of its citizens.

There is this advantage in discussing a subject of the present character at a Conference at which a large number of the most civilized States of the world are represented, that it is impossible to base an argument, either for or against a proposed measure of reform, on the presumed exclusive interest of any single State. Of course, the fact that any one State has a separate interest of its own in opposition to the measure, is not irrelevant to the controversy, because, if the interest be strong enough, and the State in question influential enough, the fact of such opposition may render all efforts at reform unprofitable or, at least, premature. It must, then, be a strictly pertinent inquiry to ascertain whether any particular State, especially one possessing considerable influence, really has the interest unfavorable to the measure which it is assumed she has. But, in an International Conference, this special inquiry into the casual attitude of a particular State is only ancillary and introductory to the consideration of the main issue, which is concerned with the general and permanent interests of all States, both individually and as a corporate community.

The subject advantageously discussed in International Conferences.

The only State which seems to assume that it has a permanent interest in favor of the capture of private persons and property at sea is England; and it is worth while considering to what extent she really has a different interest in this matter from that of the majority of other States. England has a mercantile marine exceeding (it is said) five times that of any other State. She has a naval force which is alleged to be capable of coping with the naval forces of any two other States combined. She has, moreover, a Colonial and Indian Empire of a kind to which no other State can make any pretensions, and which renders her assailable in every quarter of the globe.

English interests separately considered.

Success in War depends upon an apt combination of offensive and defensive efficiency. If England is at War, her navy has first to protect her own coasts and the coasts of her dependencies; secondly, to protect her commerce and mercantile marine generally; and, thirdly, to overpower the naval force of the enemy, or otherwise to inflict such damage on his resources as may induce him to accept the imposed conditions of Peace.

It is obvious that if the English navy could be relieved from any one of these three functions, the more disposable it would be for efficient discharge of the other two, always supposing the difficulty of discharging these did not, in the new circumstances, become proportionately increased. In other words, if England had not to protect her mercantile marine, her forces would be all the more free to defend her coasts and to overpower the naval forces of the enemy. She would not, indeed, be able to attack the mercantile marine of the enemy, but as, by the assumption, her own mercantile marine is at least five times as great as the mercantile marine of any other single State, and more than twice as great as the mercantile marine of any two States combined against her, her total gain in exemption from injury would far exceed her loss of power through the restrictions she would encounter.

Peculiar advantage to England of security for her mercantile marine.

If, again, it be argued that the mercantile marine is the natural source of supply for the navy, and therefore must be struck at as a potential arm of the national forces, then the value of rescuing such a reserve force is far greater to England than to any other State, or pair of States combined, in proportion to the vastly superior magnitude of the mercantile marine of England.

Of course, on the hypothesis that no other State but England has any navy at all, or any navy considerable enough to be worth taking into account, England would, from the present point of view, obtain only profit, and no loss, from the existing practice. But this hypothesis, imperfectly true even at the time of the height of England's naval supremacy during the wars at the close of the last century, is glaringly untrue at present, and is becoming more and more remote from the truth every day. It may be quite true that England will retain her naval supremacy; but the unwearied and gigantic efforts she is making to reconstruct her vessels after the latest type, and to press into her service the latest achievements of naval and engineering invention, show that this can only be done, in the presence of European and American competition, by an immense expenditure of capital and energy. The fact of such competition is confessed by every fresh iron-clad turned out of an English yard.

Growth of the navies of other nations.

Dependence of England on foreign countries for her food supply—

There are two other classes of facts which make the present rule of maritime capture bear far more hardly on England than on other countries. They have been so often explained at length, that they need be only summarily stated in this place. One of these classes of facts is, that if England is at War with a corn-supplying country, as Russia or America, one-third of her population, which now subsists on imported food, is either deprived of food altogether, or obtains it only at the enormously enhanced prices caused by transport through Neutral States. This, of course, is equally true of all the products of a country at War with England, on the manufacture of which large classes of the population subsist. Thus, during the Crimean War, Russian hemp, which cost during peace £30 a ton, rose during the War to £60 and even £80; and all other descriptions of Russian produce rose in the same proportion.

The other class of facts which makes the current rule bear with special hardship on England, as a trading and manufacturing State, was illustrated during the recent insurrection of the Southern States of America, when the belligerent rights enjoyed by both parties to the struggle enabled the North to deprive England—presumably an innocent Neutral—of the raw material of the manufactures in which a vast mass of her population found support. The question is not now whether the United States profited or not, on the whole, from the destruction of the commerce of the South—though as the United States Government are the main advocates of the liberty of maritime commerce in time of War, it may be presumed, at the least, that there were, even for that Government, more ways than one of looking at the subject. The point here is, that whenever two States are at War, one of which supplies England with some essential staple of its manufactures or trade, the present rule of maritime capture operates detrimentally to England, more than to any other State, in exact proportion to the greater dependence of England on a regular supply of that particular article. There are few of the leading articles of commerce and manufacture of which the demand in England is not greater than that of all other States put together; and therefore, whether England is a Belligerent or a Neutral, her economic loss by the existing rule is proved to be far greater than that of any other State, and her naval advantage less rather than greater.

Thus, so far as there is anything special in the position of England, her obvious interests are rather in favor of the proposed reform, than adverse to it. It now has to be seen wheth-

England would profit by exemption of private property from maritime capture.

er there are any considerations which should weigh with all States equally, including England, in favor of the abolition of the capture of private persons and property at sea, or whether, at least, the preponderating balance of considerations is in that direction.

There are three considerations which seem to point directly toward the abolition of the right of capture of pri-

Considerations affecting all nations equally.

vate persons and property at sea. These are (1) that exactly the same moral and economic principles apply to the respect of private property on the sea as to the respect of that on land; that (2) some principles, especially applicable to private property at sea, seem peculiarly to recommend that sort of property for exemption from capture; that (3) the exemption of that property from capture is an inevitable consequence of changes in the law which have already been made; and that (4) such exemption is likely to operate in a way to prevent the recurrence of War.

(1.) There are four distinct reasons which have recom-

Private property on land usually respected during War.

mended, and gradually brought about, the prevalent respect for private property on land. Two of these reasons are based on considerations of humanity, and two of them on considerations of self-interest. The first reason is that the indiscriminate pillage, which the capture of private property is sure to involve, and the unequal distribution of the burdens of the War it effects, are evils which, so far as they serve the purpose of the War, serve it in

Reasons for this exemption from capture.

a degree wholly disproportioned to the magnitude of those evils. The pressure on the Government which the seizure of private property occasions is, at the most, only indirect; and an incalculable amount of widely diffused mischief is inflicted without bringing to bear on the Government of the country any pressure whatever.

The second reason, also based on humane considerations, is that, whereas modern Wars are always alleged to be waged solely for the purpose of obtaining a satisfactory and lasting peaceful settlement at the earliest possible moment, the practice of capturing private property inflicts injury of a nature which, so far as the private sufferers go, no Treaty of Peace can cure. The loss extends far beyond the time of the War, and is, in fact, never made good.

The third reason is suggested by obvious considerations of policy or interest, namely, that the State to which the invading army belongs has an obvious concern in securing the good-will of the inhabitants of a traversed or occupied district, and may hereafter be found to have had a further concern in the wealth and prosperity of those who, in consequence of an acquisition of territory on a Treaty of Peace, have become its own subjects.

A fourth reason, also dictated by considerations of policy, is, that the more abiding and widespread the irritation caused by an invasion, the greater probability there is of the War being renewed at the earliest opportunity. It is thus the policy of a State which wishes to make the War final, to confine its area as much as possible, and to restrict all hostile operations to officially authorized combatants and to public property. The contest is then the more likely to assume the aspect of a mere competition of substantial strength instead of a rivalry in cruelty and passion.

There is, of course, one of these reasons which, from the difference of the subject-matter, cannot apply to sea warfare; that is, the reason based on the presumed concern a State has in the general welfare of a population, some of which may, through the events of the War, hereafter become its own subjects. But all the other reasons for respecting private property at sea apply with increased force to respecting that on land. The capture of pri-

Most of the above reasons apply with greater force to private property at sea.

vate property at sea gives rise to indiscriminate pillage under special circumstances of solitude and privacy, to which land Warfare can offer no parallel. The evil inflicted is most unequally distributed, small traders and private travellers suffering equally with great commercial firms, and the latter, often enough, through insurance devices and the heightening of prices, personally suffering least of all. The consequent pressure brought to bear on the Government is only casual and indirect, and is balanced by the pressure in the opposite direction proceeding from the home-producing classes, which, for the moment, reap rich fortunes by the depression of foreign trade. Anyway, the vast number of solitary sufferers exert no appreciable pressure at all in the direction of Peace. Again, as to the second reason, the injury to private persons is indelible, and extends far beyond the close of the War, whether it is inflicted by sea or on land; and, as to the last reason, there is no doubt that the wide-spread irritation occasioned by capture of private property at sea, as much as on land, is one of the main provocatives of enduring national hatreds.

(2.) But there are some circumstances affecting the position of private property at sea which render it far more unsuitable as an object of capture than private property on land.

Principles peculiarly applicable to exemption from capture at sea.

It is a doctrine of modern economic science that every State is enriched by the enrichment, and impoverished by the poverty, of every other State with which it has commercial dealings; and it is an equally well established doctrine, that all States, generally, are enriched in proportion to the division of labor which exists among them, or, in other words, to the degree of elaborateness in the organization of international trade. This organization demands for its conditions stability and confidence, and whatever impairs these not only to that extent weakens the organization, but goes a long way to destroy it.

But the capture of private property at sea is simply the ruin of this organization, and of all on which it depends. Were maritime Wars at all more common than they are, international trade would be impossible, and the most pacific nations would suffer equally with those most frequently belligerent. As it is, the miserable and trivial gains acquired by making maritime prizes, and the loss occasioned to the enemy's resources by hampering his commerce, make but a poor compensation for the utter disorder in which even the capturing State involves its own trade, and the wide-spread confusion and disaster it spreads on every side among Neutral trading States.

The practice of capture at sea ruinous to International trade—

In the security of which all States are concerned.

Private property on land might, indeed, with more justice, be held to be assailable, as being in a far truer sense the property of the paramount State, than are commercial goods in course of transit on the high seas the property of any particular State. Trade is the common concern of all States; and all States must co-operate to rescue it from a practice which, under the legal form of belligerent rights, is ever ready to strike a blow at it in the momentary interest of some particular State or States. Thus, not only is the same disproportion observable between the loss inflicted, and the value of the belligerent ends attained, by capturing private property at sea as by capturing it on land, but there is, over and above this excess of needless loss, the loss directly incurred by the capturing State, and by all Neutral trading States, and, indirectly, incurred by commerce generally through the paralyzing shock to public confidence imparted by such a wholly incalculable event, or rather accident, as War.

(3.) Furthermore, this exemption of private property at sea from capture is an inevitable consequence of changes in warlike usage which have been already brought about. The Declaration of Paris of 1856 has, for all States which were, or have since become, parties to it, proclaimed the double doctrine that captures of private property at sea can only be made by vessels forming part of the organized national forces, and not by commissioned privateers; and that the private property of belligerents is safe from capture if found in Neutral ships. The special circumstances amidst which this declaration was made are well known, and have, in fact, formed a subject of constantly renewed debate in the English Parliament.

<small>Changes pointing to exemption of private property from maritime capture.</small>

The most relevant facts are that, up to the commencement of the Crimean War in 1854, England had been prominent above every other State in tenaciously holding to the right of seizing belligerent goods wherever found. The general situation of the several States with which England was allied, was at War, or held relations of Neutrality, led the English Government to publish an Order in Council, on April 15th, 1854, in support of a Declaration made in the previous month to the effect that "her Majesty, being desirous of rendering the War as little onerous as possible to the Powers with whom she remains at Peace," and "in order to preserve the commerce of Neutrals from all unnecessary obstruction," was willing to waive a part of the belligerent rights appertaining to her by the Law of Nations," and that "her Majesty would waive the right of seizing enemy's property laden on board a Neutral vessel, unless it be contraband of War."

<small>The Declaration of Paris, 1856.</small>

This practice was observed throughout the War in the eyes of all Europe, and the recognition of its expediency was embodied at the close of the War in a declaration signed by the representatives of France, Austria, Prussia, Russia, Sardinia, Turkey, and England. About forty other States have since given in their adherence, and it is well known that the continued refusal to adhere on the part of the United States is solely due to their insisting on securing still greater immunities for commerce as the price of abandoning their right to use privateers.

It is irrelevant to allege at the present time, when more than

twenty years have elapsed since this Declaration was made,
either that some diplomatic, or even constitutional,
informality attached to the making of it, or that
England could, from any fresh view of her general interests,
now abjure it. So far as other States go, they have nothing to
do with constitutional irregularities in this country, whether
real or alleged, and they can only judge of the acts and intentions of England by the acts and intentions of the authorized
organs of her Government. So far as any opening for retracting the Declaration is concerned, none such exists compatible
with a decent regard to public honor. The Declaration was the
last expression and culmination of a confessedly new policy into
which England had been gradually forced, against all her instincts, her traditions, and apparent interests. For the last twenty years it has been the basis of political and military calculation
for all the States of the world; and to hint even at reconsidering it is to suggest such a public repudiation of a repeatedly
renewed engagement as would hardly have a parallel in the annals of bad faith.

Its binding character.

It thus must be assumed that the terms of the Declaration of
Paris of 1856 indicate the starting-point of a new
maritime policy for the States which are parties
to it. The purport of the Declaration is to restrict the capture of private property at sea in two directions.
It first prevents capture at all by any but the permanently organized national force. Secondly, it prevents the capture of
any private property of belligerents which is carried otherwise
than in the ships of a belligerent State.

Policy inaugurated by the Declaration of Paris.

The effect of a maritime War is thus to divert all the more
important part of its trade, that on which its commercial prosperity really depends, through the hands of Neutral carriers.
This involves just so much loss for both sides in the War as is
involved in paying for the use of a foreign vessel instead of
using a national one ready at hand, the heaviest loss falling on

the country which has the largest mercantile marine. As to all the less important trade, the passenger service and the like, its fate will be generally left to the chances of War; and yet this is the quarter from which a belligerent draws scarcely any military strength at all, while it is just here that the inconvenience, the irritation, and the abuses created are the greatest.

All this points to the fact that, owing to the changes of which the Declaration of Paris is the expression far more than the cause, the retention of the right of capturing private property is becoming an increasingly worthless belligerent right. Indeed, it is worse than worthless, for its direct operation is to enrich Neutral States at the expense of both the belligerents, and chiefly of the wealthier of the two, at the same time causing the maximum of annoyance, with the minimum of influence on the success of the War.

But there are other changes, physical, scientific, and political, which clearly indicate that the age of capturing private property at sea is passing away never to return. The colossal iron-clads, each new one outvying its predecessor in the strength of its armor-plating and the precision of its equipments; the trained engineer and the practised artillery-man, who have succeeded to the bluff and rude sailor of a by-gone generation; projectiles and torpedoes, of a kind almost wholly to supersede hand-to-hand fighting between one ship's crew and another, are phenomena which suggest how worthless for conversion to belligerent uses are untrained seamen, modern merchant-vessels, and passenger steamships, as compared with what they may have been during the ages when the doctrine of the capture of private property at sea was formulated and cherished. The general abolition of navigation laws for the artificial nursing of a nation's own mercantile marine; the recognition of colonial independence in matters of trade; and, above all, the abandonment of doctrines which sought the enrichment of one coun-

Other changes indicating that freedom of maritime commerce, in time of War, will be secured.

try in the restriction of its commerce with others, and the prosperity of each State in the impoverishment of all, are further decisive movements of an economical and social kind which make ulterior and consequential changes of the law of capture at sea irresistible.

The language in which a country loudly talks of its "naval supremacy being endangered" if it forbears to strike a blow at the commerce of its enemy, from which its enemy now suffers scarcely more than all other nations do, and certainly not more than the nation itself which inflicts the blow, is nothing more than a curiously antique legacy from an obsolete era, when Neutral ships could not carry enemies' goods; when merchantmen were still serviceable as privateers; when the differences between merchantmen and men-of-war were mostly those of size; when a monopoly of colonial trade was treated as a precious source of national wealth; and when, even in Peace, the commercial prosperity of each nation was believed to be inimical rather than helpful to the interests of all the rest. This era has passed, or is rapidly passing, away; and as soon as the new economical situation is as clearly appreciated by statesmen as it is by men of commerce, the practice of capturing private property at sea must pass away with it.

(4.) Lastly, it is impossible not to look at this whole subject from the point of view of its bearing on the prevention of War. The proposed restriction of the operation of maritime Wars to the organized national forces and the public property of the belligerents, belongs to a class of changes in the mode of conducting War which have been slowly, but surely, proceeding for some hundreds of years past.

Bearing of the question on the prevention of War.

A vast and most beneficial modification in the severity of War has been brought about through confining the area of War to the trained and responsible agents of the Governments con-

cerned. National passions are thus roused as little as possible;
military operations are throughout under effective
control, so as to admit of being summarily arrested
at any moment when Peace seems attainable; and
as little lasting loss as possible is inflicted which
might be productive of enduring acrimony, and seriously weaken the general resources of one of the markets of the world.
By restricting, too, the conduct of the War on both sides to the
official agents of the Government, such personal interests in the
continuance of the War as cannot be annihilated are at least
largely reduced in number and strength.

Advantage of restricting the conduct of War to official agents.

But the strongest reason of all for confining the conduct of a
War to the organized national forces, on both sides,
and that which especially affects Wars by sea, is,
that it is desirable in the general interests of Peace
to make War less and less a subject of chance or
gambling. All that tends to make the events of War calculable
beforehand, and its probable success or failure a matter of prediction, tends, to that extent, to prevent an actual recurrence to it.

The result of War would be more calculable, and resort to it less frequent.

When once States are content that in a military or naval point
of view great inequalities must, and do, exist between them, and
that there is no shame in admitting the fact of those inequalities,
they are likely to resort to modes of social combination among
themselves by which the Peace of the world may be made to
rest on some surer basis than the accidental self-restraint of particular States, or the problematical issue of a conflict between
any two States. The existing practice of the capture of private
property at sea makes the events of a War between two maritime States only calculable so far as trade on both sides is habitually circumscribed within rigid and clearly ascertained limits.
Such forced circumscription is fatal to mercantile prosperity,
not to say to the existence of trade itself.

Hence a choice must be made between perpetuating War as
a gambling speculation, ever presenting the readiest temptation

to the most embarrassed States, and, by getting rid of as many variable and capricious conditions as possible, allowing of War, at the best, only as a fairly calculable means of attaining a clearly definite end.

It is also to be borne in mind that, when a War is in contem-
<small>Prevention of national animosities.</small> plation, deep-laid national sympathies or antipathies go a long way in preventing or promoting it. The effect of confining the operations of War to professional soldiers and mariners, and to public property, is to do the utmost possible to prevent the growth of those ineradicable animosities which spring from War itself, and lead to each War giving birth to a new one, and so produce a progeny of fresh Wars without apparent end.

Besides the exemption of private persons and property from
<small>Other changes proposed in the interests of commerce.</small> maritime capture, a series of other co-ordinate and consequential changes have been recommended, in the interests of Peace. Such are (1) the limitation of the right of blockade to the case of naval arsenals, or places defended with an armed force; (2) the restriction of the interpretation of "contraband" to articles directly and solely conducive to the operations of War, such as rifles and ammunition; and (3) the restriction of the right of search in such a way as to reduce it within the narrowest possible limits compatible with the effective prevention of the carriage of true "contraband" articles, and of attempts to break a legitimate blockade.

The arguments in favor of all these classes of reforms may be briefly summarized as follows:

All the reforms concern trade, and a competition is thereby
<small>Small military gain and great commercial loss now occasioned by the practice of capture.</small> presented between the claims of trade and the alleged necessities of belligerency. The Declaration of the Treaty of Paris was a concession to Neutrals and belligerents alike, so far as they were traders. The limited opportunities still left by the Declaration

for destroying an enemy's trade, the complex circumstances of modern trade, and the ever-growing inter-dependence of the more important States on each other for the first necessaries of life, render the indiscriminate pillage of an enemy's trade too futile and suicidal a policy to be any longer reckoned among the necessities of naval warfare. The general loss and inconvenience to all trading nations are wholly out of proportion to the uncertain and fleeting advantages attained. International society is becoming a vast organization for mutual assurance, and the States most powerful at sea have the largest commercial marine, and, both directly and indirectly, must suffer most by the existing law and practice.

The interests of traders in favor of Peace under the present rules are counterbalanced by the new and special manufacturing and trading interests, generated by, and wholly dependent on, War; while, even among the trading classes, strong national passions soon dominate over the most clearly perceived personal interest. The extension of the War, and of its consequences, material and moral, to non-combatants, tends to prolong, to embitter, and to renew War quite as much at sea as on land, where such extension is abandoned.

If it be argued that the present rules dispose the trading classes to a general policy of Peace and conciliation at all times, it must be remembered that the pacific tendencies of the trading classes need no greater stimulus than the inevitable effects of War, in all cases, resulting from the sudden displacement of capital, the precipitate increase of taxation, the cessation of social intercourse, the impediments to free locomotion, the abnormal appearance of upstart and transient industries, and the substitution of feverish speculation for the even and healthy routine of pacific industry and commerce.

The real military gains which the present rules of warfare bring with them are too minute to be worth the prodigious sacrifice incurred. Belligerents can now transfer all their trade to

Neutrals at a trifling extra cost; the novel restriction that a blockade must be "effective," prevents any military pressure in that way on a comprehensive scale. The existing restrictions on the carriage of contraband are notoriously ineffectual for their alleged objects, while the inconvenience occasioned to Neutrals is enormous. The objections to the right of search are recognized on all sides. All that is contended for, on the plea of military necessity, would be attained by restricting the operations of maritime warfare to conflicts between the naval forces of the belligerents, and the effectual blockade of fortified harbors and ports, or towns also invested by land.

The probable influence of industrial and commercial progress on War may be thus presented in a systematic and compendious form:

I. As to the operation of the doctrine of *Free-trade*. (1) Pacific tendency of Free-trade. The substitution of the doctrine of Free-trade for the old Mercantile Theory implies the abolition of a class of restrictions favorable to the recurrence of War, and the development of a class of popular ideas and beliefs favorable to Peace. Such restrictions were those involved in the Colonial System, the Navigation Laws, and the Prohibitive Tariffs. Such popular ideas and beliefs are those which substitute reciprocity and mutual contribution between States in the place of hostile rivalry and irreconcilable opposition of interests, and which recognize that States are rich by one another's wealth, and not by one another's poverty; that the destruction of the wealth of any one State is a loss to all, and that States are being linked into a delicately-organized Society, experiencing at once, throughout all its Members, common gain or loss—common well-being or misery. (2) Free-trade, in its fullest sense, implies not merely the absence of artificial restrictions, but the positive fact that States carry out the subdivision of labor to the utmost, and that each State produces or manufactures those commodities, and those only, which it produces or manufactures with the greatest comparative cheapness. The more firmly this principle becomes established, the more fine and intricate become the commercial and monetary relationships between States, and the more disastrous and paralyzing becomes even the apprehension of War. This increasing subdivision of labor is of especial importance in respect of the growing inter-dependence of States for the supply of food. Old countries, as a rule, import food, and new countries export it. It is the old countries which, for a variety of reasons, are most prone to War; and if War does not mean famine, it must at least press—through the bread market, and even the meat market—on every part of the population of a belligerent State.

II. The modern aspects of the *Wages* question must directly affect War. Wages are rising everywhere, and the position of all classes of laborers is becoming better and more hopeful. Service in the army or navy must become comparatively less desirable, and compulsory service can only be procured at the price of an ever-increasing national cost and discontent. A keen competition is descried in the near future between the industries (so-called) of War and of Peace. The demand of labor for War, where the labor is forced, will not raise wages generally; and where the labor is not forced, it will be more and more abandoned, or else purchased only on ruinous terms.

<small>Causes operating to render War unpopular in the future.</small>

<small>Rise of wages.</small>

III. The growing *expensiveness* of War introduces a similar class of considerations to the last. When it is calculated how precious are the materials which most of the modern appliances of science to warlike purposes consume, on how vast a scale the applications take place, and what an amount of waste and loss are occasioned merely by tentative experiments, the cost of War is seen to be assuming more and more prodigious dimensions. So far as this cost is reckoned as the price of assurance, and, therefore, as akin to the necessary cost of production, the fact of War counteracts all the

<small>Increasing cost of War.</small>

other tendencies of civilization toward the cheapening of this cost.

IV. There is a manifestly growing tendency in labor to move with unparalleled facility from country to country. Thus all Europe must shortly become one labor market. The increased study of foreign languages, religious toleration, assimilation of political institutions and laws, a common postal system, projects for an International currency, and for a common fiscal system—all combine to diminish what is narrow and blindly selfish in the sense of nationality, while fortifying what is sound and precious in it; and this must operate in favor of Peace.

Growth of International Intercourse.

V. The interests and sympathies of *laborers* are thus likely to be wholly in favor of pacific relations. The interests of *land proprietors* are in favor of the condition which makes that of which they have a monopoly most in demand—that is, Peace—because Peace is indispensable to material progress. The interest of the *farmer-capitalist* is for the moment in favor of War, as raising agricultural prices; is still more decisively in favor of Peace, as favorable to trade generally, as keeping down the price of machinery and labor, and keeping open foreign markets for the disposal of produce. If the capitalist is a *trader*, his interests (except in the case of the few who draw a precarious profit from sustaining the War) are undividedly in favor of Peace.

Interests of land-owners and capitalists.

VI. The particular modes in which the interests and sentiments of all the industrial and trading classes will make themselves felt are in efforts for a modification of the Laws of War in favor of the protection of Neutral (and, ultimately, all other) trade, in promoting a conciliatory and just policy at all times between States, in humanizing the conduct of War, in rigidly preventing its extension, and in making beneficial, equal, and far-sighted Treaties.

Influence of the Industrial and commercial classes.

SECTION II.

OF THE LAWS OF WAR IN THEIR BEARING ON PEACE.

It was a maxim of the arch-thief Jonathan Wild, as record-
ed by Fielding, his biographer, that he and his
comrades should "Never do more mischief to another than was necessary to the effecting his purpose; for that mischief was too precious a thing to be thrown
away." The last twenty-five years have been distinguished by
a series of conscious efforts to give a practical application to
this doctrine; and these efforts have been made as much by the
people who delight in War as by those who have become the
reluctant victims of it.

<small>Recent efforts to limit the evil effects of War.</small>

Laws for the limitation of severity in War are of very ancient
date in European history; and it may be important to consider
the modes in which these laws originated, as well as the moral
justification on which they rest. But, before entering on the
broader inquiry, it will be convenient to recapitulate briefly the
more patent efforts that have been made of late years to establish on a firmer basis, to codify, and to amend, the chief rules
which, in practice, have long regulated and restricted the extreme use of the so-called rights of War.

The Crimean War, in 1854, which first broke up the lull of
forty years of Peace, was happily signalized, not
only by an extremity of courteous regard, on the
part of all the belligerents, for the interests of
Neutrals, but also by an almost unprecedented
consideration for the claims of non-combatants in the belligerent States, of prisoners of War, and even, in some respects, of
the private commerce conducted by citizens of the belligerent

<small>Consideration shown to Neutrals and non-combatants during the Crimean War.</small>

States themselves. This courtesy and amenity in practical action was embodied as a principle and starting-
point for the future in the Declaration annexed to
the Treaty of Paris of 1856, signed by the representatives of France, Austria, Prussia, Russia, Sardinia, Turkey, and England, and to which about forty other States have since given in their adhesion.

<small>Principles laid down in the Declaration of Paris.</small>

The immediate object of this Declaration was the conciliation of Neutral interests; but it was, in practice, impossible to conciliate these interests, so far as maritime warfare was concerned, without mitigating the severity of War in its effects on citizens of the belligerent States. The abolition of privateering, and the protection of an enemy's merchandise under a Neutral flag, as well as the stricter interpretation to be henceforward applied to blockades, were benefits conferred not only upon Neutral States, but in which the private citizens and traders of the belligerent States also have their share.

The next epoch in the republication and amendment of the Laws of War is marked by the sort of code drawn up by Professor Lieber, and—after being submitted to and approved by a committee of officers—sanctioned by President Lincoln just before the commencement of hostilities between the Northern and Southern States of America. This code is entitled "Instructions for the Government of the Armies of the United States in the Field." Professor Lieber, the author, was a Prussian by birth, and in his youth had served in the Prussian army, taking part in the campaigns of 1814 and 1815. This is a matter of some interest, because of the close relationship observable between these "Instructions" and the regulations of the so-called "Prussian Military Code"—a code which has never been published, but the substance of which can be pretty accurately collected from the constant references made to it by Prussian commanders in the proclamations and manifestoes issued in the

<small>Professor Lieber's "Instructions" for the American army.</small>

course of the late invasion of France. The Instructions here referred to were, in fact, the first attempt to make a comprehensive survey of all the exigencies to which a War of invasion is likely to give rise; and it is said on good authority that, with one exception (that of concealing in an occupied district arms or provisions for the enemy), no case presented itself during the Franco-German War of 1870 which had not been provided for in the American Instructions.

The interval between the outbreak of hostilities in America and the Franco-German War was marked by two generous and successful efforts, known as the Conventions of Geneva and St. Petersburg, to mitigate, by systematic compromises and arrangements, the effects of warfare on the sick and wounded, and to discourage the use of barbarous implements, which might inflict torturing pain in excess of any military advantage to be gained by the use of them.

Conventions of Geneva and St. Petersburg.

The Convention of Geneva was signed on August 22d, 1864, by the Plenipotentiaries of Switzerland, Baden, Belgium, Denmark, France, Hesse, Italy, the Netherlands, Portugal, Prussia, Spain, Würtemburg, and, subsequently, Great Britain. The Convention provided, in a series of Articles, for the Neutralization of ambulances and military hospitals, and of all persons engaged in the medical service or the transport of the wounded, and also of chaplains. A distinctive flag and arm-badge were to be adopted, which were to bear a red cross on a white ground.

The Convention of St. Petersburg, in 1868, was entered into, on the proposition of Russia, by Great Britain, Austria and Hungary, Bavaria, Belgium, Denmark, France, Greece, Italy, the Netherlands, Persia, Portugal, Prussia and the North German Confederation, Russia, Sweden and Norway, Switzerland, Turkey, and Würtemburg. The instrument recited that "the only legitimate object which States should endeavor to accomplish during War is to weaken the military forces of the enemy;

that for this purpose it is sufficient to disable the greatest possible number of men; that this object would be exceeded by the employment of arms which uselessly aggravate the sufferings of disabled men, or render their death inevitable; that the employment of such arms would, therefore, be contrary to the laws of humanity." The contracting parties thereupon "engage to renounce, in case of War among themselves, the employment by their military or naval troops of any projectile of a weight below 400 grammes, which is either explosive or charged with fulminating or inflammable substances."

The most ambitious effort which has been made in recent times to review and include in a general survey all the chief branches of the Laws of War was inaugurated in 1874 by the Society for the Amelioration of the Condition of Prisoners of War, and was greatly advanced by the proceedings of the Brussels Conference, convoked by the Emperor of Russia in the course of the same year. The Society owed its existence to the Universal Alliance Congress, which sat at Paris in June, 1872; and its scheme was mainly confined to carrying still further, in the interests of prisoners of War, the beneficent projects to which the Conventions of Geneva and St. Petersburg had already given substantial effect.

<small>Society for Ameliorating the Condition of Prisoners of War.</small>

In the original circular letter addressed by the Comte de Hondetot, President of the Executive Committee of the Society, to Foreign Governments, soliciting them to send delegates to a Conference to be opened at Paris in May, 1874, it was said that "the disparity in the rules already existing relative to the treatment of soldiers who become prisoners of War, and the absence of any rule whatever in most countries, have suggested the formation of a Society, composed of members of various nationalities, with the view of moving the Governments to conclude an agreement upon a question so highly interesting to civilization and humanity."

This letter was dated March 28th, 1874; and on the 6th of April the Russian Government, in the person of Prince Gortchakow, sent a communication to the Foreign Governments, announcing the answer which it had already returned to the proposal of the Society, and further declaring that it had arrived at the intention of "laying before the cabinets a project for an International Code, with the object of determining the laws and usages of warfare." The words of Prince Gortchakow in this despatch are noticeable. He encloses the project therewith, and adds: "The motive by which it is inspired is one of humanity; which, we are convinced, will meet a general feeling, a general interest, and a general need. The more that solidarity becomes developed which tends in these times to bring together, to unite, nations as the members of one family, the more their military organization tends to give to their Wars the character of conflicts between armed nations; the more necessary does it become, therefore, to determine, with greater precision than in past times, the laws and usages admissible in a state of War, in order to limit the consequences and to diminish the calamities attendant upon it, so far as it may be possible and desirable. With this end in view, it seems indispensable to establish, by common accord, upon a basis of complete reciprocity, rules which may be made binding on all Governments and their armies. We believe this to be both the duty and the interest of every State. The project which we submit to the examination of the cabinets is only a starting-point for ulterior deliberations, which we trust will prepare the way for a general understanding. To this end, we are of opinion that a Conference of special Plenipotentiaries might be convoked to discuss these questions, and to decide upon a definite code, which might thenceforth be clothed with an international character."

Prince Gortchakow goes on to suggest the City of Brussels as particularly appropriate for such a Congress, and names the

15th of July as a convenient date of meeting. The Congress met, accordingly, at Brussels in July, the English Government having specially guarded itself against doing more than "sending a military officer as delegate, who would not be invested with any plenipotentiary powers, and who would simply report the proceedings, reserving to Her Majesty's Government entire liberty of action in regard to them." Lord Derby, the British Foreign Secretary, had also expressly stipulated that such a delegate could only be sent upon his Government receiving from the Russian Government, as well as from the Governments of all the Powers invited to take part in the Conference, the most positive and distinct assurance "that their delegates at the Conference should be instructed to confine themselves to the consideration of details of military operations, of the nature of those dealt with in the Project of the Russian Government, and should not entertain in any shape, directly or indirectly, anything relating to maritime operations or naval warfare."

The Brussels Congress.

The results of the Congress are of the highest interest, though no actual convention has, as yet, resulted from them. The discussions between the representatives of the larger and of the smaller States served to bring to light many of the inherent, but scarcely suspected, obstacles to unanimity in the attempt to codify the Laws of War at the present time, and to expose in the clearest light some insuperable difficulties in the way of conciliating opposing interests, owing to the mere transitory influence of passions already excited by recent Wars. A careful review of the original text for the amendment of the Laws of War proposed by the Russian Government, of the text as finally "modified by the Conference," and of the arguments, or almost desultory conversations, in which the different representatives expressed their views on every part of the scheme, will be found to afford the best attainable instruction on the whole subject of

Result of the Congress in modifying and codifying the Laws of War.

the Laws of War, as applicable, and in fact applied, to the present circumstances of European States. The text, as modified by the Conference, embodies in clear and legal, though not technical, language all the best recognized, as well as all the unwritten, rules and usages relating to the conduct of land warfare.

In two clauses it summarily includes all the regulations of the Conventions of Geneva and St. Petersburg. It further reduces to precise expression the least vague and uncertain of the rules of practice which the more modern requirements of War had already suggested and partially enforced. The distinction between combatants and non-combatants, the treatment by an invading army of invaded territory and of its inhabitants, the conduct of sieges and bombardments, and, according to the original purport of the whole movement, the situation of prisoners of War, form a series of topics, each of which is handled with minuteness, but not prolixity. Taken together, they present a code which, whatever its legally binding force, cannot be henceforth left out of account in any attempt to ascertain the actual customs and usages, as well as the moral sentiments, of many of the most enlightened Governments of the world at the present time. Specimens of the enactments of this code are given at a later page.

Two deductions from the value of this code have to be made.

Unwillingness of England to co-operate in a second Congress.

One is, the persistent reluctance of England, in the interests, as asserted by the Foreign Secretary, Lord Derby, of all the smaller States, and of England itself, to assent to the renewal of the Conference in the following year (1875), for the purpose of giving more cogent effect to its recommendations. Lord Derby went so far as to say that "the result of the Brussels Conference had been to prove that it was not possible to create an understanding with respect to the really important articles of the Russian project; that the interests of the invading and of the invaded State are irreconcilable; and that, even could certain Laws of War be published in terms which admitted of general adhesion, they would only exercise in fact that fictitious influence which the Russian Government had protested against at the opening of the Conference. In these circumstances Her Majesty's Government could not consent to pursue the matter, nor to take any part in further negotiations or Conferences on the subject."

The second deduction from the value of the results of the Congress, is the glaring imperfection of those results in some important respects. This is manifested, for instance, in the total omission from the modified text of the subject of reprisals, which was a prominent topic of the original scheme, and was discussed at the sittings of the Congress. This omission seems to have been owing to the strong feelings, not yet abated, which had been aroused in the late Franco-German War. The language in which Baron Jomini, the Russian delegate, expressed his regret for the total omission of the topic is interesting, as pointing out the expectations and conceptions which the Russian Government, at all events, professed to have entertained:

The work of the Congress incomplete.

Topic of reprisals omitted.

"I regret that the uncertainty of silence is to prevail with respect to one of the most bitter necessities of War. If the practice could be suppressed by this reticence, I could but approve of this course. But if it is still to exist, this reticence may, it is to be feared, remove any limits to its exercise. Nevertheless, I believe that the mere mention in the protocol that the committee, after having endeavored to regulate, to soften, and to restrain reprisals, has shrunk from the task before the general repugnance felt with regard to the subject, will have a most serious moral bearing. It will, perhaps, be the best limitation we have been able to affix to the practice, and especially to the use which may be made of it in future."

Without considering too minutely the motives of the various States which took part in this celebrated Congress, or weighing the amount of the separate interests they may be presumed to have had in its issue, it may be broadly laid down that both the most military and the most pacific States are deeply concerned in the adjustment, in one direction or another, of Laws of War. During the last quarter of a century War has been conducted on a scale of magnitude, and with the help of scientific inventions, wholly unknown in former times. The notion of an "armed nation" is no longer confined to the attitude of a country at the exceptional crisis of suffering an invasion. The notion has been extended, and is being increasingly extended, to the chronic condition of all the leading States in times of what is, apparently, the most profound Peace. Thus, whenever War actually takes place, its effects on life, limb, commerce, wealth, and honor radiate to a far wider circumference, and are intensified at every point to which they reach. The provision for the circumscription of War to the combatants professionally engaged, laboriously as it is attempted in form, rather expresses the ever-increasing difficulty of such circumscription, than indicates any natural tendency toward the separation of the fighting from the non-fighting part of the population.

Laws of War matter of universal concern.

Magnitude of modern armies, and—

The German *landsturm* may be taken as one of the most modern instances of the possible extension of the area of organized warfare. Every member of this force is liable to serve in the national army of defence, up to the age of sixty years—the organized German army to be encountered by an invader being thereby raised, it is said, to three millions of men.

extension of the area effected by Laws of War.

It is obvious, then, that such questions as the treatment of prisoners of War, the modes of dealing with occupied districts, villages, and towns, and their inhabitants, as well as the manner in which an invading army may support itself in a hostile territory, and even the kind of warlike instruments employed, must henceforth come home to private persons in obscure and outlying quarters, such as, even in the most ruinous Wars of former times, have themselves had little to fear from the shock of arms. Thus it comes about that the modern inquiry as to what are, or ought to be, the Laws of War, becomes in time of War, and so far as the belligerent States are concerned, an inquiry into the whole political constitution under which the population of those States is liable to be, for the time, compelled to live.

By the fact of invasion, which, by the hypothesis, may be presumed as likely to befall the one State as the other, the male population may be converted into a standing army, martial law be substituted for the laws and customs of Peace, and all the ordinary provisions for personal liberty, for the security of property, for the just and orderly trial of offenders, be instantly overruled by regulations conceived in the interests of the War, and over which the smallest possible amount of popular control can at any time be exercised. The severer side of Laws of War has been rather epigrammatically expressed by Mr. Sutherland Edwards, one of the *Times* correspondents during the Franco-German War. "Laws are not silent in the midst of arms, but the laws made to replace ordinary laws are of a primitive and barbarous type. In principle they might not unfairly be summed up as follows:

"1. For every offence punish some one; the guilty if possible, but some one.

"2. Better a hundred innocents should suffer than that one guilty man should escape.

"3. When in doubt, shoot the prisoner."

It does not need any circuitous reasoning to show that, even apart from all considerations of humanity, States which, whether voluntarily or compulsorily, are devoting themselves to a military career, have a strong concern and private interest in ascertaining the limitations which are to be imposed on severity in War. The larger the army, and the shorter and more superficial the

It is to the interest of military States to conciliate non-combatants.

training its magnitude involves, the more indispensable it is for commanders in the field to be able to apply the sternest rules to the conduct of their own troops.

The Government to which an invading army belongs can have no interest whatever in exacerbating on every side the feelings of the population among which the army comes. Beyond the necessity of preventing opposition and securing supplies in the most economic fashion, all the interests of the invaders are in favor of conciliating the friendship, or at least the respect, of those not engaged in the War, and of sparing to the uttermost public as well as private property, upon which they have an opportunity of laying their hands. These principles are now so fully acknowledged, that the only difficulty remaining is where to draw a line between those persons who are and those who are not engaged in opposing the invasion, and how to impose efficient penalties on persons who disobey the military code in its spirit or its letter.

It may thus be expected that, for the purpose of conducting warfare in the most civilized manner compatible with fighting at all, much will yet be done by conventions, and by more or less clearly understood practice, to circumscribe in every way now possible the area of War, to reduce its severity, and to substitute the notion of War as a means, rough, but necessary, for the attainment of some worthy end, for the notion of War as a casual and ferocious struggle, in which no other end is even plausibly put forward than the satisfaction of cupidity, or the indulgence of national animosities.

Probability of further limitations of the severity of War.

There are those, however, who are far from content even with this description of the prospect in view for the more civilized countries of the world. Educate your soldiers to the utmost pitch of moral self-restraint, or even of national heroism; take from them all that imparts to them the character of butchers, and clothe them with all that is most worthy of admiration in the occupations of Peace; give them the highest spirit of self-sacrifice, unmarred, even in the heat of conflict, by any taste for bloodshed or rapine, or delight in the miseries of their fellow-men; make your armies models of organization, of individual consecration to the corporate interest, and of loyalty to the State they serve, and to the military end which that State has in view. When all this is accomplished, as it might be one day, and as, perhaps, it has been already in one army or another at different epochs, it may still be asked whether Wars are likely to become any the less frequent, and whether a reign of permanent Peace is any nearer than it was before. For those who attach practical importance to so momentous an issue as this, not only is the more general investigation here suggested one not too remote to attract immediate interest, but, inasmuch as every detailed and progressive amendment of the Laws of War prepares the way for a total reconstruction of practices now looked upon with approval, the most far-sighted philanthropist must condescend to discuss even military details, for which he naturally may have little taste.

<small>Question of permanent Peace.</small>

<small>The development of the Laws of War as bearing upon the ultimate abolition of War.</small>

From the times of Livy, writing at the epoch of the Christian era, to those of Grotius, whose great work owed its origin to the felt horror of the Thirty Years' War, which closed in 1648, the coexistence on the battle-field of two systems of obligation, one to the claims of military necessity, the other to the claims of abstract morality, has been recognized by all the leading writers on the subject, and by those who have been responsible for the actual conduct of War. The story told by Livy of Camillus, when besieging the city of the Falixi, was no doubt an anachronism, to the extent that the historian imputed to a far earlier age sentiments which had only been formulated in his own time. But the fact of sentiments so memorable being prevalently acknowledged even at that time—intervening be-

<small>Co-existing claims of military necessity and of morality.</small>

<small>Recognized by Livy.</small>

tween the Wars of the Republic and those of the Empire—points out how congenial they are to the instincts of even the most bellicose human nature. In reply to the school-master, who in the course of the siege had treacherously delivered into his hands the sons of the chief men of the city, Camillus answers that it was true that "the Romans and the Falixi were bound to one another by no obligations created by man, but by the obligations which nature had created they were both of them bound, and ever should be; there were rights of War as well as of Peace, and in conformity to them they had been taught to do all that justice, as well as all that courage, prompted."

Grotius, always loyally, if not servilely, following the examples of former times, distinguishes, in different chapters, all that a military commander is licensed to do by the actual inhuman practice of War, and the modifications of the severity so permitted which a higher morality, or the desultory humanity of particular commanders, seem to recommend as doctrine or precedent. Mr. Ward, in his "History of the Law of Nations," fills up the chasm between the times of Livy and Grotius, and points out, with the aid of copious illustrations, how all the institutions and events, through the operation of which the modern States of Europe acquired their existing political form, combined to modify the severity of War, and to circumscribe its effects.

By Grotius.

Influences which have modified the character of War.

Mr. Ward passes in review the effect of chivalry, of ecclesiastical institutions, and of the feudal system, and throughout the whole region of International Law he demonstrates that while one series of influences tended to produce dislocation and animosities among the nascent States, another series, far more potent, more continuous, and more universal, was tending to bind the States together, and to make their Governments entertain sentiments of friendliness to one another. The conflict of these two classes of influences, uncertain and spasmodic as it appears on a narrow inspection of it, forms a large part of the history of

European civilization; and the whole of this process is mirrored in the gradual changes which have been brought about in the art and practice of War.

These historical considerations might of themselves suggest that there is some close, though hidden, connection between improvements in the practice of War, looked at merely from a military point of view, and the growth of those civilized habits which are the only augury of the final establishment of Peace. The amendments of the Laws of War have two distinct aspects and origins. These amendments either have in view the mere increase of efficiency of the army, by preventing insubordination, controlling licentious dispositions, maintaining discipline in exceptional and unforeseen circumstances, and generally securing that the soldier shall only differ from the most manageable of mechanical agencies in his ability to understand and act upon the word of command, and in the power of self-adjustment by which he can mould his own actions in conformity with a common plan; or they have in view the benefit of those, whether combatants or non-combatants, who belong to the State against which the War is waged. The most highly elaborated system of Laws of War would succeed, as far as is possible, in rendering the attainment of these two objects not incompatible; and looking at the most recent codes, previously adverted to, it would appear that both have floated simultaneously before the minds of those who have revised the laws, and, in fact, little discrimination has been attempted between them. There must, then, be some ground of unity on which all these amendments rest, and in view of which their value and bearing must be judged.

Improvements in the practice of War correspond with progress in civilization.

This ground of unity may perhaps be found in the fact that, whatever are the laws for the restraint and direction of those who carry on War, the differences between one class or kind of laws and another are of infinitely less importance than the difference which exists be-

Observance of any laws in War an immense gain.

tween a system of warfare in which Laws of War of some sort are recognized, and a system in which the will of one who is going forth conquering and to conquer is the supreme and final rule of action for him and his. During this terrific period of some thousands of years, in which the nations of the world are being made perfect through the suffering of War, the hope of ever attaining the perfection compatible with the natural condition of human life must wholly rest upon the perpetual sustenance of those moral ties between man and man, and between nation and nation, from which all promising growths can alone spring. There can be no doubt but that by the union, in the way of alliances and of co-operation, which it has promoted, War has done something toward educating and preserving some moral instincts of the most precious kinds. But there can also be no doubt but that, so far as warfare has become habitual in a State, or as particular Wars have lasted long and had their area widely and indefinitely extended, the most flourishing shoots of all moral unity between the populations to which the law has reached have been previously threatened. So far as Wars have incidentally favored fellowship and brotherhood, it has been by force of those very Laws of War, on the subsistence of which all durable alliances, all effective concentration of purpose, have depended.

Savages, indeed, make occasional combinations and alliances, and the Book of Judges presents a picture of a more advanced stage, in which a momentary co-operation is secured for a definite end, and a brief warfare is followed by an anarchy of Peace, in which everybody does what is right in his own eyes. But in all gradations of warlike practice, from the time of the most primitive and casual expeditions to the modern era of "armed nations," using up in times of Peace most of the public revenue and the best physical resources of the country in preparation for ever-renewed War, there are still present the two counter agencies, by which mankind is separated on the one hand, and is bound together on the other. The hope of progress has turned, and will turn, upon the narrowing within the smallest possible compass what is casual, accidental, or capricious in warfare. It is in this region that individual passions, national prejudices, the indulgence of narrow and short-sighted selfishness, find their home and pasture-ground.

When once it is recognized that War is the most serious of *Restraints in the practice of War may prepare the way for its abolition.* all pursuits in which man can ever presume to engage, and calls for the contribution of all that legislative science and educated habits of self-restraint can yield, the field is at least partially cleared for the natural play of those orderly instincts which belong to conditions of Peace. It is in disorder, irregularity, hurry, and confusion that what is truly bellicose, ferocious, and purely animal in man can best range at large. It being assumed that the moral ties which bind man to man, as God's common creatures and children, are not matters of artificial and laborious construction, but are real and innate, only needing the order of social and political existence to discover them, and to call them into their appropriate activity, it may follow that they may be hidden or destroyed by one sort of warfare, while they may live and even flourish by the help of another. Thus, improvements in the mere technical regularity of warfare, which must imply restrictions upon an aimless and reckless severity, may be silently nurturing the very moral sentiments which, in time, will become the direct agency for the abolition of War itself.

For the main hope of permanent Peace turns not so much *Growing sense of solidarity the chief ground of hope for Peace.* on the casual adoption of more convenient, less expensive, and less circuitous processes than War for the defence of rights, as on the ultimate preponderance, diffusion, and strength of the sentiments which bind men together, as contrasted with the force of those which separate them. The conspicuous and alarming organization of War in the present day, with all the material appliances employed, and with all the special political and quasi-legal administration to which it gives rise, are far more patent to the eyes of all men than facts of another class, not, indeed, so startling and lurid, but of far deeper and more lasting import. It is certain that the mere introduction of free, popular institutions in two States, and a single glance or reminiscence of brotherly sentiment between the populations of those States, might supersede in a day all the elaborate contrivances for War which military dynasties had for years before laboriously collected together. It is not so much that novel expedients for terminating differences would be resorted to, as that the differences themselves, where existing in any portentous form, would be of a wholly novel kind. So-called national honor would have a very different interpretation put upon it when the alternative of fighting for it was so repugnant as to seem impossible. All questions capable of reference to arbitration would not be tardily and hesitatingly referred to it, but such references would be eagerly sought for in anticipation, and as few unsettled questions left open as remain in an assize town after a general jail delivery.

The impulse toward Peace, or rather the dominant repulsion from War, would be favored by a number of circumstances, some of them slight in themselves and almost evading attention, but which in the aggregate would have long prepared the populations of the two States for concord, and indisposed them for quarrels or physical conflicts. Many of these circumstances are negative rather than positive, but not the less influential on that account.

Circumstances favorable to Peace.

Such are the total abandonment of the lust of territory, an easy forgetfulness of transient animosities or disputes, the absence of dynastical apprehensions, the impossibility of those secret diplomatic mismanagements which so frequently generate widespread misunderstandings.

Chief among the more positive influences favoring a pacific

disposition is a growing concern for the freedom of commercial intercourse, for unrestricted opportunities of travel and mutual acquaintance, and, in fact, for all that zealous co-operation which, as existing among the citizens of any one State, is the source of its vitality and growth.

These relations, which, stated in this abstract form, seem rather to wear the color of a gorgeous prophecy than the duller drapery of facts which meet the eye, are really already found to exist between more than one pair of States in the civilized world, of equal political importance, and, so far as can be conjectured, military or naval strength. They have been described here for the purpose of clearly showing what is the state of things where the true moral ties, which everywhere, in truth, bind men and States together, have succeeded in attaining a supreme ascendency over the accidental elements of selfishness, distrust, or mere dislike, the force of which is represented in armies and navies.

The exact antithesis of the above picture—that is, where the dislocating elements have attained a supreme ascendency over the moral ties—has been, and still is, too faithfully imaged in such abuse of military strength as characterized the English in their Chinese Wars, and in some of their Asiatic expeditions, the English, again, in their barbarous conflicts with the aboriginal tribes in the neighborhood of some of their colonies, and the French in some of their exploits in the north of Africa.

Wars in which legal and moral obligations have been ignored.

The effect of conduct such as is here alluded to, in which all Laws of War are superseded in the name of military necessity, or are treated as good enough for one hemisphere or country but not for another, operates as an annihilation of the very idea of moral ties existing between belligerents. The very defence put forward for this unscrupulous indulgence in War is that moral duties are not necessarily binding on one army unless they are acknowledged and performed by the combatants on the other side. But this plea rests the performance of moral duties upon the basis of choice, caprice, charity, or bargain, and is nothing else than a repudiation of the absolute obligation of morality, and a denial of the moral constitution of every single combatant on either side.

<small>Mischievous results.</small> What, however, is important to notice for the purpose of the present argument is, that where Laws of War, instead of being made, or held, obligatory on all combatants on both sides, are merely introduced so far as they are accidentally convenient for the purposes of one, the utmost is done to destroy the basis on which alone real pacific relations can be resumed and permanently maintained. Especially in conflicts with half-civilized races, it is in the exciting moments of battle that the most distinct lessons are taught by those who represent the best moral attainment of the civilized world. If the lessons taught are such as to misrepresent the moral responsibilities of the teacher, every War, or even every engagement, must only plunge the combatants on one side into a deeper abyss of hostility to all civilized institutions, and of general savagery, and react fatally on the other side, by teaching the army, and those who follow its movements at home, that duties generally have only to be performed so far and so long as it is safe and convenient to perform them.

<small>War under legal restraint a stage toward permanent Peace.</small> Thus, by taking two extreme cases, it has been shown that War, as modified by the laws and restrictions which the conscience of the civilized world, working in concurrence with the dictates of military and political convenience, imposes, marks an intermediate and, it may be hoped, transitory stage, between an absolute oblivion of moral obligations, and such an ascendency of the sense of these obligations as would render the cruel hardships and bitter passions which are inevitable, even in the best conducted Wars, an anachronism. From this point of view it would be interesting to notice the real effect of some of the

leading doctrines and regulations by which the conduct of War is now, so far as Europe is concerned, surrounded by limitations conceived in the interest of humanity, and therefore, as has been shown, of Peace.

The "modified text" of the Brussels Congress may be taken as an approximate statement, if not of the actual practice now habitual in European Wars, at least of the theoretical rules already either well established or on the verge of receiving such general approval as must lead to their being established. Take, for instance, the leading topic of prisoners of War. According to the resolutions of the Congress, prisoners of War are "lawful and disarmed enemies;" "they are in the power of the enemy's Government, but not of the individuals or of the corps who made them prisoners;" "they should be treated with humanity;" "all their personal effects, except their arms, are to be considered their own property;" while "liable to internment in a town, fortress, camp, or in any locality whatever, under an obligation not to go beyond certain fixed limits," they "may not be placed in confinement, unless absolutely necessary as a measure of security;" they may be "employed on certain public works which have no immediate connection with the operations on the theatre of War, provided the employment be not excessive, nor humiliating to their military rank if they belong to the army, or to their official or social position if they do not belong to it;" "the pay they receive will go toward ameliorating their position, or will be put to their credit at the time of their release;" their maintenance is to be provided for by the Government in whose power they are, and, in default of a mutual understanding on the subject between the belligerents, and as a "general principle," they are to be "treated, as regards food and clothing, on the same footing as the troops of the Government who made them prisoners."

"Modified text" of the Brussels Congress—

upon prisoners of War.

Take, again, the modified text agreed to, after a rather fiery

discussion between the German delegate on the one side, and the representatives of the Netherlands, Belgium, and Switzerland on the other, respecting the relations of an invading army to the population of the invaded country.

Leaving on one side, as presenting insuperable difficulties, the vexed question of the right of the population of occupied territory to rise in arms against the invader without being treated as rebels and traitors, the modified text confines itself to the following rules, which seem to have been treated as of indisputable authority: "The population of an occupied territory cannot be compelled to take part in military operations against their own country. The population of occupied territories cannot be compelled to swear allegiance to the enemy's power. The honor and rights of the family, the life and property of individuals, as well as their religious convictions and the exercise of their religion, should be respected. Private property cannot be confiscated. Pillage is expressly forbidden." With respect to the last two clauses, the modified text introduces some explanations and definitions for the purpose of regulating the mode of exacting forced contributions for the support of the invading army.

<small>Relations of invaders to the invaded.</small>

The text, indeed, though reproducing the actual practice in recent Wars of invasion on the European continent, is behind the requirements of some of the most competent authorities on the subject, and, as will be seen lower down, the strong recommendations and experience of the Duke of Wellington. The text says that the enemy, in levying contributions, should proceed, as far as possible, according to the rules for the distribution and assessment of the taxes in force in the occupied territory; that for every contribution a receipt should be given to the person furnishing it; that requisition should be made only by the authority of the commandant of the locality occupied; and that for every requisition an indemnity should be granted or receipt given. The text says nothing about the kind of materials to which requisitions may extend, and is certainly most unsatisfactory in respect of the modes of payment which it contemplates. The passage of the text in which it introduces the necessities of War as a ground for determining the sorts of payments and services which may be demanded from parishes and their inhabitants, in fact does nothing more than leave the whole matter to the irresponsible will of the officer in command.

Before leaving this last-mentioned topic, it may be well to recall more precisely the views held by the Duke of Wellington in 1815, as reported by Lord Palmerston on his visit to Paris, in September of that year. The Duke told Lord Palmerston that "the system of individual plunder had been the ruin of the French army, and would be the destruction of the Prussian. When officers were allowed to make requisitions for their troops, they soon began to make them for themselves; and those who demanded provisions to-day would call for money to-morrow. War then assumed a new character; the profession of arms became a mercenary speculation, and the officers' thoughts grew to be directed to the acquisition of plunder instead of the attainment of glory."

The Duke of Wellington upon requisitions by an invading army.

Lord Palmerston adds that the Duke had succeeded in keeping his army well in hand; no officer was permitted to make any requisition himself, but was obliged to state his wants to the commissary, who applied to the agents of the French Government for the articles required; and the supply being made through channels known to the people, and by authorities recognized by them, the burden was not felt to be so oppressive as if the exaction had been made by the immediate order of an enemy, and at the caprice of individual officers. The consequence was, that though both the Prussians and the English lived equally at the expense of the country, the first were detested and the latter liked.

The general reasoning is applicable to all cases of invasion, though the passage of the allied armies through France could only be called an invasion in a special sense.

In citing the above extracts from the amendments of the Laws of War agreed to at the Brussels Conference, it is not here even so much as hinted that they are anything more than imperfect and tentative approximations to the rules which a pure regard to the interests of humanity would enact, and still less that the rules themselves represent the actual practice even of those States which have been most loud in the vindication of them. It is notorious that in the Franco-German War the most cruel hardships were inflicted on the French nation, not from the want of sufficient rules for restricting severities, or of a sincere desire on the part of the Germans to conduct the War in a civilized manner, but from the wide scope for license which, in the hurry and confusion of an invasion, the strictest rules still leave open, and from the unscrupulous rigor with which an observance of the rules affecting the invaded population was enforced.

Rules of the Brussels Conference imperfect:

Impossibility of applying them in all the emergencies of actual War.

The mode, indeed, of enforcing Laws of War must always leave a dangerous latitude of discretion to commanders in the field, where it is quite impracticable to substitute for prompt and rough remedies the tardy and dignified procedure of Peace. It is in this region of discretion that the perplexed question of reprisals, and of what are called military executions—which in fact are nothing else than the punishment of the innocent with or for the guilty—would seem destined always to lurk.

A special hardship is also involved in the fact that the new crimes which the Laws of War invent are measured on a wholly different principle from the crimes recognized in legislation for Peace, and their magnitude bears very little proportion to moral guilt. Thus, in the new circumstances of modern War, there are scarcely any offences which it is more indispensable

Some offences acquire a criminal character which is new to them.

for an invading army to repress, by every method within its reach, than those of taking up railway lines, destroying railway bridges, and cutting telegraph wires. Such offences have effects far more serious than the old-fashioned offences of creating impediments on roads of march, or of casually intercepting individual messengers. The whole safety of an army and the success of an expedition may be involved in the possibility of a sure reliance on rapid conveyance from point to point, or on communication being maintained hour by hour between widely removed detachments of the army.

These criticisms point to the fact that, in discussing the bearing of Laws of War, it must be borne in mind that (1) all imaginable Laws of War are imperfect from a purely humanitarian point of view; and however near they approach to perfection from a point of view which is at once military and humanitarian, they must, by their very nature, leave open wide gaps to be filled by the discretion of individual commanders, or the peculiar emergencies which the changing events of the War may from time to time present; that (2) the laws now actually in existence are very far from approaching even the degree of perfection which the philanthropist might be entitled to demand of the military legislator, and express, in fact, nothing more than the maximum amount of agreement which, in the present circumstances of Europe, the European States, great and small, can, in view of all the separate interests involved, or supposed to be involved, arrive at; and that (3), so far as recent experience has gone — an experience which involves Wars conducted on the European continent on a wholly unprecedented scale of magnitude — the laws themselves are most imperfectly obeyed, often scandalously outraged, and, if the conflict long endure, more and more cast on one side and forgotten.

Defects of Laws of War.

Nevertheless, with all these deductions, the existence of such Laws for the mitigation of severities in War as professedly govern the conduct of modern armies is a great boon to humanity, and affords the best of all guarantees for the gradual abolition of War itself. Over and above the public and constant testimony which any laws for the limitation of War present to the moral ties which, in spite of the War itself, continue to bind together the citizens and soldiers of both States, some more particular effects of these Laws on the promotion and maintenance of Peace are brought about in certain distinctly intelligible ways, which may be recapitulated as follows:

They have, nevertheless, great value.

1. Laws of War, whatever their character and merit, have, at least, the effect of assigning limits, lines, and boundaries to the conduct of War. If ferocity or individual license cannot be eradicated, they are, at least in outward form, put into fetters. If the distinction between the private citizen and the armed soldier is drawn recklessly or hastily, at any rate the notion of such a distinction is persistently maintained. War, in profession at least, as the Emperor William said at Forbach in his proclamation on entering France, is made on soldiers, and not upon citizens. In this proclamation the Emperor added that French citizens would "continue to enjoy entire security for their persons and property so long as they did not themselves deprive him, by hostile enterprises against the German troops, of the right of granting them his protection." Even if the humane treatment of prisoners of War cannot be absolutely insured, the moral duty of securing their persons from outrage, and of providing for them with all the care due to the stranger and the guest, is openly confessed. Even if private property is exposed to the utmost risks, and, in spite of every restraint, is still recklessly stolen or injured under the name of requisitions, still a distinct protest continues to be made against the supposition that War can be waged for the purposes of self-enrichment, or that unpermitted

Legal rules tend to eliminate the element of passion from War—

spoliation is any less robbery in a time of War than in a time of Peace.

<small>Cause War to be regarded as a means to an end—</small> All these lines and boundaries, imperfect, uncertain, fluctuating, and often undecipherable as they are, at least have the effect of sustaining the idea that War is only made in order to promote a distinct political object outside itself, and not for the purpose of giving vent to those passions and dispositions which are in truth, or ought to be, the disfigurements and not the characteristic features of War.

<small>and may suggest the substitution of other means.</small> The general result must be to bring into ever clearer view the notion of War as merely a means to an end, and, therefore, possibly one among many other means to the same end. The political use of War is thus constantly encroaching on the mere military appetite for it; and simultaneously, the various defects of War, as an instrument the most costly, the most uncertain, the most injurious to both belligerents, and the most outrageous to humanity, become matter of grave political consideration in the course of calculating the worth of the object to be attained, and the material or moral expensiveness of various competing means at hand for attaining it. It is obvious, then, that to the extent that War is, in public profession and even in desultory practice, restricted and circumscribed, the arguments for choosing the alternative of Peace obtain a better chance of being heard and deliberately weighed. The issue in the course of time can hardly be doubtful.

2. A minor consequence of the imposition of bounds and <small>Laws of War prevent the generation of fresh animosities and the consequent prolongation of Wars.</small> limits to War by the laws introduced for the mitigation of its severity, is that commanders in the field, and their Governments, thereby retain in their hands the only effective means for bringing the War to an instant close so soon as the political object is attained. The history of long Wars, such as the

11

Hundred Years' War of the English in France, the Thirty Years' War in Germany, and even the Bonapartist Wars, shows how hard it is to maintain from the outset one steady political purpose, or limited assemblage of purposes, as the cause of the War, without the War itself, and its events, generating in their progress an ever-enlarged variety of new purposes, which themselves tend to give to the War an indefinite perpetuity, only prevented, in fact, by total exhaustion on one side or on both. It is one of the hardest problems of diplomatists, and exercises all the self-restraint of commanders in the field, upon whom are always cast diplomatic functions of the first importance, to prevent this incessant generation of fresh causes of dispute; and, of all causes, those due to the license of individual soldiers, or the reckless violation and destruction of property, are among the most potent. So far as Laws of War are wisely conceived, strictly interpreted, and sternly as well as impartially administered, the original objects of the War are kept free from all perplexing or confusing images, which, mostly unreal, are of the fruit rather of passion and hatred than of any genuine political differences.

3. It has sometimes been said by the most thoughtless writers on War, that the more cruelly and recklessly War is conducted, the more likely it is to become matter of general abomination, and, therefore, the more effectually are the ultimate interests of Peace provided for. Such persons would reduce Laws of War to the narrowest proportions, and would do little more than provide against usages familiar only among the lowest of the savage races. They would connive at, if not applaud, the indiscriminate use of all the implements and all the force in the hands of a commander; unrestricted violence, even amounting to depopulation, is looked upon with approval as likely to wean the suffering nation forever from a warlike career; and even the hor-

Error of the theory that unrestricted severity in War hinders resort to it.

rors of a long siege, followed by bombardment and barbarous assault, are counted among the necessities of War, the absence of which might make it only too pleasant and attractive a pastime.

Those who write and speak in this way can only have taken a most superficial view of the meaning of St. James's account of why "Wars and fightings" come. They come not from any studied preference for War as an occupation, nor from any misapprehension as to the sufferings it causes, nor even from any forgetfulness of the losses and calamities which a very recent War may have brought with it. So far as War is used as any other than the roughest, the nearest, and the most familiar instrument for the attainment of political ends, it owes its sustenance to the force of those brutal and unbridled passions which St. James designates as the lusts which war in our members.

It is not most, it may be even least of all, the soldier who is easily possessed with the uncontrollable desire to fight. It needs, under the modern conditions of easy communication, but a few paragraphs in any largely circulated daily newspaper about some alleged violation of the national honor, prestige, or what not, or even the narrative of some accidental conflict on the frontiers between the inhabitants of outlying villages, to rouse, throughout a whole country, the most vindictive and savage passions of which human nature is capable, and which years of civilization and centuries of Christianity seem only to have cloaked and never disciplined. These feelings become, by means of civil and domestic association, and of all the facile machinery for ascertaining and concentrating public opinion, a dominant rage, of a strength far greater and more lasting than is possible in the isolated brute beast. Governments are perforce led or driven by the incendiary vehemence of those they rule; and they can only maintain their own existence by finding some diplomatic artifice for precipitating a War, and glutting the popular thirst for blood.

Marginal note: Wars result from reckless passion, which is indifferent to the suffering inflicted.

In such a state of things as this, the recurrence of which at frequent intervals is one of the most harrowing phenomena of modern times, it is far more the severities of War than the mitigations of it, which are its recommendation to the popular mind. If the people have themselves suffered in previous Wars, they wish now to make others suffer equally, and in the same way. The strength and blindness of passion make them callous to the possible sufferings of themselves and their countrymen; the familiar experience of the murderer who, with the certainty of conviction and of bringing on himself a shameful death, takes no count of the future in the presence of the enemy who for the moment is before him, is repeated and multiplied over half a continent.

If this be a true explanation of the deep-lying causes which, in the teeth of all the civilizing influences operating directly the other way, continue to make War possible and popular, the remedies for it must be in the exactly opposite direction from that to which the advocates of reckless severity are looking.

The main and only hope for maintaining throughout large populations a balance of mind and moral self-restraint in the presence of irritating instruments and diplomatic controversies, is to be found in such a popular training as shall bring the brutal passions of an associated crowd under exactly the same chronic discipline as the civilized individual man, not to say the Christian, has long learned to exercise in the culture of his own spirit. Human society in a single country could never have existed, or its artificial maintenance would be an intolerable burden, if every occasion of discord, every act, or suspicion of an act, of wrong-doing, every question of disputed rights, were instantly to call into action, offensive or defensive, the strongest passions of the human breast.

Moral control over national passion the only means of attaining lasting Peace.

The progress of civilization has been marked, not by the annihilation, nor even the weakening, of these passions, but by the effective subordination and use of them to the loftiest ends.

Progress in the past a ground for hope in the future. The disuse of private Wars, of trial by battle, and of duelling, has marked the gradual and more overt steps of this great moral achievement. It is only in the relations between nation and nation that it is still believed that brutality, passionateness, cruelty, and selfishness may not only riot to the uttermost, but may legitimately begin to riot on the very slightest provocation. It is impossible for any believer in the progress of the human race, and in the redemption which, day by day, and century by century, is searching out all the dark places of the earth, and bringing them under a truly Divine dominion, to admit that War represents more than one transient spasm, be it of hard necessity or of still untamed passion, which the world will in no long time have outgrown and, except for purposes of wholesome reminder, have forgotten. So far as Laws of War exist and operate, their action has been shown to help forward the arrival of this kingdom which cannot be moved, and which alone can hold its own in those moments when "the heathen rage, and the people imagine a vain thing."

INDEX.

A.

	PAGE
Abolition of War	10
" " desire of, must be assumed	97
Abolition of War a political aim	99
Aggression a cause of War	54
Aix-la-Chapelle, Protocol of	87
"Alabama" Case	88
" Claims, loose wording of	128
Ambassadors, precedence of	87
Ambition a cause of War	54
Ameliorating condition of Prisoners of War, Society for	219
Amity, traditional, between States	56
Animosity, traditional, of States	56
Arbitration	118–123
" Court of, need for, 87 *seq.*	
" Geneva	89, 127
Argyle, Duke of, on Prerogative	31, 32, *note.*
Armies, Standing	79–83
" Peace and War footing of	170 *seq.*
Armies, Effect of their magnitude	173
Armies, Localization in	176
" Mobilization in	176
Armies, size of in Peace and in War	170–175
Army, Active, distinguished from Reserve	163
Army, English	162
" " Reconstruction of	81
" French	164, 171
" " Exemptions from Service in	165
Army, German	80, 163, 171, 176
" Russian	172
" Regulation Act, territorial principle in	178
Attractions of military life	81
Augustus, testamentary instructions of	64
Austin, Mr., on International Law	84
Austria, universal service in	164

B.

Balance of Power	58, 67
" " Recent references to	137 *seq.*
Balance of Power, present inefficiency of doctrine of	142
Ballot, Conscription by	163
" Modifying universal service	163

INDEX.

Belgium, Independence of........ 66
" Neutrality of......153, 154
Bentham, Jeremy.............. 34
Bernard, Rt. Hon. Mountague, on phraseology of Treaty of Washington............... 128
Bernard, Rt. Hon. Mountague, on Treaty Obligations....... 133
Bishops, attitude of, toward War 37
Black Sea, Neutralization of.... 146
Blockade, restrictions upon..... 211
Bosphorus, partial Neutralization of....................... 146
Brussels Conference.....8, 190, 191, 219, 221–223
" " Modified text of.................... 235–237

C.

Canadian Fishery dispute...... 90
Canal, Panama, Neutralization of....................... 147
Canal, Suez..............149, 150
Canning, Non-intervention policy of......................... 112
Capitalists, interests of........ 215
Capture, Maritime.........196–215
" " English policy with regard to............. 197
Capture, Maritime, English interests with regard to.......... 199
Cardwell, Lord, Scheme of Army, Reconstruction of........... 178
Castlereagh, Lord, upon Conference of Troppau.........184, 185
Causes of War.............45, 94
" " obsolete........ 94
Changes in the character of War..................12–14, 17

Changes, Political, effected by War....................... 53
China War.................. 37
Chinese Wars................ 233
Christianity, influence of......35–42
Church of England, attitude of, toward War.............37 *seq.*
Citizens of Foreign States, Laws relating to.................. 91
Civilization, progress of, antagonistic to War.............17, 18
Civilized and uncivilized States, Wars between............. 14
Civil Wars.................. 15
Clayton-Bulwer Convention..... 147
Cobden, Non-intervention advocated by................... 112
Colonial system.............. 213
Comte on International morality 34
" on natural policy of England..................... 67
Comte, System of European policy of...................... 98
Comte, Scheme of 120 Republics of....................... 134
Conferences and Congresses, International.............182–195
Conferences and Congresses, attitude of England toward.191, 192
Conferences and Congresses, conditions essential to success of 192
Conferences on Greek affairs.185, 186
" of Troppau.....184, 193
Conference proposed by France, 1863..................187, 189
Congress, Brussels.189–191, 194, 219 220
" " modified text of....................235–237

INDEX.

Congress, Universal Alliance.... 219
" Vienna..........183, 193
" Verona............. 183
Conscription by Ballot......... 163
Conspirators against Foreign States, Laws relating to...... 91
Contraband, restrictions upon use of term.................. 211
Convention of Geneva......... 218
" St. Petersburg... 218
Co-operation, International....43, 44
Correspondence, War, of Daily Papers..................26-28
Court, International, need for... 68
Cracow, Neutralization of...... 156
Crimean War............... 38
" " Causes of........ 93
" " Alliance between England and France during.. 107
Crimean War, consideration shown to Neutrals during.... 216
Cuba, Intervention in.......... 59

D.

Dardanelles, partial Neutralization of................... 146
Darien, Isthmus of............ 147
Declaration of Paris... 206-208, 217
Derby, Lord, on Winslow Extradition Case................ 90
Derby, Lord, on Intervention... 113
" " Action of, in reference to the Brussels Congress, 190, 191, 221, 222
Diplomacy, publicity of........ 76
Duelling, disappearance of..... 11

E.

Economic Science antagonistic to War................... 18-25

Education antagonistic to War.. 21
" Military, development of..................... 82
Edwards, Mr. Sutherland, on harshness of Laws of War... 225
Ellicott, Bishop, attitude of, toward War................ 38
Emperor of Germany, Proclamation of, on entering France... 240
Equal States, Wars between.... 16
Equality of States, theory of...48 seq.
Equal rights, disputes upon..... 48
Equilibrium of States......138 seq.
Erckmann-Chatrian........... 29
Exemption of private property from capture at sea ......196 seq.
Exemption of private property from capture on land.....202, 203

F.

Fishery, Canadian, dispute..... 90
France, universal service in.... 164
Franco-Prussian War, cause of, 54, 76, 94
" " shortness of 174
Franco-Prussian War, Newspaper Correspondence during... 27
Free-trade.........18, 112, 213 seq.

G.

Geneva, Convention of........ 218
Germany, military organization of..................... 80
Germany, universal service in.... 163
Gortchakow, Prince, Brussels Congress, proposed by....189, 220
Greece, Conferences upon...185-187
Grotius on International morality...................... 71

Grotius on just and unjust Wars. 72
" Moral obligations in War recognized by..........227, 228

H.

Hegel on International Morality. 34
Holms, Mr., Scheme of Army Improvement of.............. 163
Holy Alliance..........58, 103, 106
Hondetot, Comte de........... 219
Honduras, Treaty with........ 148
Honor, morbid sentiment of...75–77
House of Commons, share taken by, in conduct of Foreign Affairs.................... 62

I.

Inequality of States..........49, 50
Instruments of Warfare, changes in...................... 180
Instructions of Professor Lieber. 217
Internal growth of States.....51–54
International Association, pacific effect of..................42–44
International Congresses....182–195
" " Intercourse, growth of........... 215
International Law, aims of..... 9
" " State of, a cause of War.............84–95
International Law, nature of.... 84
" " Sources of... 85
" " Vagueness of 85
International Lawyer, functions of........................ 7, 8
Intervention........57–61, 101, 117
" Legal right of..... 103
" " Duty of..... 105
" Morality of....... 109

Intervention, practised by England..................... 111
Intervention in Internal affairs of other States............. 114
Intervention in foreign disputes. 115
Invaders, relations of, to invaded population................ 236
Inventions, application of, to military purposes........ 23, 180
Ionian Islands, Neutralization of 157
Italy, universal service in...... 164

J.

Jealousies, hereditary, between States.................... 55
Jomini, Baron 223
Judaism, warlike temper of.... 40
Judicial combat, disappearance of........................ 11

K.

Kant on International morality.. 34
Kingsley, Charles, sympathy with the War spirit of...... 38

L.

Land-owners, interests of...... 215
Landsturm, German.......... 224
Laws of War, variations of.... 8
" objects of...... 9
" as bearing on Peace 216–245
Legal restraints in War....... 229
" " " Neglect of...................... 233
Legal restraints in War a stage toward permanent Peace..... 234
Lesseps, M. de.............. 150
Liberalism, spread of......... 29

Lieber, Professor, instructions of, for American Army...... 217
Livy, recognition of moral obligations in War, by.......... 227
Localization, principle of, in armies.................. 176–179
Luxemburg, Neutralization of 154–156

M.

Magee, Bishop, sympathy of, with War................ 38
Mechanical skill, diversion of, to military purposes........... 23
Mediation................117, 118
Mercantile Marine, English, advantage to it of security from capture.................... 199
Mercantile theory, substitution of Free-trade for........... 213
Merchant-ships, disputes relating to................... 92
Military establishments, evils of. 23
" life, attractions of..... 81
Mill, on International morality.. 33
" " revision of Treaties.... 131
Mobilization of armies.....176–179
Modified text of Brussels Congress................... 235–237
Monarchy, connection of, with Church.................... 38
Monroe doctrine...........66, 104
Morality, International.......69–78
Mozley, Professor, lecture of, in defence of War............ 38

N.

Nature, law of................ 85
Naval warfare, changes in..... 208
" " restrictions upon 210

Navies, growth of European.... 200
Navigation Laws, abolition of.. 213
Navy, English, supremacy of... 200
Netherlands, independence of... 66
Neutralization........... 143–159
" of seas, rivers, etc. 145
" the Rhine....... 145
" the Black Sea ... 146
" Canals, railways, etc...................... 147
Neutralization of the Panama Canal..................... 147
Neutralization Suez Canal...... 149
" Switzerland..... 151
" Belgium........ 153
" Luxemburg 155
" Cracow......... 156
" Ionian Islands... 157
Neutrals, interests and duties of 116
Newspapers, War Correspondence of.................... 25
Non-conformists, pacific principles of.................... 37
Non-intervention, advocated by England.................. 58
Non-intervention, growth of party of................... 112

O.

Origin and history of Law of Nations, Mr. Ward's........ 35
Organization, military, in Germany..................... 80
Orsini conspiracy............. 76

P.

Palmerston, Lord, China War initiated by his Government... 37
Palmerston, Lord, on maritime capture.................197, 198

INDEX.

Peace, Influences favorable to.. 232
Peter the Great's will......... 64
Philosophy, modern, opposed to
    War.................... 33, 35
Plunder, by invading army..236–238
Popular assemblies, attitude of,
    toward War.............. 32
Popular Government, effect of,
    upon traditional policy...... 62
Press, influence of........... 26–28
Prisoners of War............. 235
    "   " Society for
ameliorating condition of.... 219
Private Wars, disappearance of. 11
Property, private, at sea, capture
    of...................... 196–215
Property, private, on land... 202–204
    "   " of invaded population.................... 236
Prussia, Wars of............ 52, 53
    " universal service originated by................. 166
Publicity of diplomacy, its effects
on sensitiveness on points of
honor..................... 76, 77

Q.

Quakers, peace principles of.... 36

R.

Railways, destruction of....... 239
    " Neutralization of..... 147
Recruiting for army, modes of,
    162–170
Religion, influences of....... 35–42
Remedies for War.......... 96 seq.
Reprisals, topic omitted at Brussels Conference............ 223
Requisitions of invading force.. 236

Restrictions upon naval warfare 210
Revolution, French, Wars of.... 52
Rhine, Neutrality of. 145
Roman Catholic Church....... 37
Russell, Earl, on proposal of International Congress..... 188, 189
Russia, policy of, in Asia and
    Europe................... 66
Russo-Turkish War........... 52
    "   " Newspaper Correspondence during......... 27

S.

Sardinia, rights of............ 152
Savoy, Neutralization of....... 152
Science applied to military purposes.................... 23, 82
Search, restrictions upon right
of........................ 211
Senate of United States, share
of, in making treaties....... 132
Sensibility, mutual, of States...55–57
Service, universal............. 163
Seven Years' War............ 52
Slavery denounced in Vienna
Congress.................. 183
Slavery denounced in Verona
Congress.................. 183
Social progress hindered by War 24
Sovereignty of States, as affected by Intervention.......... 103
Standing armies..........160–182
    "   " a cause of War.79–84
State, growth of moral ideas in
reference to............... 69
States, internal growth of, incompatible with external relations.................... 51–55
States, mutual relations of..... 109

INDEX. 253

	PAGE
States, Mutual distrust of	121
" Magnitude of	133
" Consolidation of	134
" Disintegration of	134
" Large and small, advantage of	135
States, equilibrium of	137
St. Petersburg, Convention of	218
Switzerland, Independence of	66
" Neutralization of	151
Systems of policy	61–68

T.

Tariffs, prohibitive, abolition of	213
Telegraph Wires, cutting of	239
Territorial principle in armies.	176 *seq.*
Thirty Years' War	141
Trade, influence of War upon,	196–215
" Foreign, of England, injury to from maritime capture	199
Trade, International, injury to from maritime capture	200
Treaties	123–133
" Obligations of	71, 74
" Enforcement of	106
" of General Alliance	107
" of general settlement	107
" of Münster and Osnaburg	108, 141
Treaties of Neutralization	108
" Phraseology of	127
" Remedies for defects of	128
" of peace, unsuitable occasions for general settlements	129
Treaties, revision of	131
" Discussion of in popular assemblies	132

	PAGE
Treaties, references to Balance of Power in	137–140
Treaty of Berlin	60
" " Paris, 1856	60, 108
" " Revision of demanded by Russia	71, *note*, 131
Treaty of Paris, Neutralization of Black Sea provided for by	146
Treaty of Paris, 1814, Neutralization of Switzerland	151
Treaty of Utrecht	106, 141
" of Vienna	60, 105
" " " Neutralization of Rhine, provided for in	145
Treaty of Washington	71, *note*, 89, 90
Trochu, General, account of territorial principle by	177
Troppeau, Conferences of	184, 193
Turkey, Intervention in	59

U.

United States, advocacy of freedom of maritime commerce by	201
United States, conduct of foreign relations by Government of	77, 132
United States, foreign disputes of, "Trent" Case	88
United States, foreign disputes of, "Alabama" Case	88, 127
United States, foreign disputes of, "Virginius"	89
Universal Alliance Congress	219
Utilitarians, English	34

V.

Verona Congress	183

Vices, pacific.................. 41	Ward, Mr., on Christian Church
Vienna Congress............... 183	in Middle Ages............ 35
" Protocol of............ 87	Ward, Mr., on precedence of
" Treaty of............60, 106	ambassadors............... 87
"Virginius," case of........... 89	Ward, Mr., on modifications in
Virtues, military.............. 41	warfare.................... 228
Voluntary enlistment.......... 162	Wars, civil.................. 15
Volunteer system.............. 81	Washington, Treaty of. 71, *note*, 89, 90
	Weak and strong States, Wars
W.	between..................13, 14
Wages, rise of................ 214	Wellington, Duke of, upon req-
War, appreciation of evils of... 121	uisitions.................. 237
" Expense of.............. 214	Westphalia, Peace of......... 108
" Waste of............23, 173	Winslow, Extradition Case..... 90

THE END.

VALUABLE AND INTERESTING WORKS

FOR

PUBLIC & PRIVATE LIBRARIES,

PUBLISHED BY HARPER & BROTHERS, NEW YORK.

☞ *For a full List of Books suitable for Libraries published by HARPER & BROTHERS, see HARPER'S CATALOGUE, which may be had gratuitously on application to the publishers personally, or by letter enclosing Nine Cents in Postage stamps.*

☞ HARPER & BROTHERS *will send their publications by mail, postage prepaid, on receipt of the price.*

MACAULAY'S ENGLAND. The History of England from the Accession of James II. By THOMAS BABINGTON MACAULAY. New Edition, from new Electrotype Plates. 8vo, Cloth, with Paper Labels, Uncut Edges and Gilt Tops, 5 vols. in a Box, $10 00 per set. Sold only in Sets. Cheap Edition, 5 vols. in a Box, 12mo, Cloth, $2 50; Sheep, $3 75.

MACAULAY'S LIFE AND LETTERS. The Life and Letters of Lord Macaulay. By his Nephew, G. OTTO TREVELYAN, M.P. With Portrait on Steel. Complete in 2 vols., 8vo, Cloth, Uncut Edges and Gilt Tops, $5 00; Sheep, $6 00; Half Calf, $9 50. Popular Edition, two vols. in one, 12mo, Cloth, $1 75.

HUME'S ENGLAND. The History of England, from the Invasion of Julius Cæsar to the Abdication of James II., 1688. By DAVID HUME. New and Elegant Library Edition, from new Electrotype Plates. 6 vols. in a Box, 8vo, Cloth, with Paper Labels, Uncut Edges and Gilt Tops, $12 00. Sold only in Sets. Popular Edition, 6 vols. in a Box, 12mo, Cloth, $3 00; Sheep, $4 50.

GIBBON'S ROME. The History of the Decline and Fall of the Roman Empire. By EDWARD GIBBON. With Notes by Dean MILMAN, M. GUIZOT, and Dr. WILLIAM SMITH. New Edition, from new Electrotype Plates. 6 vols., 8vo, Cloth, with Paper Labels, Uncut Edges and Gilt Tops, $12 00. Sold only in Sets. Popular Edition, 6 vols. in a Box, 12mo, Cloth, $3 00; Sheep, $4 50.

HILDRETH'S UNITED STATES. History of the United States. FIRST SERIES: From the Discovery of the Continent to the Organization of the Government under the Federal Constitution. SECOND SERIES: From the Adoption of the Federal Constitution to the End of the Sixteenth Congress. By RICHARD HILDRETH. Popular Edition, 6 vols. in a Box, 8vo, Cloth, with Paper Labels, Uncut Edges and Gilt Tops, $12 00. Sold only in Sets.

MOTLEY'S DUTCH REPUBLIC. The Rise of the Dutch Republic. A History. By JOHN LOTHROP MOTLEY, LL.D., D.C.L. With a Portrait of William of Orange. Cheap Edition, 3 vols. in a Box, 8vo, Cloth, with Paper Labels, Uncut Edges and Gilt Tops, $6 00. Sold only in Sets. Original Library Edition, 3 vols., 8vo, Cloth, $10 50; Sheep, $12 00; Half Calf, $17 25.

MOTLEY'S UNITED NETHERLANDS. History of the United Netherlands: from the Death of William the Silent to the Twelve Years' Truce—1584-1609. With a full View of the English-Dutch Struggle against Spain, and of the Origin and Destruction of the Spanish Armada. By JOHN LOTHROP MOTLEY, LL.D., D.C.L. Portraits. Cheap Edition, 4 vols. in a Box, 8vo, Cloth, with Paper Labels, Uncut Edges and Gilt Tops, $8 00. Sold only in Sets. Original Library Edition, 4 vols., 8vo, Cloth, $14 00; Sheep, $16 00; Half Calf, $23 00.

MOTLEY'S LIFE AND DEATH OF JOHN OF BARNEVELD. The Life and Death of John of Barneveld, Advocate of Holland: with a View of the Primary Causes and Movements of "The Thirty Years' War." By JOHN LOTHROP MOTLEY, LL.D., D.C.L. Illustrated. Cheap Edition, 2 vols. in a Box, 8vo, Cloth, with Paper Labels, Uncut Edges and Gilt Tops, $4 00. Sold only in Sets. Original Library Edition, 2 vols., 8vo, Cloth, $7 00; Sheep, $8 00; Half Calf, $11 50.

GEDDES'S HISTORY OF JOHN DE WITT. History of the Administration of John De Witt, Grand Pensionary of Holland. By JAMES GEDDES. Vol. I.—1623-1654. With a Portrait. 8vo, Cloth, $2 50.

SKETCHES AND STUDIES IN SOUTHERN EUROPE. By JOHN ADDINGTON SYMONDS. In Two Volumes. Post 8vo, Cloth, $4 00.

SYMONDS'S GREEK POETS. Studies of the Greek Poets. By JOHN ADDINGTON SYMONDS. 2 vols., Square 16mo, Cloth, $3 50.

BENJAMIN'S CONTEMPORARY ART. Contemporary Art in Europe. By S. G. W. BENJAMIN. Illustrated. 8vo, Cloth, $3 50.

BENJAMIN'S ART IN AMERICA. Art in America. By S. G. W. BENJAMIN. Illustrated. 8vo, Cloth, $4 00.

HUDSON'S HISTORY OF JOURNALISM. Journalism in the United States, from 1690 to 1872. By FREDERIC HUDSON. 8vo, Cloth, $5 00; Half Calf, $7 25.

JEFFERSON'S LIFE. The Domestic Life of Thomas Jefferson: Compiled from Family Letters and Reminiscences, by his Great-granddaughter, SARAH N. RANDOLPH. Illustrated. Crown 8vo, Cloth, $2 50.

KINGLAKE'S CRIMEAN WAR. The Invasion of the Crimea; its Origin, and an Account of its Progress down to the Death of Lord Raglan. By ALEXANDER WILLIAM KINGLAKE. With Maps and Plans. Three Volumes now ready. 12mo, Cloth, $2 00 per vol.

LAMB'S COMPLETE WORKS. The Works of Charles Lamb. Comprising his Letters, Poems, Essays of Elia, Essays upon Shakspeare, Hogarth, etc., and a Sketch of his Life, with the Final Memorials, by T. NOON TALFOURD. With Portrait. 2 vols., 12mo, Cloth, $3 00.

LAWRENCE'S HISTORICAL STUDIES. Historical Studies. By EUGENE LAWRENCE. Containing the following Essays: The Bishops of Rome.—Leo and Luther.—Loyola and the Jesuits.—Ecumenical Councils.—The Vaudois.—The Huguenots.—The Church of Jerusalem.—Dominic and the Inquisition.—The Conquest of Ireland.—The Greek Church. 8vo, Cloth, Uncut Edges and Gilt Tops, $3 00.

LOSSING'S FIELD-BOOK OF THE REVOLUTION. Pictorial Field-Book of the Revolution: or, Illustrations by Pen and Pencil of the History, Biography, Scenery, Relics, and Traditions of the War for Independence. By BENSON J. LOSSING. 2 vols., 8vo, Cloth, $14 00; Sheep or Roan, $15 00; Half Calf, $18 00.

LOSSING'S FIELD-BOOK OF THE WAR OF 1812. Pictorial Field-Book of the War of 1812; or, Illustrations by Pen and Pencil of the History, Biography, Scenery, Relics, and Traditions of the last War for American Independence. By BENSON J. LOSSING. With several hundred Engravings on Wood by Lossing and Barritt, chiefly from Original Sketches by the Author. 1088 pages, 8vo, Cloth, $7 00; Sheep, $8 50; Roan, $9 00; Half Calf, $10 00.

FORSTER'S LIFE OF DEAN SWIFT. The Early Life of Jonathan Swift (1667-1711). By JOHN FORSTER. With Portrait. 8vo, Cloth, Uncut Edges and Gilt Tops, $2 50.

GREEN'S ENGLISH PEOPLE. History of the English People. By JOHN RICHARD GREEN, M.A. 3 volumes ready. 8vo, Cloth, $2 50 per volume.

SHORT'S NORTH AMERICANS OF ANTIQUITY. The North Americans of Antiquity. Their Origin, Migrations, and Type of Civilization Considered. By JOHN T. SHORT. Illustrated. 8vo, Cloth, $3 00.

SQUIER'S PERU. Peru: Incidents of Travel and Exploration in the Land of the Incas. By E. GEORGE SQUIER, M.A., F.S.A., late U. S. Commissioner to Peru. With Illustrations. 8vo, Cloth, $5 00.

MYERS'S LOST EMPIRES. Remains of Lost Empires: Sketches of the Ruins of Palmyra, Nineveh, Babylon, and Persepolis. By P. V. N. MYERS. Illustrated. 8vo, Cloth, $3 50.

4   *Valuable Works for Public and Private Libraries.*

HALLAM'S MIDDLE AGES. View of the State of Europe during the Middle Ages. By HENRY HALLAM. 8vo, Cloth, $2 00; Sheep, $2 50.

HALLAM'S CONSTITUTIONAL HISTORY OF ENGLAND. The Constitutional History of England, from the Accession of Henry VII. to the Death of George II. By HENRY HALLAM. 8vo, Cloth, $2 00; Sheep, $2 50.

HALLAM'S LITERATURE. Introduction to the Literature of Europe during the Fifteenth, Sixteenth, and Seventeenth Centuries. By HENRY HALLAM. 2 vols., 8vo, Cloth, $4 00; Sheep, $5 00.

SCHWEINFURTH'S HEART OF AFRICA. The Heart of Africa. Three Years' Travels and Adventures in the Unexplored Regions of the Centre of Africa—from 1868 to 1871. By Dr. GEORG SCHWEINFURTH. Translated by ELLEN E. FREWER. With an Introduction by WINWOOD READE. Illustrated by about 130 Wood-cuts from Drawings made by the Author, and with two Maps. 2 vols., 8vo, Cloth, $8 00.

M'CLINTOCK & STRONG'S CYCLOPÆDIA. Cyclopædia of Biblical, Theological, and Ecclesiastical Literature. Prepared by the Rev. JOHN M'CLINTOCK, D.D., and JAMES STRONG, S.T.D. 9 *vols. now ready.* Royal 8vo. Price per vol., Cloth, $5 00; Sheep, $6 00; Half Morocco, $8 00. (*Sold by Subscription.*)

MOHAMMED AND MOHAMMEDANISM: Lectures Delivered at the Royal Institution of Great Britain in February and March, 1874. By R. BOSWORTH SMITH, M.A., Assistant Master in Harrow School; late Fellow of Trinity College, Oxford. With an Appendix containing Emanuel Deutsch's Article on "Islam." 12mo, Cloth, $1 50.

MOSHEIM'S ECCLESIASTICAL HISTORY, Ancient and Modern; in which the Rise, Progress, and Variation of Church Power are considered in their connection with the State of Learning and Philosophy, and the Political History of Europe during that Period. Translated, with Notes, etc., by A. MACLAINE, D.D. Continued to 1826, by C. COOTE, LL.D. 2 vols., 8vo, Cloth, 4 00; Sheep, $5 00.

HARPER'S NEW CLASSICAL LIBRARY. Literal Translations. The following volumes are now ready. 12mo, Cloth, $1 50 each.

CÆSAR.—VIRGIL.—SALLUST.—HORACE.—CICERO'S ORATIONS.—CICERO'S OFFICES, etc.—CICERO ON ORATORY AND ORATORS.—TACITUS (2 vols.).— TERENCE. — SOPHOCLES. — JUVENAL. — XENOPHON.— HOMER'S ILIAD.—HOMER'S ODYSSEY.—HERODOTUS.—DEMOSTHENES (2 vols.). — THUCYDIDES. — ÆSCHYLUS. — EURIPIDES (2 vols.).— LIVY (2 vols.).—PLATO [Select Dialogues].

NICHOLS'S ART EDUCATION. Art Education applied to Industry. By GEORGE WARD NICHOLS. Illustrated. 8vo, Cloth, $4 00; Half Calf, $6 25.

PARTON'S CARICATURE. Caricature and Other Comic Art, in All Times and Many Lands. By JAMES PARTON. With 203 Illustrations. 8vo, Cloth, Uncut Edges and Gilt Tops, $5 00; Half Calf, $7 25.

VINCENT'S LAND OF THE WHITE ELEPHANT. The Land of the White Elephant: Sights and Scenes in Southeastern Asia. A Personal Narrative of Travel and Adventure in Farther India, embracing the Countries of Burma, Siam, Cambodia, and Cochin-China (1871-2). By FRANK VINCENT, Jr. Illustrated with Maps, Plans, and Wood-cuts. Crown 8vo, Cloth, $3 50.

LIVINGSTONE'S SOUTH AFRICA. Missionary Travels and Researches in South Africa: including a Sketch of Sixteen Years' Residence in the Interior of Africa, and a Journey from the Cape of Good Hope to Loanda on the West Coast; thence across the Continent, down the River Zambesi, to the Eastern Ocean. By DAVID LIVINGSTONE, LL.D., D.C.L. With Portrait, Maps, and Illustrations. 8vo, Cloth, $4 50; Sheep, $5 00; Half Calf, $6 75.

LIVINGSTONE'S ZAMBESI. Narrative of an Expedition to the Zambesi and its Tributaries, and of the Discovery of the Lakes Shirwa and Nyassa, 1858-1864. By DAVID and CHARLES LIVINGSTONE. Map and Illustrations. 8vo, Cloth, $5 00; Sheep, $5 50; Half Calf, $7 25.

LIVINGSTONE'S LAST JOURNALS. The Last Journals of David Livingstone in Central Africa, from 1865 to his Death. Continued by a Narrative of his Last Moments and Sufferings, obtained from his Faithful Servants Chuma and Susi. By HORACE WALLER, F.R.G.S., Rector of Twywell, Northampton. With Portrait, Maps, and Illustrations. 8vo, Cloth, $5 00; Sheep, $5 50; Half Calf, $7 25. Cheap Popular Edition, 8vo, Cloth, with Map and Illustrations, $2 50.

GROTE'S HISTORY OF GREECE. 12 vols., 12mo, Cloth, $18 00; Sheep, $22 80; Half Calf, $39 00.

RECLUS'S EARTH. The Earth: a Descriptive History of the Phenomena of the Life of the Globe. By ÉLISÉE RECLUS. With 234 Maps and Illustrations, and 23 Page Maps printed in Colors. 8vo, Cloth, $5 00.

RECLUS'S OCEAN. The Ocean, Atmosphere, and Life. Being the Second Series of a Descriptive History of the Life of the Globe. By ÉLISÉE RECLUS. Profusely Illustrated with 250 Maps or Figures, and 27 Maps printed in Colors. 8vo, Cloth, $6 00.

VAN-LENNEP'S BIBLE LANDS. Bible Lands: their Modern Customs and Manners Illustrative of Scripture. By the Rev. HENRY J. VAN-LENNEP, D.D. With upward of 350 Wood Engravings and two Colored Maps. 838 pp., 8vo, Cloth, $5 00; Sheep, $6 00; Half Morocco or Half Calf, $8 00.

NORDHOFF'S COMMUNISTIC SOCIETIES OF THE UNITED STATES. The Communistic Societies of the United States, from Personal Visit and Observation; including Detailed Accounts of the Economists, Zoarites, Shakers, the Amana, Oneida, Bethel, Aurora, Icarian, and other existing Societies. With Particulars of their Religious Creeds and Practices, their Social Theories and Life, Numbers, Industries, and Present Condition. By CHARLES NORDHOFF. Illustrations. 8vo, Cloth, $4 00.

NORDHOFF'S CALIFORNIA. California: for Health, Pleasure, and Residence. A Book for Travellers and Settlers. Illustrated. 8vo, Cloth, $2 50.

NORDHOFF'S NORTHERN CALIFORNIA AND THE SANDWICH ISLANDS. Northern California, Oregon, and the Sandwich Islands. By CHARLES NORDHOFF. Illustrated. 8vo, Cloth, $2 50.

SHAKSPEARE. The Dramatic Works of William Shakspeare. With Corrections and Notes. Engravings. 6 vols., 12mo, Cloth, $9 00. 2 vols., 8vo, Cloth, $4 00; Sheep, $5 00. In one vol., 8vo, Sheep, $4 00.

STRICKLAND'S (MISS) QUEENS OF SCOTLAND. Lives of the Queens of Scotland and English Princesses connected with the Regal Succession of Great Britain. By AGNES STRICKLAND. 8 vols., 12mo, Cloth, $12 00; Half Calf, $26 00.

BAKER'S ISMAILÏA. Ismailïa: a Narrative of the Expedition to Central Africa for the Suppression of the Slave-trade, organized by Ismail, Khedive of Egypt. By Sir SAMUEL WHITE BAKER, PASHA, F.R.S., F.R.G.S. With Maps, Portraits, and Illustrations. 8vo, Cloth, $5 00; Half Calf, $7 25.

BOSWELL'S JOHNSON. The Life of Samuel Johnson, LL.D., including a Journal of a Tour to the Hebrides. By JAMES BOSWELL, Esq. Edited by JOHN WILSON CROKER, LL.D., F.R.S. With a Portrait of Boswell. 2 vols., 8vo, Cloth, $4 00; Sheep, $5 00; Half Calf, $8 50.

SAMUEL JOHNSON: HIS WORDS AND HIS WAYS; what he Said, what he Did, and what Men Thought and Spoke Concerning him. Edited by E. T. MASON. 12mo, Cloth, $1 50.

JOHNSON'S COMPLETE WORKS. The Works of Samuel Johnson, LL.D. With an Essay on his Life and Genius, by ARTHUR MURPHY, Esq. 2 vols., 8vo, Cloth, $4 00; Sheep, $5 00; Half Calf, $8 50.

GRIFFIS'S JAPAN. The Mikado's Empire: Book I. History of Japan, from 660 B.C. to 1872 A.D. Book II. Personal Experiences, Observations, and Studies in Japan, 1870-1874. By WILLIAM ELLIOT GRIFFIS, A.M., late of the Imperial University of Tōkiō, Japan. Copiously Illustrated. 8vo, Cloth, $4 00; Half Calf, $6 25.

SMILES'S HISTORY OF THE HUGUENOTS. The Huguenots: their Settlements, Churches, and Industries in England and Ireland. By SAMUEL SMILES. With an Appendix relating to the Huguenots in America. Crown 8vo, Cloth, $2 00.

SMILES'S HUGUENOTS AFTER THE REVOCATION. The Huguenots in France after the Revocation of the Edict of Nantes; with a Visit to the Country of the Vaudois. By SAMUEL SMILES. Crown 8vo, Cloth, $2 00.

SMILES'S LIFE OF THE STEPHENSONS. The Life of George Stephenson, and of his Son, Robert Stephenson; Comprising, also, a History of the Invention and Introduction of the Railway Locomotive. By SAMUEL SMILES. With Steel Portraits and numerous Illustrations. 8vo, Cloth, $3 00.

RAWLINSON'S MANUAL OF ANCIENT HISTORY. A Manual of Ancient History, from the Earliest Times to the Fall of the Western Empire. Comprising the History of Chaldæa, Assyria, Media, Babylonia, Lydia, Phœnicia, Syria, Judæa, Egypt, Carthage, Persia, Greece, Macedonia, Parthia, and Rome. By GEORGE RAWLINSON, M.A., Camden Professor of Ancient History in the University of Oxford. 12mo, Cloth, $1 25.

THE VOYAGE OF THE "CHALLENGER." The Atlantic: an Account of the General Results of the Voyage during 1873, and the Early Part of 1876. By Sir WYVILLE THOMSON, K.C.B., F.R.S. With numerous Illustrations, Colored Maps, and Charts, from Drawings by J. J. Wyld, engraved by J. D. Cooper, and Portrait of the Author, engraved by C. H. Jeens. 2 vols., 8vo, Cloth, $12 00.

ALISON'S HISTORY OF EUROPE. FIRST SERIES: From the Commencement of the French Revolution, in 1789, to the Restoration of the Bourbons in 1815. [In addition to the Notes on Chapter LXXVI., which correct the errors of the original work concerning the United States, a copious Analytical Index has been appended to this American Edition.] SECOND SERIES: From the Fall of Napoleon, in 1815, to the Accession of Louis Napoleon, in 1852. 8 vols., 8vo, Cloth, $16 00; Sheep, $20 00; Half Calf, $34 00.

WALLACE'S GEOGRAPHICAL DISTRIBUTION OF ANIMALS. The Geographical Distribution of Animals. With a study of the Relations of Living and Extinct Faunas, as Elucidating the Past Changes of the Earth's Surface. By ALFRED RUSSEL WALLACE. With Maps and Illustrations. In 2 vols., 8vo, Cloth, $10 00.

WALLACE'S MALAY ARCHIPELAGO. The Malay Archipelago: The Land of the Orang-Utan and the Bird of Paradise. A Narrative of Travel, 1854-1862. With Studies of Man and Nature. By A. R. WALLACE. Maps and Illustrations. Crown 8vo, Cloth, $2 50.

BOURNE'S LIFE OF LOCKE. The Life of John Locke. By H. R. Fox BOURNE. 2 vols., 8vo, Cloth, Uncut Edges and Gilt Tops, $5 00.

8   *Valuable Works for Public and Private Libraries.*

BLUNT'S BEDOUIN TRIBES OF THE EUPHRATES. Bedouin Tribes of the Euphrates. By LADY ANNE BLUNT. Edited, with a Preface and some Account of the Arabs and their Horses, by W. S. B. Map and Sketches by the Author. 8vo, Cloth, $2 50.

BROUGHAM'S AUTOBIOGRAPHY. Life and Times of Henry, Lord Brougham. Written by Himself. 3 vols., 12mo, Cloth, $6 00.

THOMPSON'S PAPACY AND THE CIVIL POWER. The Papacy and the Civil Power. By the Hon. R. W. THOMPSON, Secretary of the U. S. Navy. Crown 8vo, Cloth, $3 00.

THE POETS AND POETRY OF SCOTLAND: From the Earliest to the Present Time. Comprising Characteristic Selections from the Works of the more Noteworthy Scottish Poets, with Biographical and Critical Notices. By JAMES GRANT WILSON. With Portraits on Steel. 2 vols., 8vo, Cloth, $10 00; Sheep, $12 00; Half Calf, $14 50; Full Morocco, $18 00.

THE STUDENT'S SERIES. With Maps and Illustrations. 12mo, Cloth.

FRANCE.—GIBBON.—GREECE.—ROME (by LIDDELL).—OLD TESTAMENT HISTORY.—NEW TESTAMENT HISTORY.—STRICKLAND'S QUEENS OF ENGLAND (Abridged).—ANCIENT HISTORY OF THE EAST.—HALLAM'S MIDDLE AGES.—HALLAM'S CONSTITUTIONAL HISTORY OF ENGLAND. —LYELL'S ELEMENTS OF GEOLOGY.—MERIVALE'S GENERAL HISTORY OF ROME.—COX'S GENERAL HISTORY OF GREECE.—CLASSICAL DICTIONARY. Price $1 25 per volume.

LEWIS'S HISTORY OF GERMANY.—ECCLESIASTICAL HISTORY.— HUME'S ENGLAND. Price $1 50 per volume.

CAMERON'S ACROSS AFRICA. Across Africa. By VERNEY LOVETT CAMERON, C.B., D.C.L., Commander Royal Navy, Gold Medalist Royal Geographical Society, etc. With a Map and numerous Illustrations. 8vo, Cloth, $5 00.

BARTH'S NORTH AND CENTRAL AFRICA. Travels and Discoveries in North and Central Africa: being a Journal of an Expedition undertaken under the Auspices of H.B.M.'s Government, in the Years 1849-1855. By HENRY BARTH, Ph.D., D.C.L. Illustrated. 3 vols., 8vo, Cloth, $12 00; Sheep, $13 50; Half Calf, $18 75.

ADDISON'S COMPLETE WORKS. The Works of Joseph Addison, embracing the whole of the *Spectator*. 3 vols., 8vo, Cloth, $6 00; Sheep, $7 50; Half Calf, $12 75.

TENNYSON'S COMPLETE POEMS. The Poetical Works of Alfred Tennyson, Poet-Laureate. With numerous Illustrations by Eminent Artists, and Three Characteristic Portraits. 8vo, Paper, $1 00; Cloth, $1 50.

THE REVISION OF THE ENGLISH VERSION OF THE NEW TESTAMENT. With an Introduction by the Rev. P. SCHAFF, D.D. 618 pp., Crown 8vo, Cloth, $3 00.

This work embraces in one volume:

I. ON A FRESH REVISION OF THE ENGLISH NEW TESTAMENT. By J. B. LIGHTFOOT, D.D., Canon of St. Paul's, and Hulsean Professor of Divinity, Cambridge. Second Edition, Revised. 196 pp.

II. ON THE AUTHORIZED VERSION OF THE NEW TESTAMENT in Connection with some Recent Proposals for its Revision. By R. C. TRENCH, D.D., Archbishop of Dublin. 194 pp.

III. CONSIDERATIONS ON THE REVISION OF THE ENGLISH VERSION OF THE NEW TESTAMENT. By C. J. ELLICOTT, D.D., Bishop of Gloucester and Bristol. 178 pp.

ANNUAL RECORD OF SCIENCE AND INDUSTRY. The Annual Record of Science and Industry. Edited by Professor SPENCER F. BAIRD, of the Smithsonian Institution, with the Assistance of Eminent Men of Science. The Yearly Volumes for 1871, 1872, 1873, 1874, 1875, 1876, 1877, 1878 are ready. 12mo, Cloth, $2 00 per vol.; $15 00 per set of 8 vols.

BULWER'S HORACE. The Odes and Epodes of Horace. A Metrical Translation into English. With Introduction and Commentaries. By LORD LYTTON. With Latin Text from the Editions of Orelli, Macleane, and Yonge. 12mo, Cloth, $1 75.

BULWER'S KING ARTHUR. King Arthur. A Poem. By LORD LYTTON. 12mo, Cloth, $1 75.

BULWER'S MISCELLANEOUS PROSE WORKS. The Miscellaneous Prose Works of Edward Bulwer, Lord Lytton. 2 vols., 12mo, Cloth, $3 50. Also, in uniform style, *Caxtoniana*. 12mo, Cloth, $1 75.

DAVIS'S CARTHAGE. Carthage and her Remains: being an Account of the Excavations and Researches on the Site of the Phœnician Metropolis in Africa and other Adjacent Places. Conducted under the Auspices of Her Majesty's Government. By Dr. N. DAVIS, F.R.G.S. Profusely Illustrated with Maps, Wood-cuts, Chromo-Lithographs, etc. 8vo, Cloth, $4 00; Half Calf, $6 25.

CRUISE OF THE "CHALLENGER." Voyages over many Seas, Scenes in many Lands. By W. J. J. SPRY, R. N. With Map and Illustrations. Crown 8vo, Cloth, $2 00.

EATON'S CIVIL SERVICE IN GREAT BRITAIN. Civil Service in Great Britain. A History of Abuses and Reforms, and their Bearing upon American Politics. By DORMAN B. EATON. 8vo, Cloth, $2 50.

CARLYLE'S FREDERICK THE GREAT. History of Friedrich II., called Frederick the Great. By THOMAS CARLYLE. Portraits, Maps, Plans, etc. 6 vols., 12mo, Cloth, $12 00; Sheep, $14 40; Half Calf, $22 50.

CARLYLE'S FRENCH REVOLUTION. The French Revolution: a History. By THOMAS CARLYLE. 2 vols., 12mo, Cloth, $3 50; Sheep, $4 30; Half Calf, $7 00.

CARLYLE'S OLIVER CROMWELL. Oliver Cromwell's Letters and Speeches, including the Supplement to the First Edition. With Elucidations. By THOMAS CARLYLE. 2 vols., 12mo, Cloth, $3 50; Sheep, $4 30; Half Calf, $7 00.

DRAPER'S CIVIL WAR. History of the American Civil War. By JOHN W. DRAPER, M.D., LL.D. 3 vols., 8vo, Cloth, Beveled Edges, $10 50; Sheep, $12 00; Half Calf, $17 25.

DRAPER'S INTELLECTUAL DEVELOPMENT OF EUROPE. A History of the Intellectual Development of Europe. By JOHN W. DRAPER, M.D., LL.D. New Edition, Revised. 2 vols., 12mo, Cloth, $3 00; Half Calf, $6 50.

DRAPER'S AMERICAN CIVIL POLICY. Thoughts on the Future Civil Policy of America. By JOHN W. DRAPER, M.D., LL.D. Crown 8vo, Cloth, $2 00; Half Morocco, $3 75.

McCARTHY'S HISTORY OF ENGLAND. A History of Our Own Times, from the Accession of Queen Victoria to the Berlin Congress. By JUSTIN McCARTHY. Vol. I.; 12mo, Cloth, $1 25. (*Vol. II. Nearly Ready.*)

PERRY'S HISTORY OF THE CHURCH OF ENGLAND. A History of the English Church, from the Accession of Henry VIII. to the Silencing of Convocation in the Eighteenth Century. By G. G. PERRY, M.A., Canon of Lincoln and Rector of Waddington. With an Appendix containing a Sketch of the History of the Protestant Episcopal Church in the United States of America, by J. A. SPENCER, S.T.D. Crown 8vo, Cloth, $2 50.

BARTLETT'S FROM EGYPT TO PALESTINE. From Egypt to Palestine: Through Sinai, the Wilderness, and the South Country. Observations of a Journey made with Special Reference to the History of the Israelites. By S. C. BARTLETT, D.D., LL.D., President of Dartmouth College, and lately Professor in the Chicago Theological Seminary. With Maps and Illustrations. 8vo, Cloth, $3 50.

THE FIRST CENTURY OF THE REPUBLIC. A Review of American Progress. 8vo, Cloth, $5 00.

www.ingramcontent.com/pod-product-compliance
Lightning Source LLC
Chambersburg PA
CBHW032144230426
43672CB00011B/2443